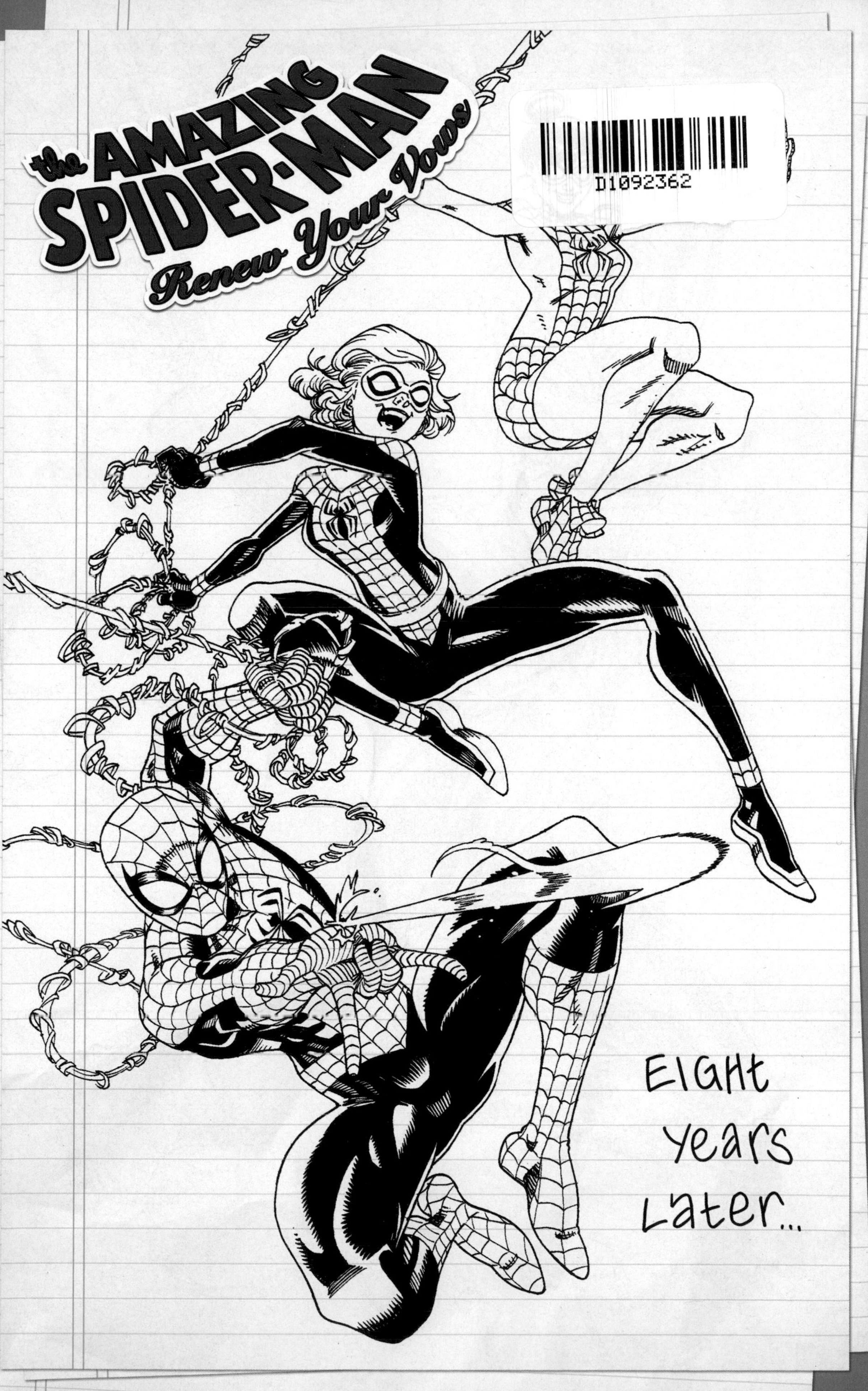
the AMAZING SPIDER-MAN
Renew Your Vows
EIGHt years Later...

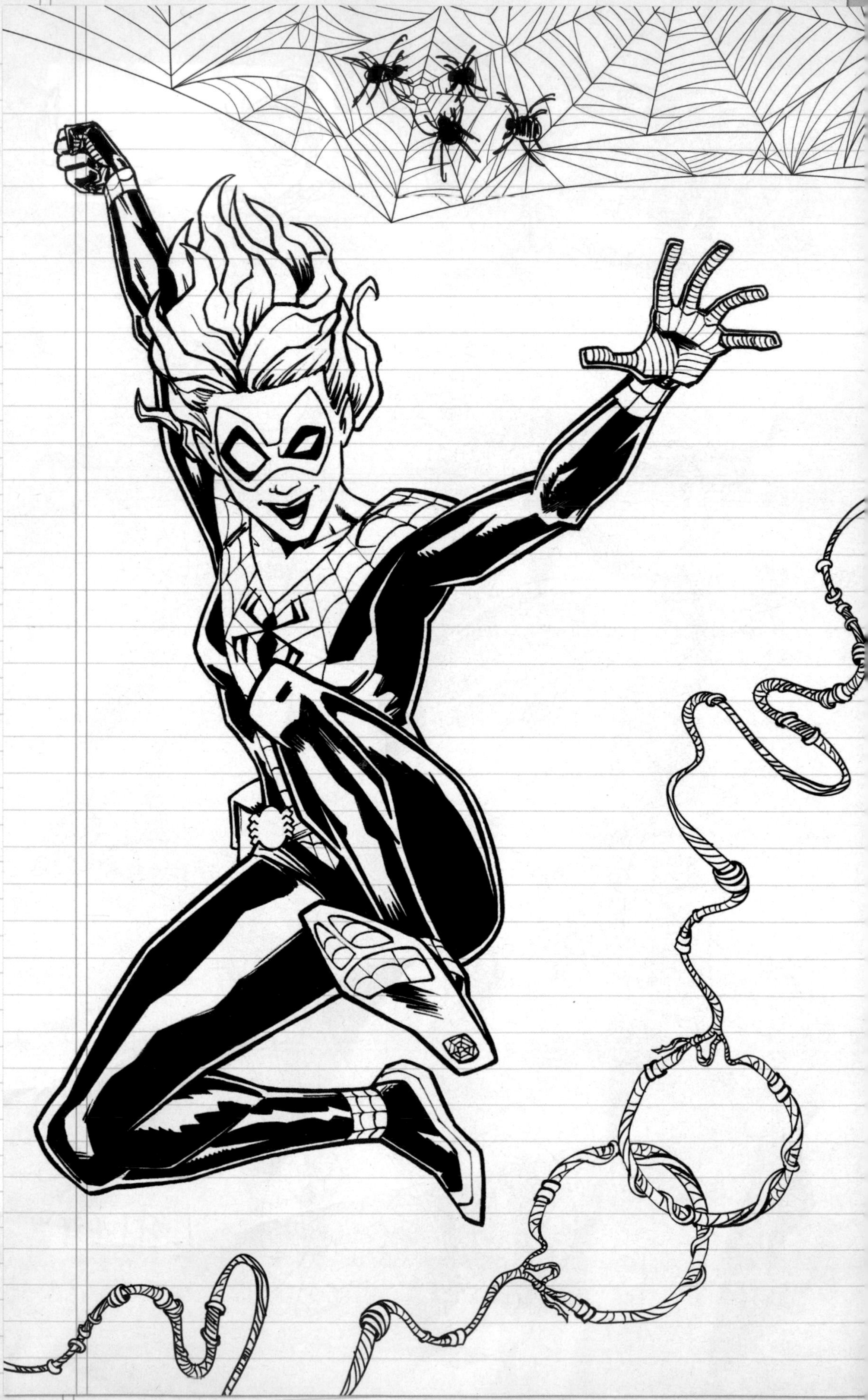

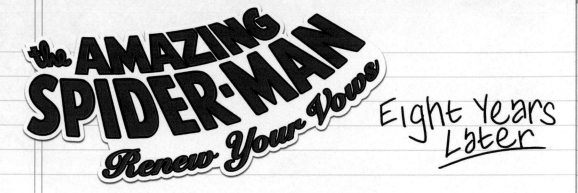

the AMAZING SPIDER-MAN Renew Your Vows

Eight Years Later

writer: JODY HOUSER

artists: NICK ROCHE (#13-15) & NATHAN STOCKMAN (#16-18)

color artist: RUTH REDMOND

letterer: VC's JOE CARAMAGNA

cover art: RYAN STEGMAN with JESUS ABURTOV (#13) & BRIAN REBER (#14-18)

editors: HEATHER ANTOS & KATHLEEN WISNESKI

supervising editor: JORDAN D. WHITE

Spider-Man created by STAN LEE & STEVE DITKO

collection editor: JENNIFER GRÜNWALD
assistant editor: CAITLIN O'CONNELL
associate managing editor: KATERI WOODY
editor, special projects: MARK D. BEAZLEY
vp production & special projects: JEFF YOUNGQUIST
svp print, sales & marketing: DAVID GABRIEL
book designer: ADAM DEL RE

editor in chief: C.B. CEBULSKI
chief creative officer: JOE QUESADA
president: DAN BUCKLEY
executive producer: ALAN FINE

AMAZING SPIDER-MAN: RENEW YOUR VOWS VOL. 3 — EIGHT YEARS LATER. Contains material originally published in magazine form as AMAZING SPIDER-MAN: RENEW YOUR VOWS #13-18. First printing 2018. ISBN 978-1-302-90582-8. Published by MARVEL WORLDWIDE, INC., a subsidiary of MARVEL ENTERTAINMENT, LLC. OFFICE OF PUBLICATION: 135 West 50th Street, New York, NY 10020. **Printed in Canada.** DAN BUCKLEY, President, Marvel Entertainment; JOHN NEE, Publisher; JOE QUESADA, Chief Creative Officer; TOM BREVOORT, SVP of Publishing; DAVID BOGART, SVP of Business Affairs & Operations, Publishing & Partnership; DAVID GABRIEL, SVP of Sales & Marketing, Publishing; JEFF YOUNGQUIST, VP of Production & Special Projects; DAN CARR, Executive Director of Publishing Technology; ALEX MORALES, Director of Publishing Operations; DAN EDINGTON, Managing Editor; SUSAN CRESPI, Production Manager; STAN LEE, Chairman Emeritus. For information regarding advertising in Marvel Comics or on Marvel.com, please contact Vit DeBellis, Custom Solutions & Integrated Advertising Manager, at vdebellis@marvel.com. For Marvel subscription inquiries, please call 888-511-5480. **Manufactured between 4/6/2018 and 5/8/2018 by SOLISCO PRINTERS, SCOTT, QC, CANADA.**

10 9 8 7 6 5 4 3 2 1

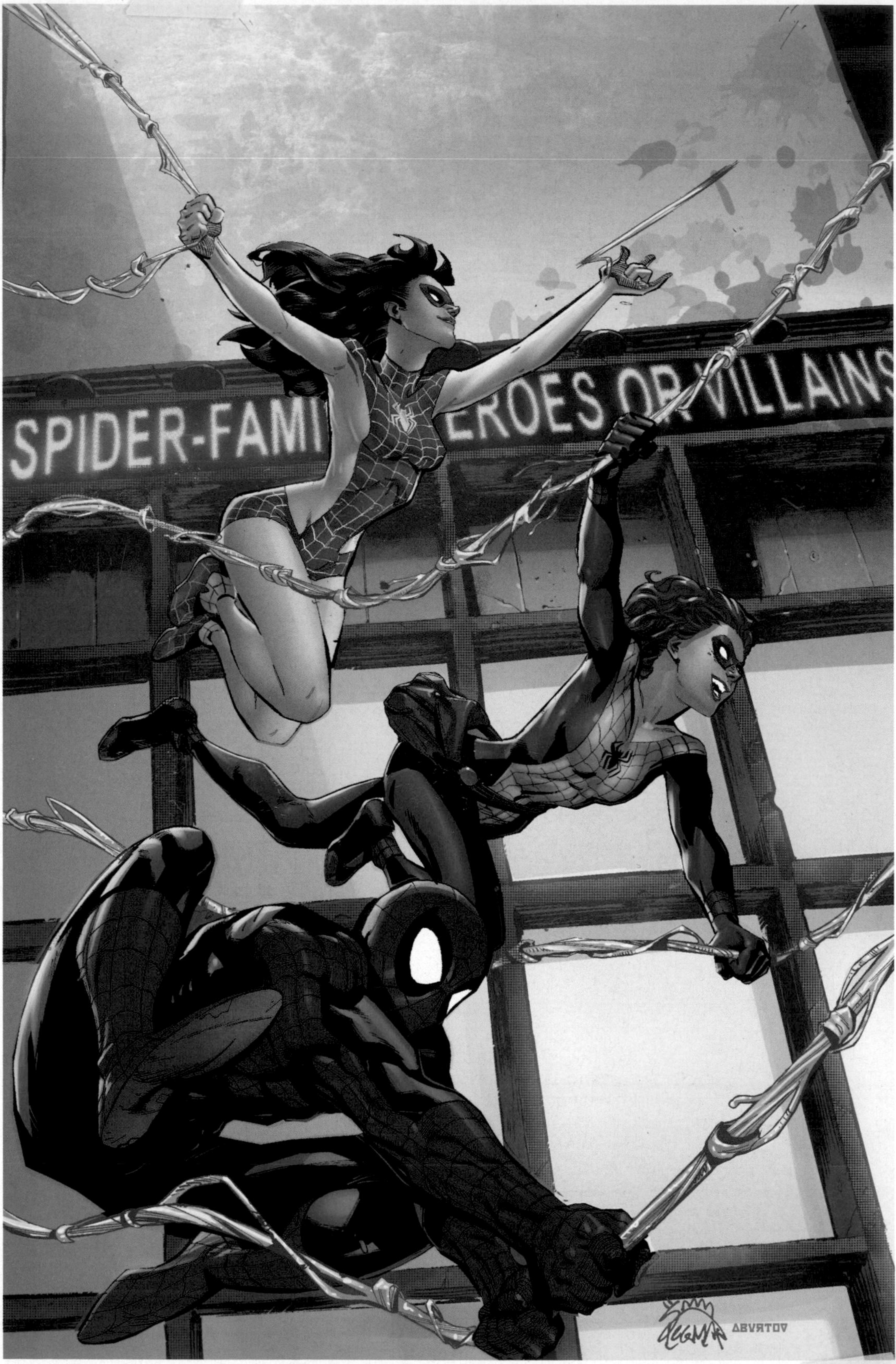
SPIDER-FAMI EROES OR VILLAINS

13: EIGHT YEARS LATER — PART 1

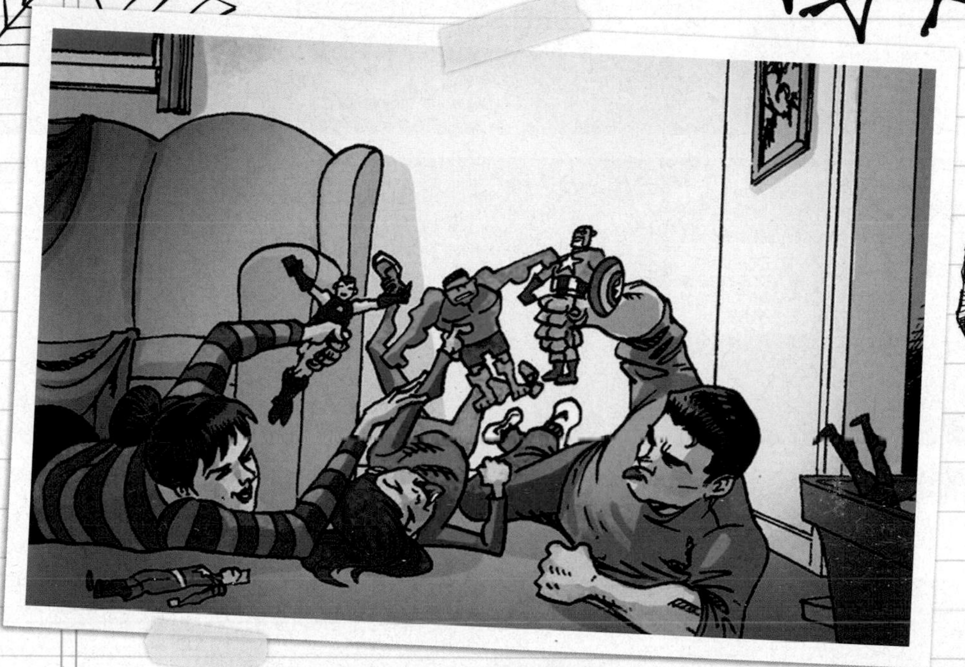

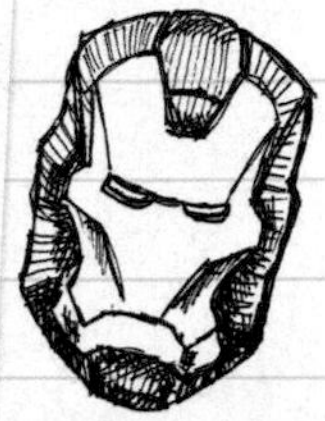

When **PETER PARKER** was bitten by a radioactive spider, he gained the proportional speed, strength and agility of a spider. Learning that with great power there must also come great responsibility, he became the crimefighting super hero **SPIDER-MAN**! With his wife, **MARY JANE**, and their teenage daughter, **ANNIE MAY**, the Parker family has become a force to be reckoned with!

- BACK 2 SCHOOL SHOPPING
- CONVINCE PARENTS 2 CHANGE CURFEW
- GET CLASS SCHEDULE
- PICK UP BOOKS

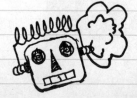

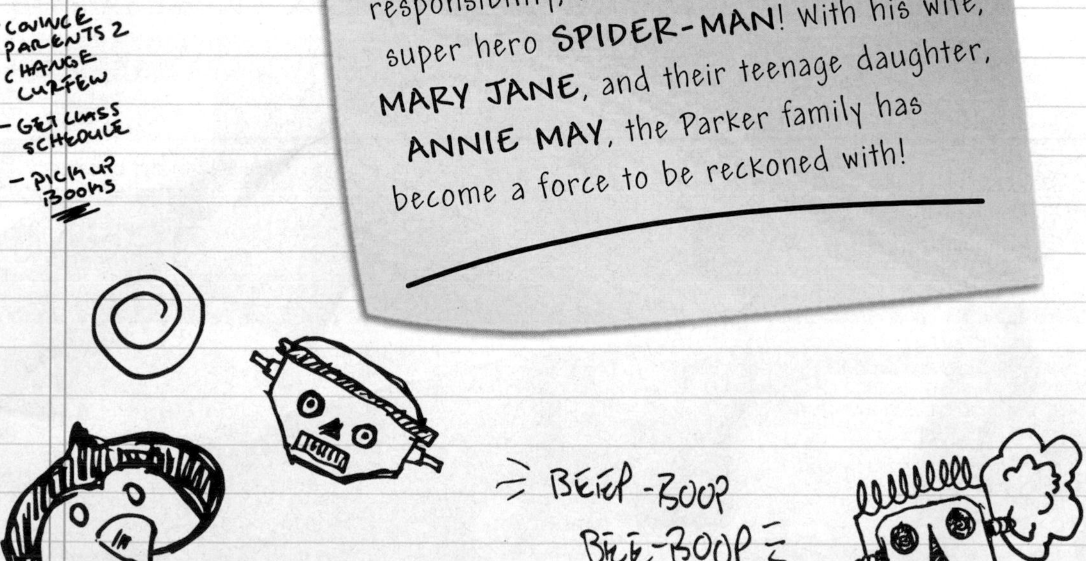
BEEP-BOOP
BEE-BOOP

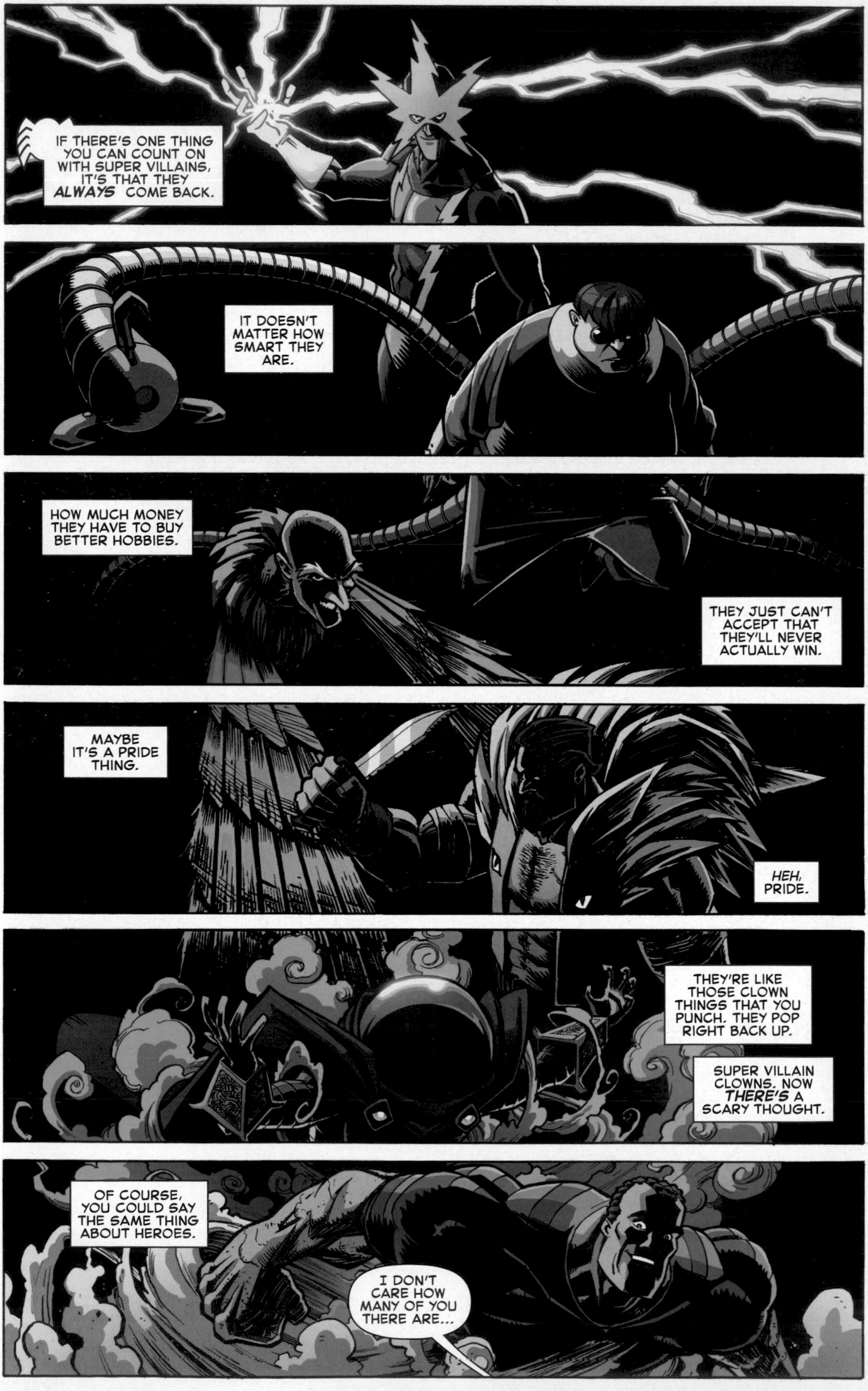
IF THERE'S ONE THING YOU CAN COUNT ON WITH SUPER VILLAINS, IT'S THAT THEY *ALWAYS* COME BACK.
IT DOESN'T MATTER HOW SMART THEY ARE.
HOW MUCH MONEY THEY HAVE TO BUY BETTER HOBBIES.
THEY JUST CAN'T ACCEPT THAT THEY'LL NEVER ACTUALLY WIN.
MAYBE IT'S A PRIDE THING.
HEH, PRIDE.
THEY'RE LIKE THOSE CLOWN THINGS THAT YOU PUNCH. THEY POP RIGHT BACK UP.
SUPER VILLAIN CLOWNS. NOW *THERE'S* A SCARY THOUGHT.
OF COURSE, YOU COULD SAY THE SAME THING ABOUT HEROES.
I DON'T CARE HOW MANY OF YOU THERE ARE...

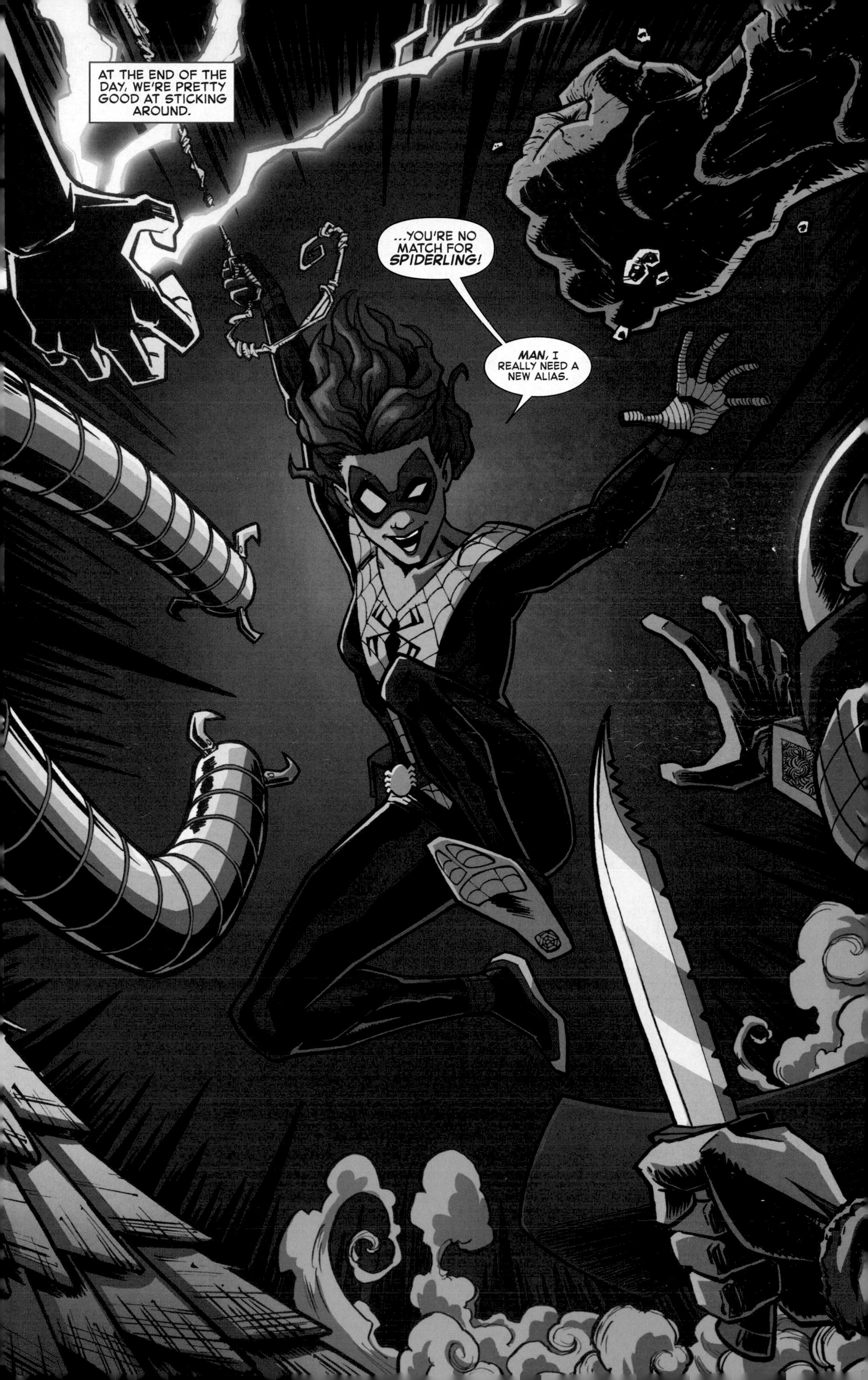
AT THE END OF THE DAY, WE'RE PRETTY GOOD AT STICKING AROUND.
...YOU'RE NO MATCH FOR SPIDERLING!
MAN, I REALLY NEED A NEW ALIAS.

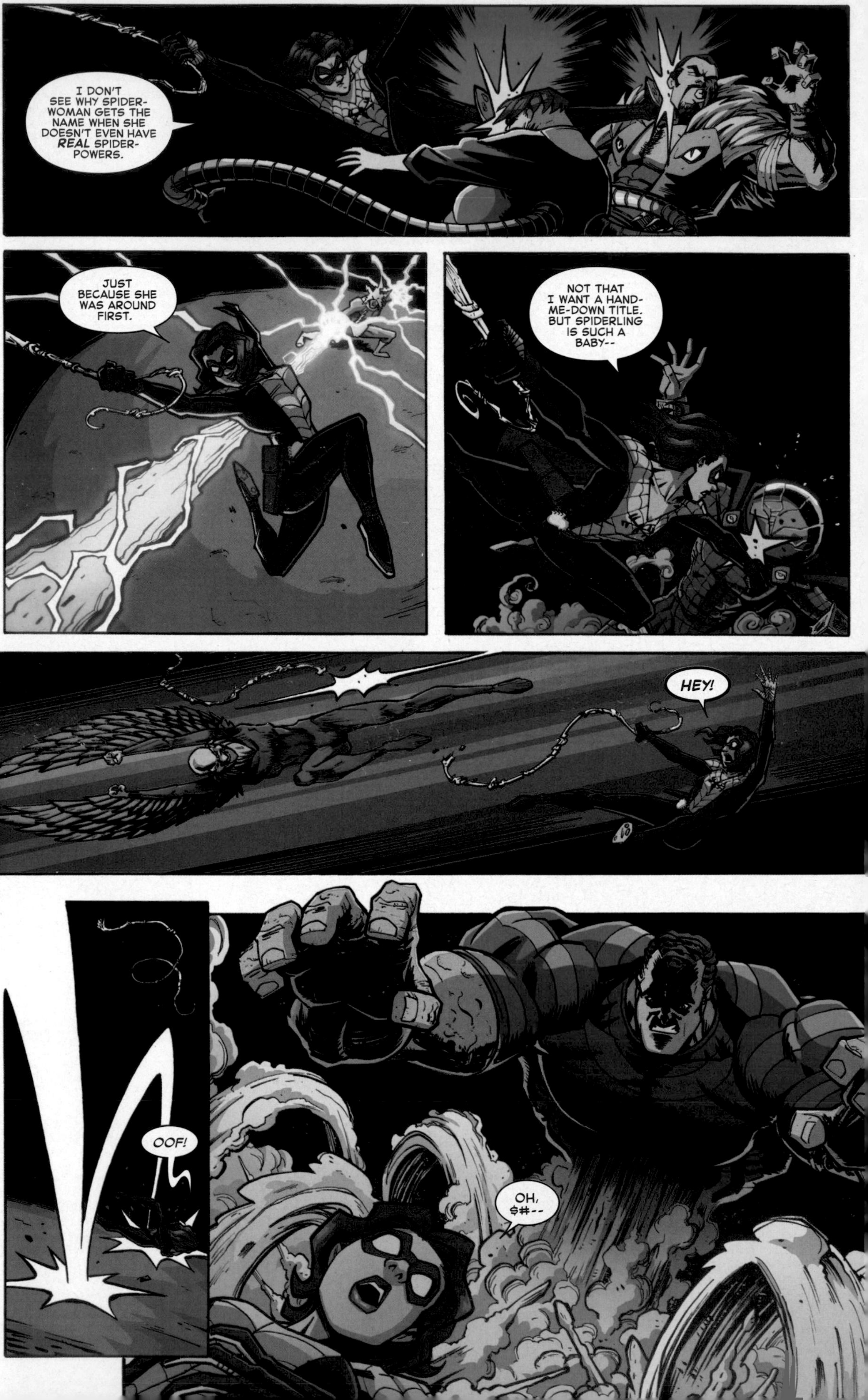
I DON'T SEE WHY SPIDER-WOMAN GETS THE NAME WHEN SHE DOESN'T EVEN HAVE *REAL* SPIDER-POWERS.
JUST BECAUSE SHE WAS AROUND FIRST.
NOT THAT I WANT A HAND-ME-DOWN TITLE. BUT SPIDERLING IS SUCH A BABY--
HEY!
OOF!
OH, $#--

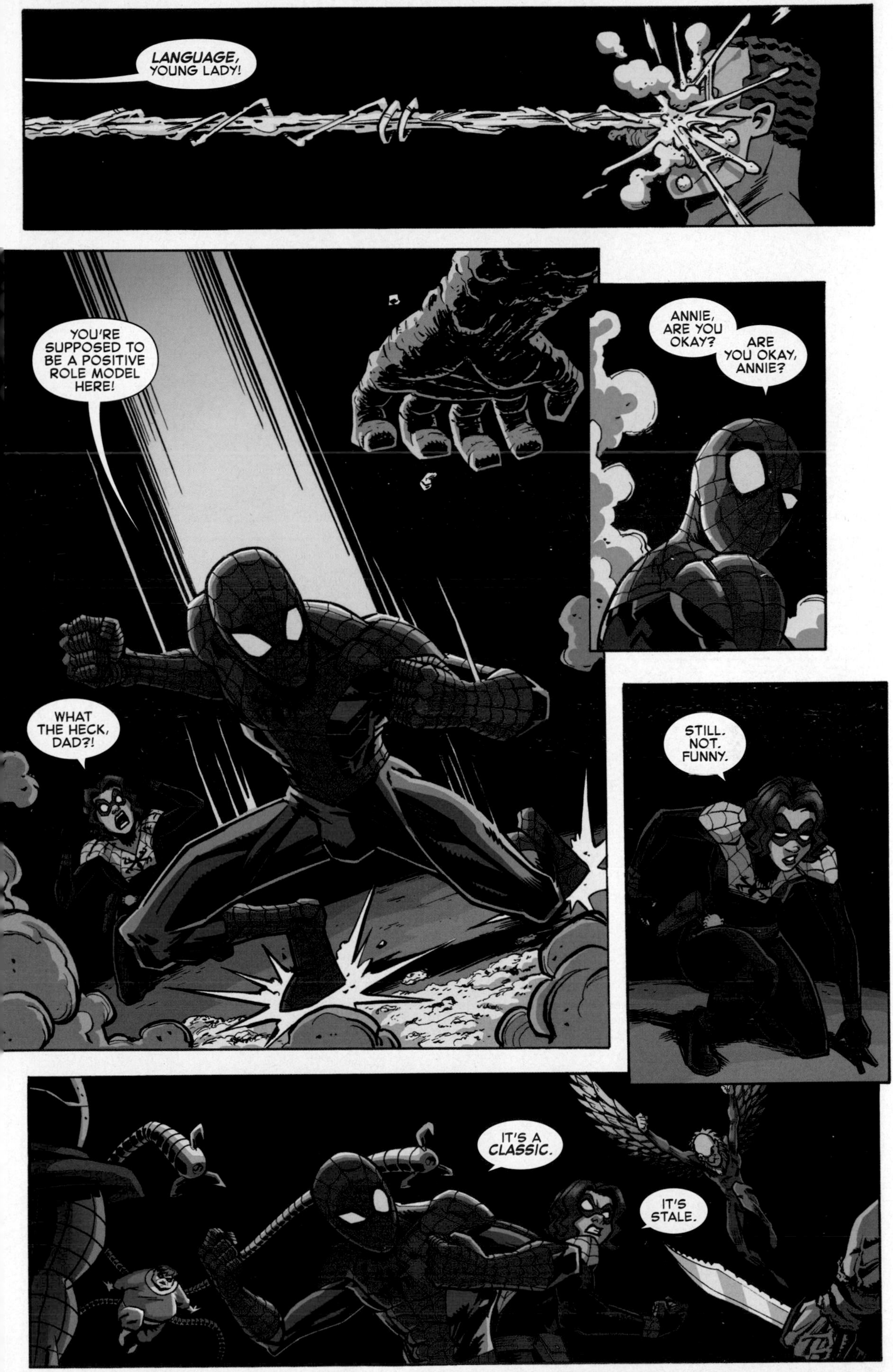
LANGUAGE, YOUNG LADY!
YOU'RE SUPPOSED TO BE A POSITIVE ROLE MODEL HERE!
WHAT THE HECK, DAD?!
ANNIE, ARE YOU OKAY?
ARE YOU OKAY, ANNIE?
STILL. NOT. FUNNY.
IT'S A CLASSIC.
IT'S STALE.

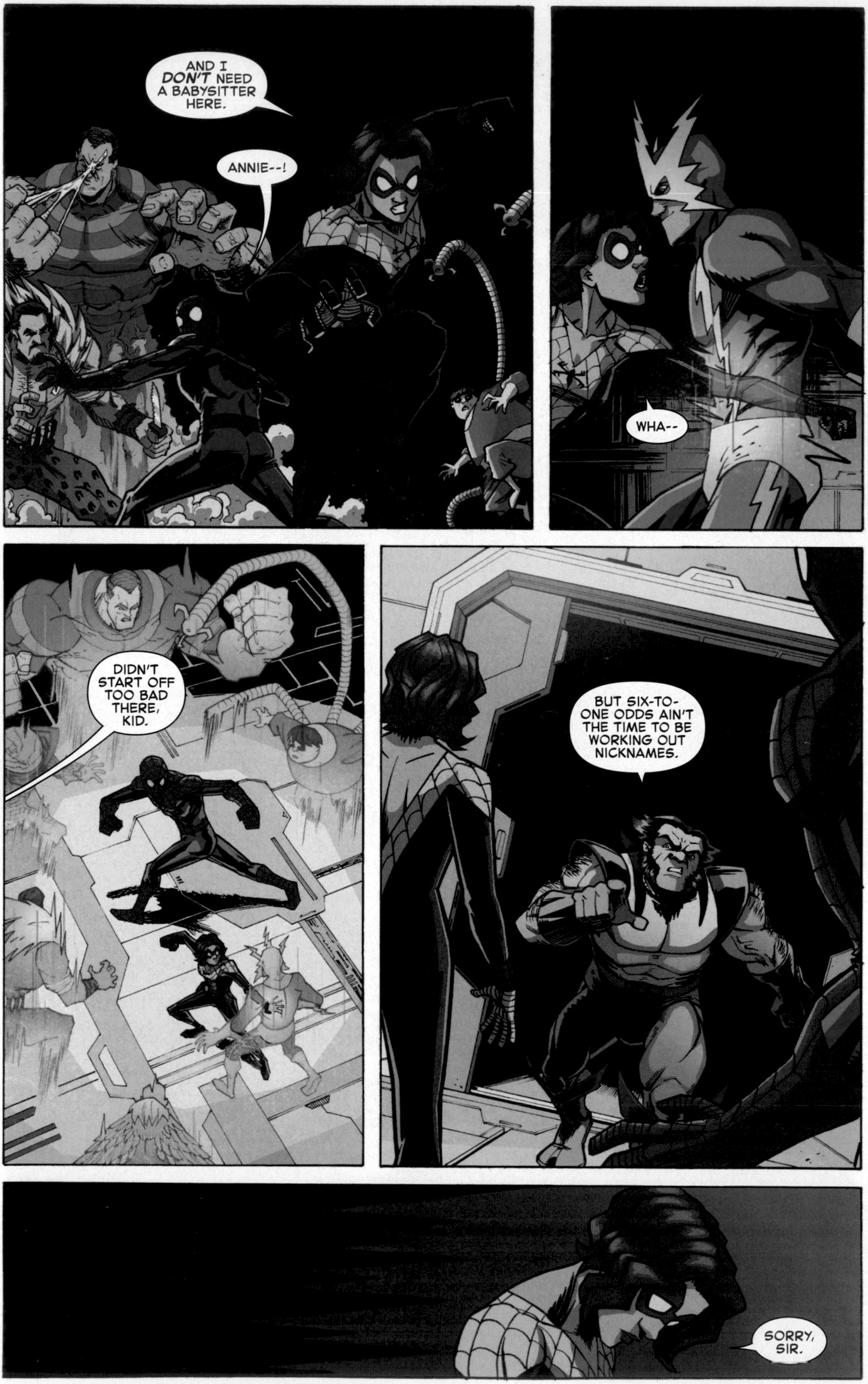
AND I *DON'T* NEED A BABYSITTER HERE.
ANNIE--!
WHA--
DIDN'T START OFF TOO BAD THERE, KID.
BUT SIX-TO-ONE ODDS AIN'T THE TIME TO BE WORKING OUT NICKNAMES.
SORRY, SIR.

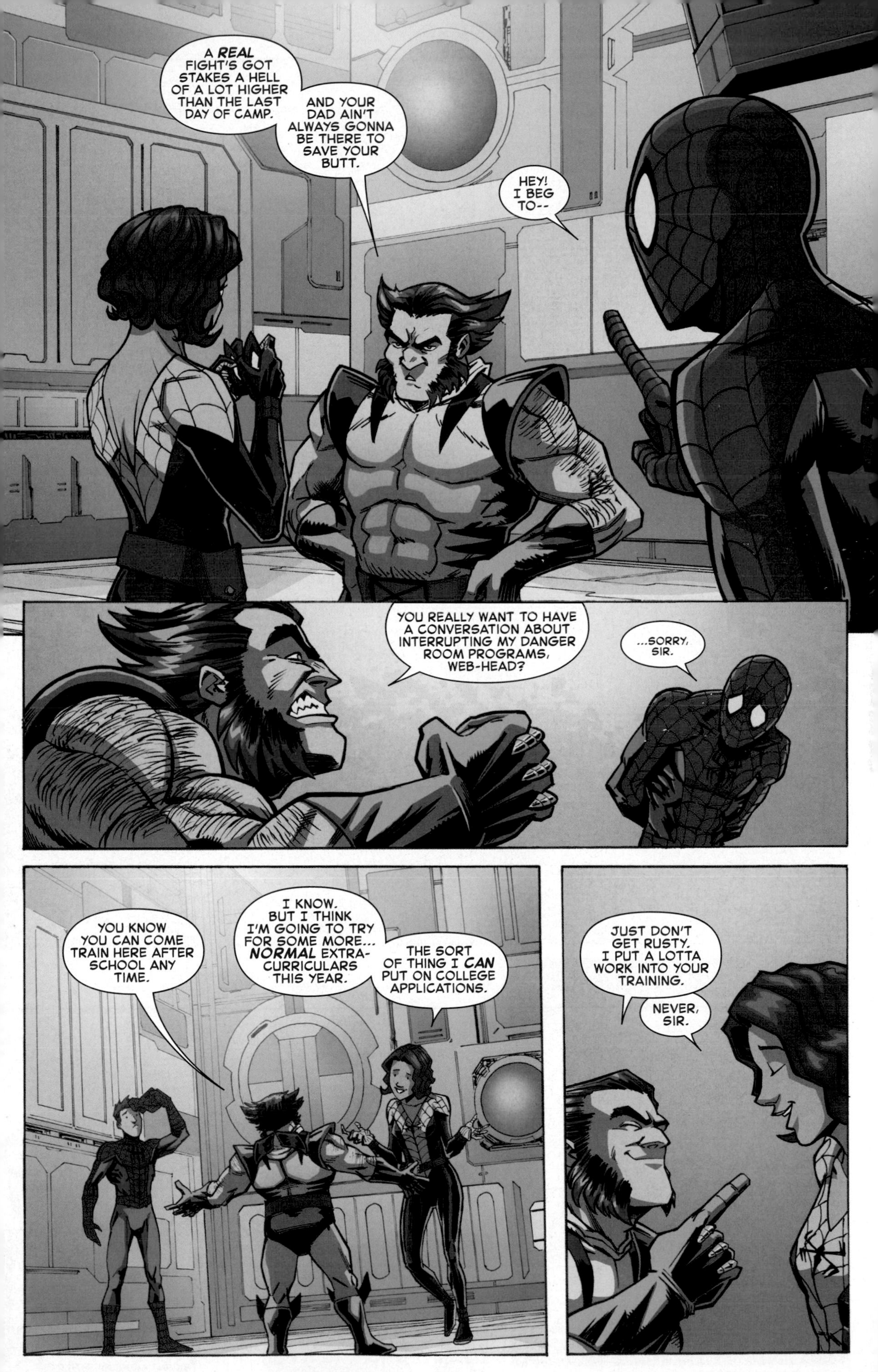
A *REAL* FIGHT'S GOT STAKES A HELL OF A LOT HIGHER THAN THE LAST DAY OF CAMP.
AND YOUR DAD AIN'T ALWAYS GONNA BE THERE TO SAVE YOUR BUTT.
HEY! I BEG TO--
YOU REALLY WANT TO HAVE A CONVERSATION ABOUT INTERRUPTING MY DANGER ROOM PROGRAMS, WEB-HEAD?
...SORRY, SIR.
YOU KNOW YOU CAN COME TRAIN HERE AFTER SCHOOL ANY TIME.
I KNOW. BUT I THINK I'M GOING TO TRY FOR SOME MORE... *NORMAL* EXTRA-CURRICULARS THIS YEAR.
THE SORT OF THING I *CAN* PUT ON COLLEGE APPLICATIONS.
JUST DON'T GET RUSTY. I PUT A LOTTA WORK INTO YOUR TRAINING.
NEVER, SIR.

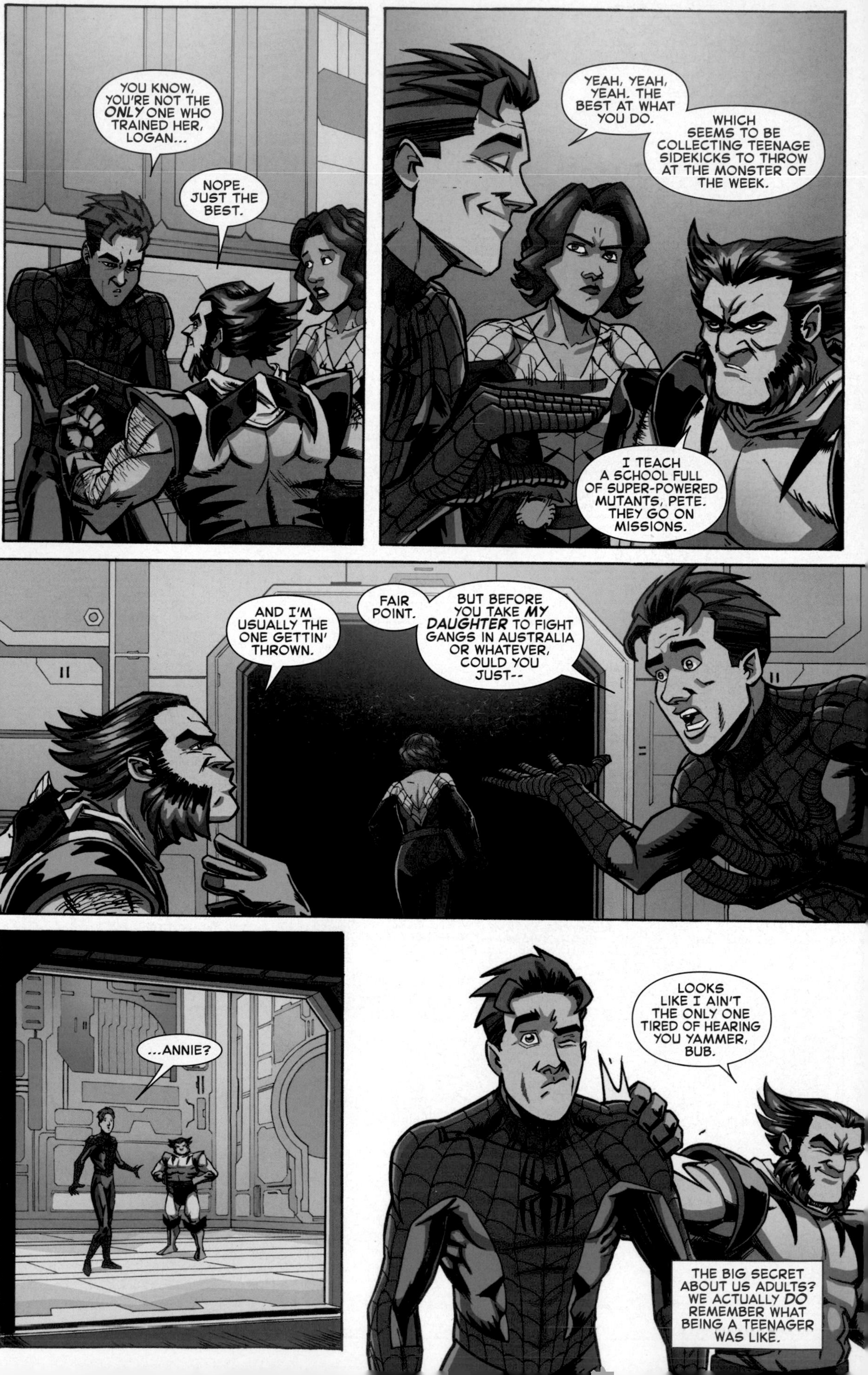
YOU KNOW, YOU'RE NOT THE ONLY ONE WHO TRAINED HER, LOGAN...
NOPE. JUST THE BEST.
YEAH, YEAH, YEAH. THE BEST AT WHAT YOU DO.
WHICH SEEMS TO BE COLLECTING TEENAGE SIDEKICKS TO THROW AT THE MONSTER OF THE WEEK.
I TEACH A SCHOOL FULL OF SUPER-POWERED MUTANTS, PETE. THEY GO ON MISSIONS.
AND I'M USUALLY THE ONE GETTIN' THROWN.
FAIR POINT.
BUT BEFORE YOU TAKE MY DAUGHTER TO FIGHT GANGS IN AUSTRALIA OR WHATEVER, COULD YOU JUST--
...ANNIE?
LOOKS LIKE I AIN'T THE ONLY ONE TIRED OF HEARING YOU YAMMER, BUB.
THE BIG SECRET ABOUT US ADULTS? WE ACTUALLY DO REMEMBER WHAT BEING A TEENAGER WAS LIKE.

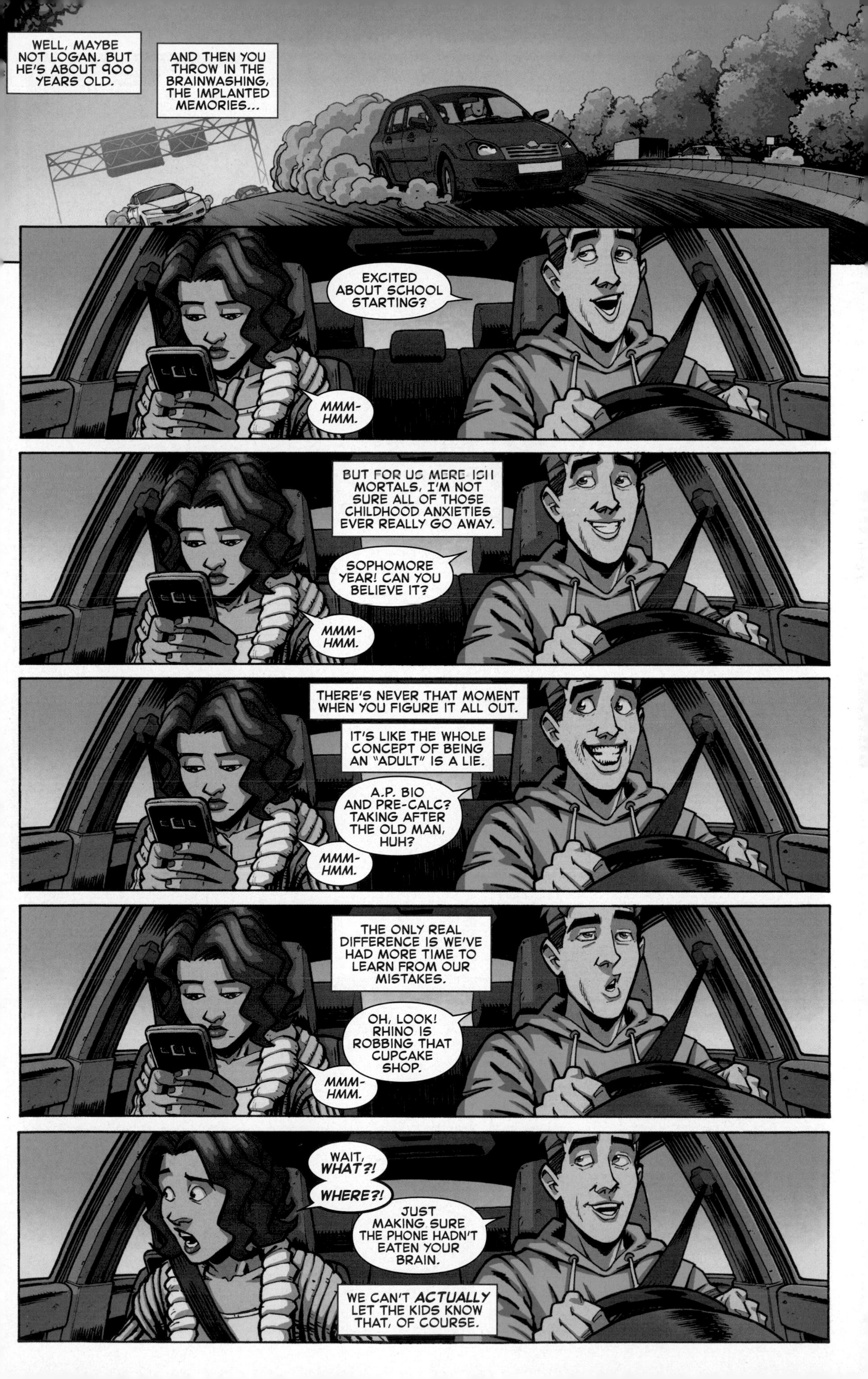
WELL, MAYBE NOT LOGAN. BUT HE'S ABOUT 900 YEARS OLD.
AND THEN YOU THROW IN THE BRAINWASHING, THE IMPLANTED MEMORIES...
EXCITED ABOUT SCHOOL STARTING?
MMM-HMM.
BUT FOR US MERE ISH MORTALS, I'M NOT SURE ALL OF THOSE CHILDHOOD ANXIETIES EVER REALLY GO AWAY.
SOPHOMORE YEAR! CAN YOU BELIEVE IT?
MMM-HMM.
THERE'S NEVER THAT MOMENT WHEN YOU FIGURE IT ALL OUT.
IT'S LIKE THE WHOLE CONCEPT OF BEING AN "ADULT" IS A LIE.
A.P. BIO AND PRE-CALC? TAKING AFTER THE OLD MAN, HUH?
MMM-HMM.
THE ONLY REAL DIFFERENCE IS WE'VE HAD MORE TIME TO LEARN FROM OUR MISTAKES.
OH, LOOK! RHINO IS ROBBING THAT CUPCAKE SHOP.
MMM-HMM.
WAIT, WHAT?!
WHERE?!
JUST MAKING SURE THE PHONE HADN'T EATEN YOUR BRAIN.
WE CAN'T ACTUALLY LET THE KIDS KNOW THAT, OF COURSE.

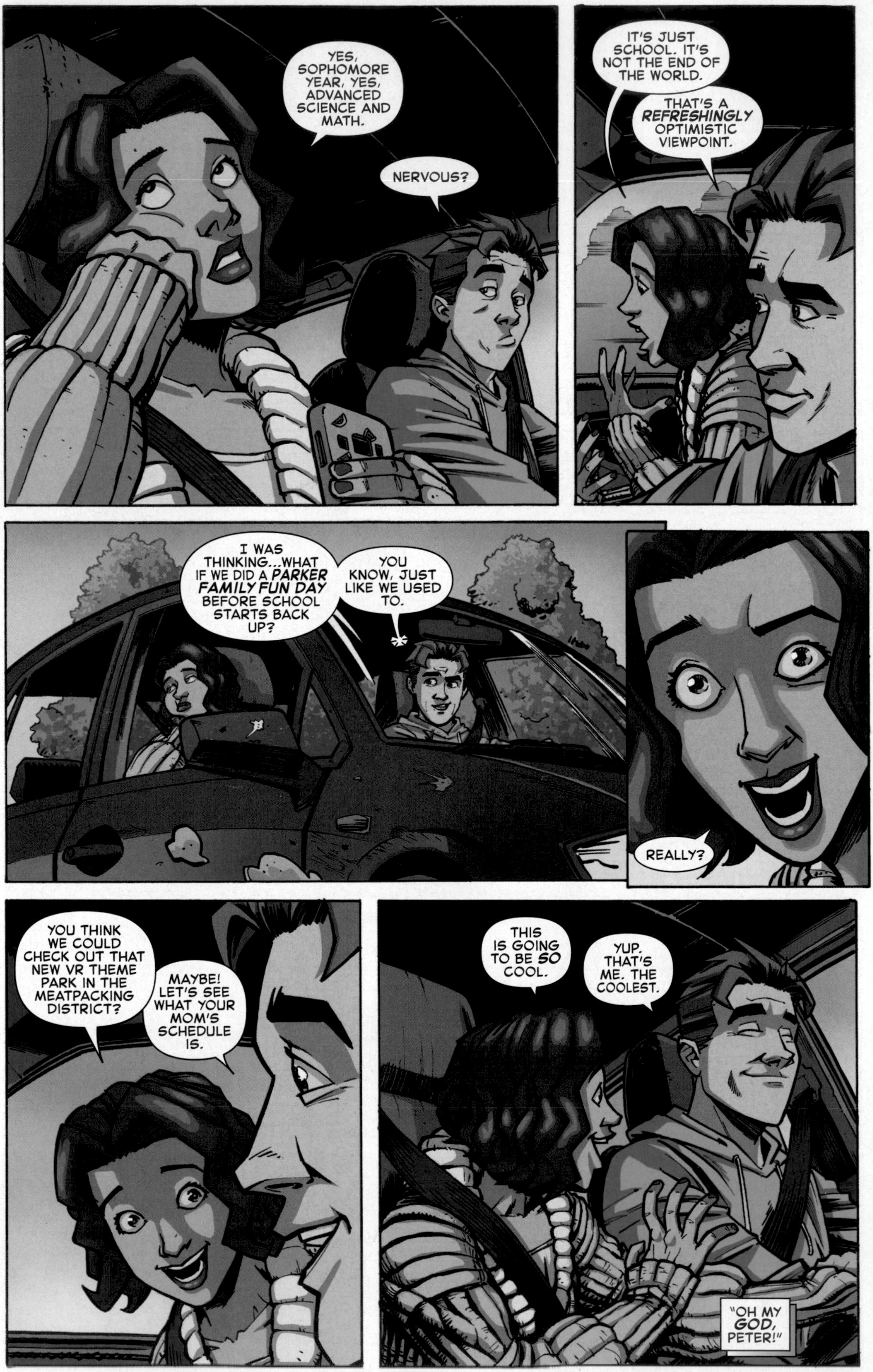
YES, SOPHOMORE YEAR, YES, ADVANCED SCIENCE AND MATH.
NERVOUS?
IT'S JUST SCHOOL. IT'S NOT THE END OF THE WORLD.
THAT'S A REFRESHINGLY OPTIMISTIC VIEWPOINT.
I WAS THINKING...WHAT IF WE DID A PARKER FAMILY FUN DAY BEFORE SCHOOL STARTS BACK UP?
YOU KNOW, JUST LIKE WE USED TO.
REALLY?
YOU THINK WE COULD CHECK OUT THAT NEW VR THEME PARK IN THE MEATPACKING DISTRICT?
MAYBE! LET'S SEE WHAT YOUR MOM'S SCHEDULE IS.
THIS IS GOING TO BE SO COOL.
YUP. THAT'S ME. THE COOLEST.
"OH MY GOD, PETER!"

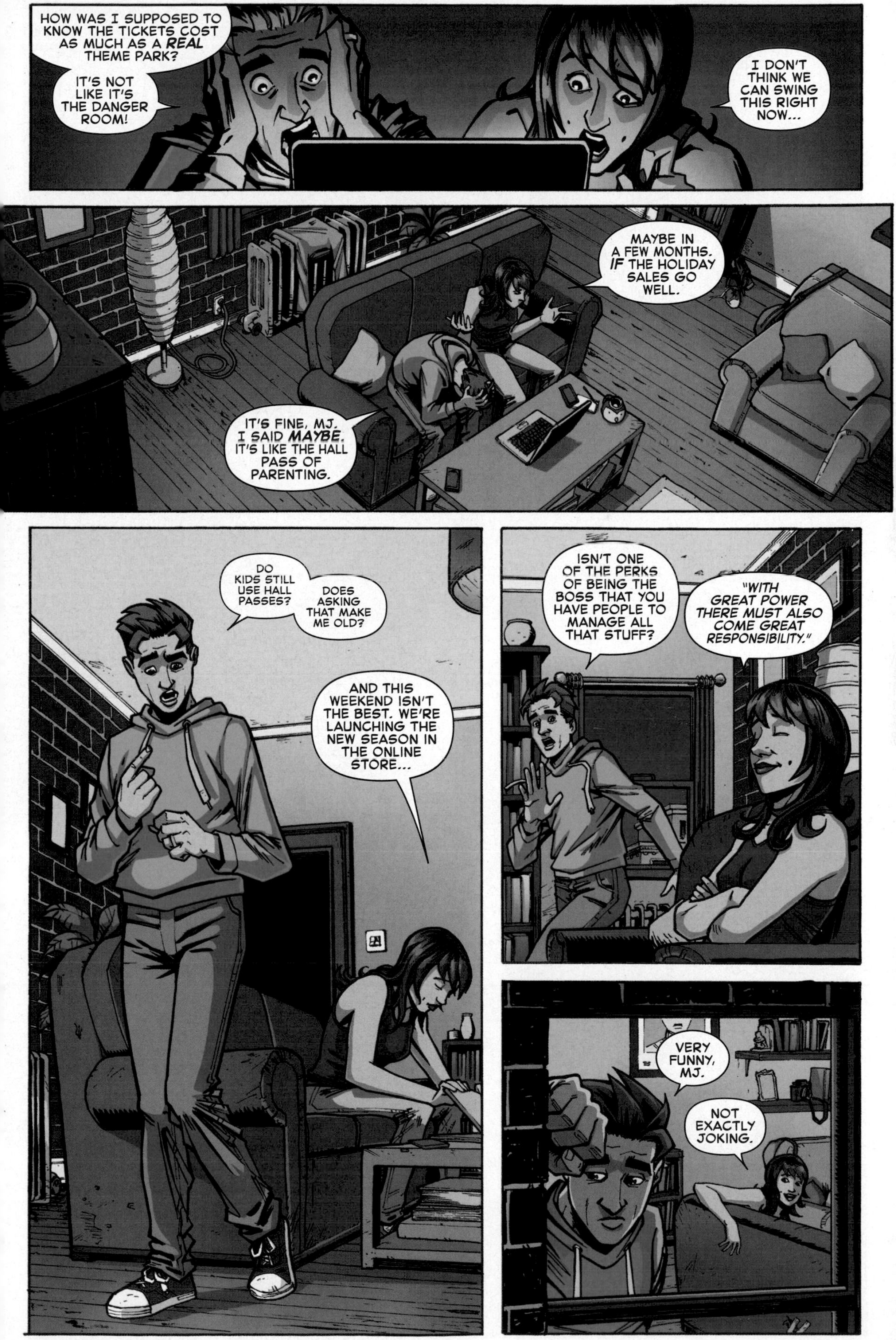
HOW WAS I SUPPOSED TO KNOW THE TICKETS COST AS MUCH AS A REAL THEME PARK?
IT'S NOT LIKE IT'S THE DANGER ROOM!
I DON'T THINK WE CAN SWING THIS RIGHT NOW...
MAYBE IN A FEW MONTHS. IF THE HOLIDAY SALES GO WELL.
IT'S FINE, MJ. I SAID MAYBE. IT'S LIKE THE HALL PASS OF PARENTING.
DO KIDS STILL USE HALL PASSES?
DOES ASKING THAT MAKE ME OLD?
AND THIS WEEKEND ISN'T THE BEST. WE'RE LAUNCHING THE NEW SEASON IN THE ONLINE STORE...
ISN'T ONE OF THE PERKS OF BEING THE BOSS THAT YOU HAVE PEOPLE TO MANAGE ALL THAT STUFF?
"WITH GREAT POWER THERE MUST ALSO COME GREAT RESPONSIBILITY."
VERY FUNNY, MJ.
NOT EXACTLY JOKING.

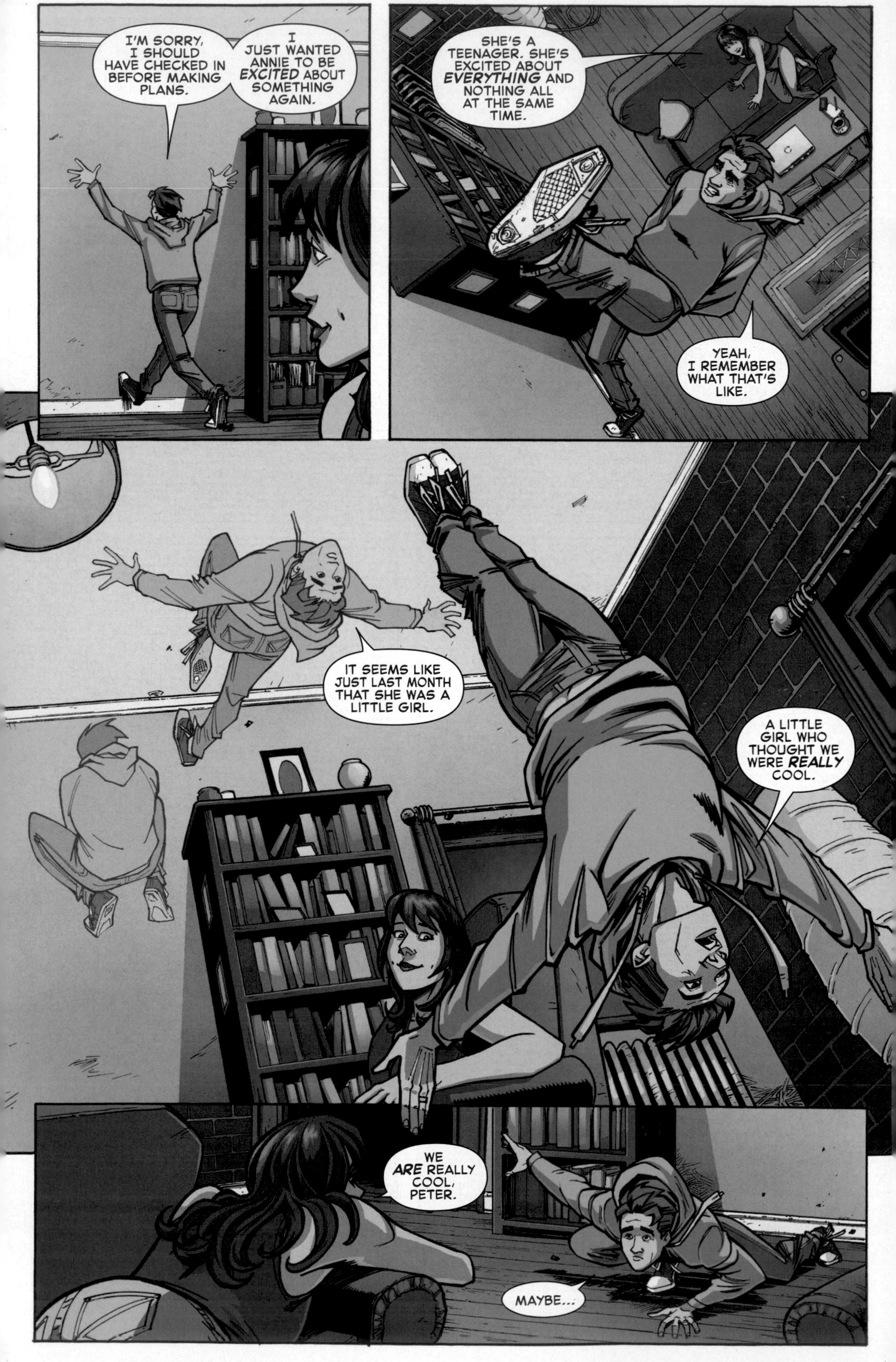
I'M SORRY, I SHOULD HAVE CHECKED IN BEFORE MAKING PLANS.
I JUST WANTED ANNIE TO BE EXCITED ABOUT SOMETHING AGAIN.
SHE'S A TEENAGER. SHE'S EXCITED ABOUT EVERYTHING AND NOTHING ALL AT THE SAME TIME.
YEAH, I REMEMBER WHAT THAT'S LIKE.
IT SEEMS LIKE JUST LAST MONTH THAT SHE WAS A LITTLE GIRL.
A LITTLE GIRL WHO THOUGHT WE WERE REALLY COOL.
WE ARE REALLY COOL, PETER.
MAYBE...

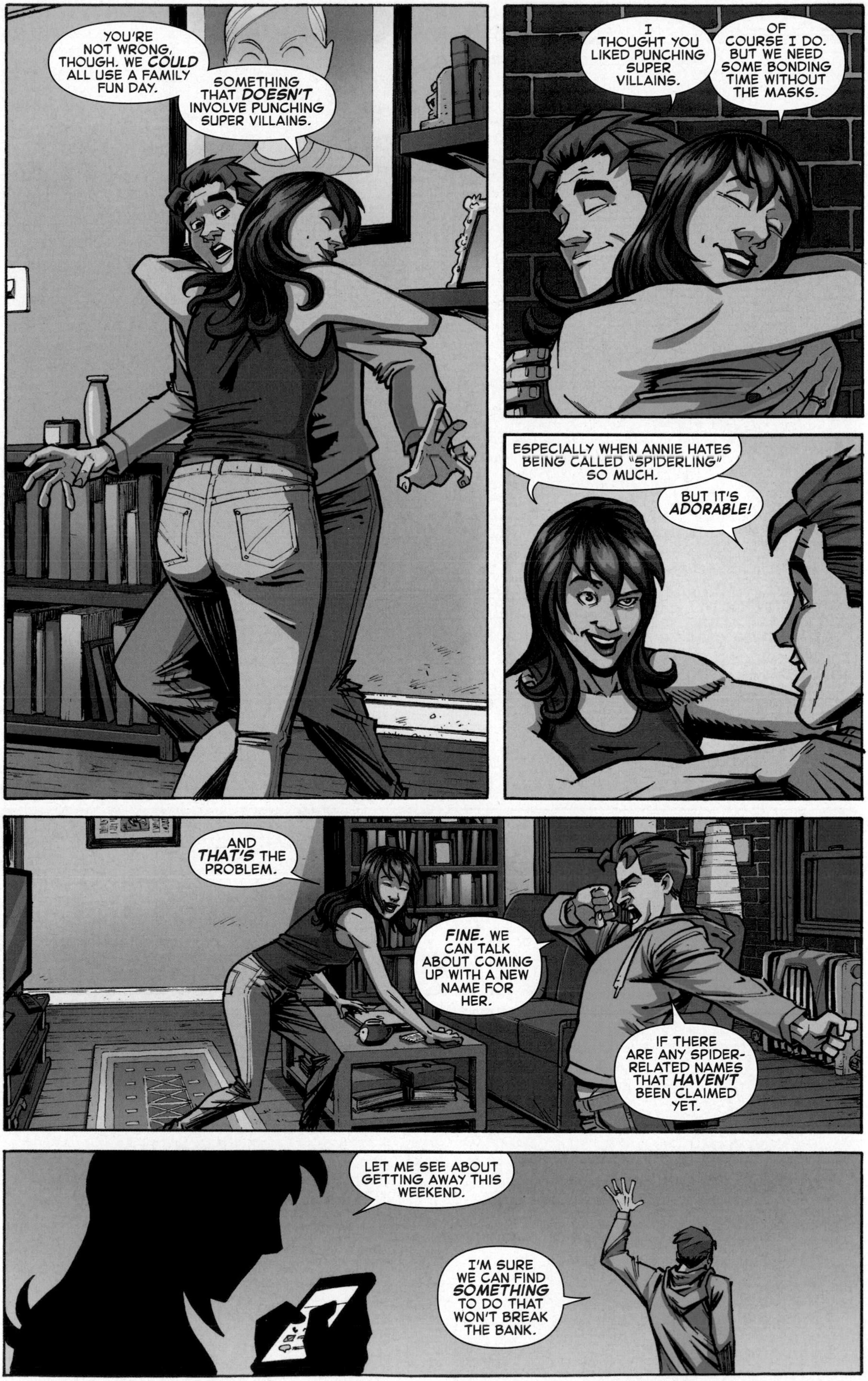
YOU'RE NOT WRONG, THOUGH. WE COULD ALL USE A FAMILY FUN DAY.
SOMETHING THAT DOESN'T INVOLVE PUNCHING SUPER VILLAINS.
I THOUGHT YOU LIKED PUNCHING SUPER VILLAINS.
OF COURSE I DO. BUT WE NEED SOME BONDING TIME WITHOUT THE MASKS.
ESPECIALLY WHEN ANNIE HATES BEING CALLED "SPIDERLING" SO MUCH.
BUT IT'S ADORABLE!
AND THAT'S THE PROBLEM.
FINE. WE CAN TALK ABOUT COMING UP WITH A NEW NAME FOR HER.
IF THERE ARE ANY SPIDER-RELATED NAMES THAT HAVEN'T BEEN CLAIMED YET.
LET ME SEE ABOUT GETTING AWAY THIS WEEKEND.
I'M SURE WE CAN FIND SOMETHING TO DO THAT WON'T BREAK THE BANK.

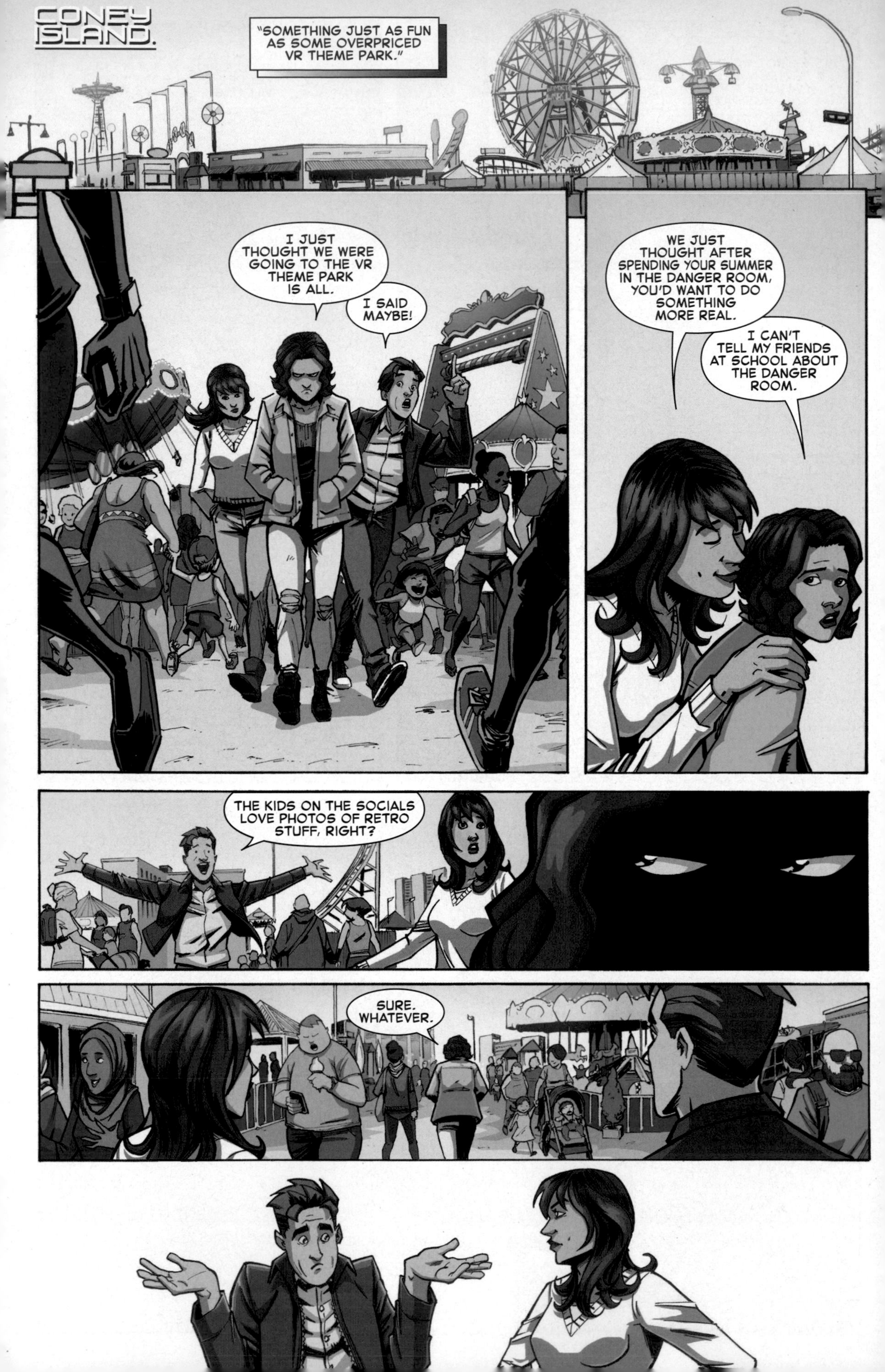
CONEY ISLAND.
"SOMETHING JUST AS FUN AS SOME OVERPRICED VR THEME PARK."
I JUST THOUGHT WE WERE GOING TO THE VR THEME PARK IS ALL.
I SAID MAYBE!
WE JUST THOUGHT AFTER SPENDING YOUR SUMMER IN THE DANGER ROOM, YOU'D WANT TO DO SOMETHING MORE REAL.
I CAN'T TELL MY FRIENDS AT SCHOOL ABOUT THE DANGER ROOM.
THE KIDS ON THE SOCIALS LOVE PHOTOS OF RETRO STUFF, RIGHT?
SURE. WHATEVER.

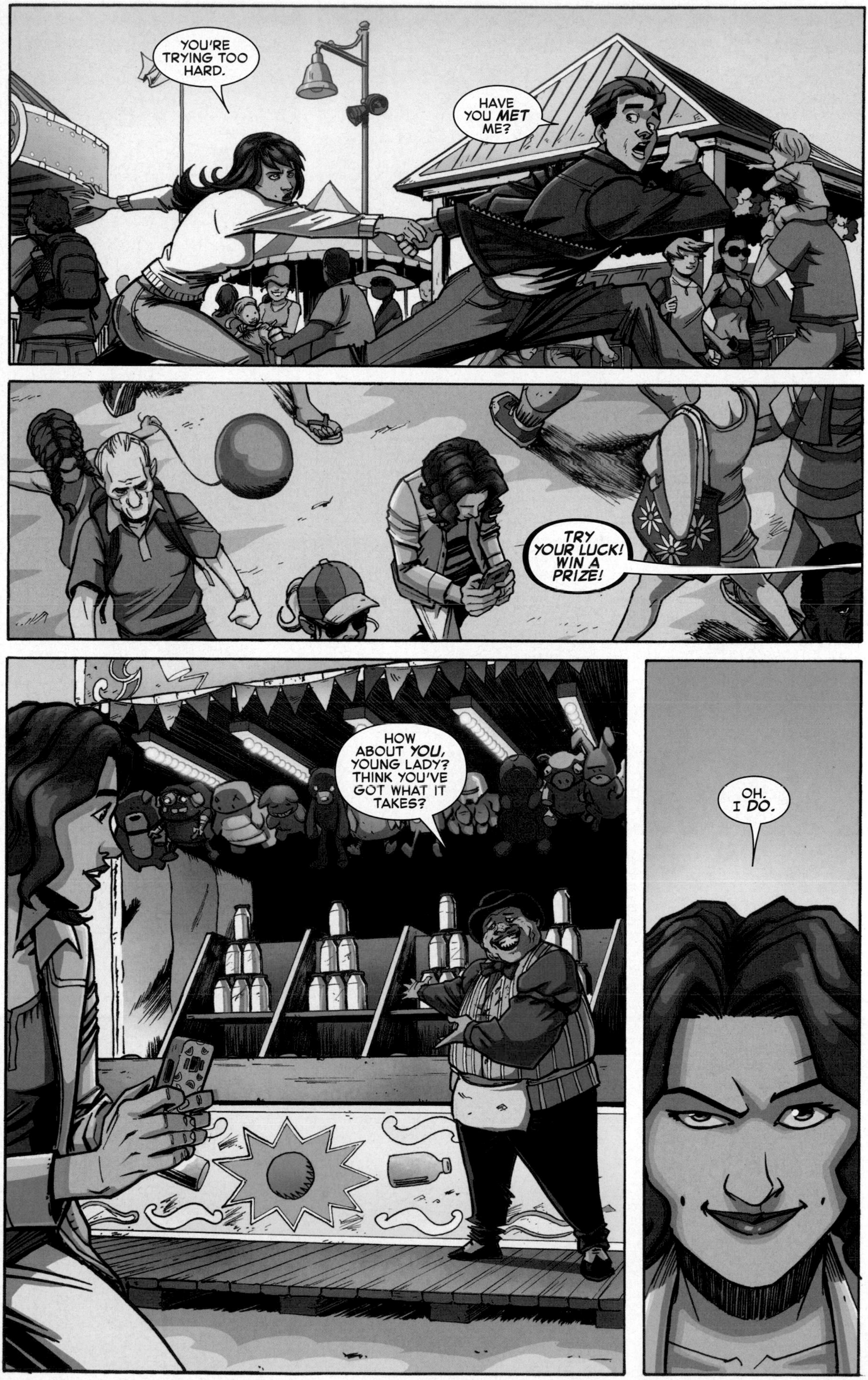
YOU'RE TRYING TOO HARD.
HAVE YOU MET ME?
TRY YOUR LUCK! WIN A PRIZE!
HOW ABOUT YOU, YOUNG LADY? THINK YOU'VE GOT WHAT IT TAKES?
OH. I DO.

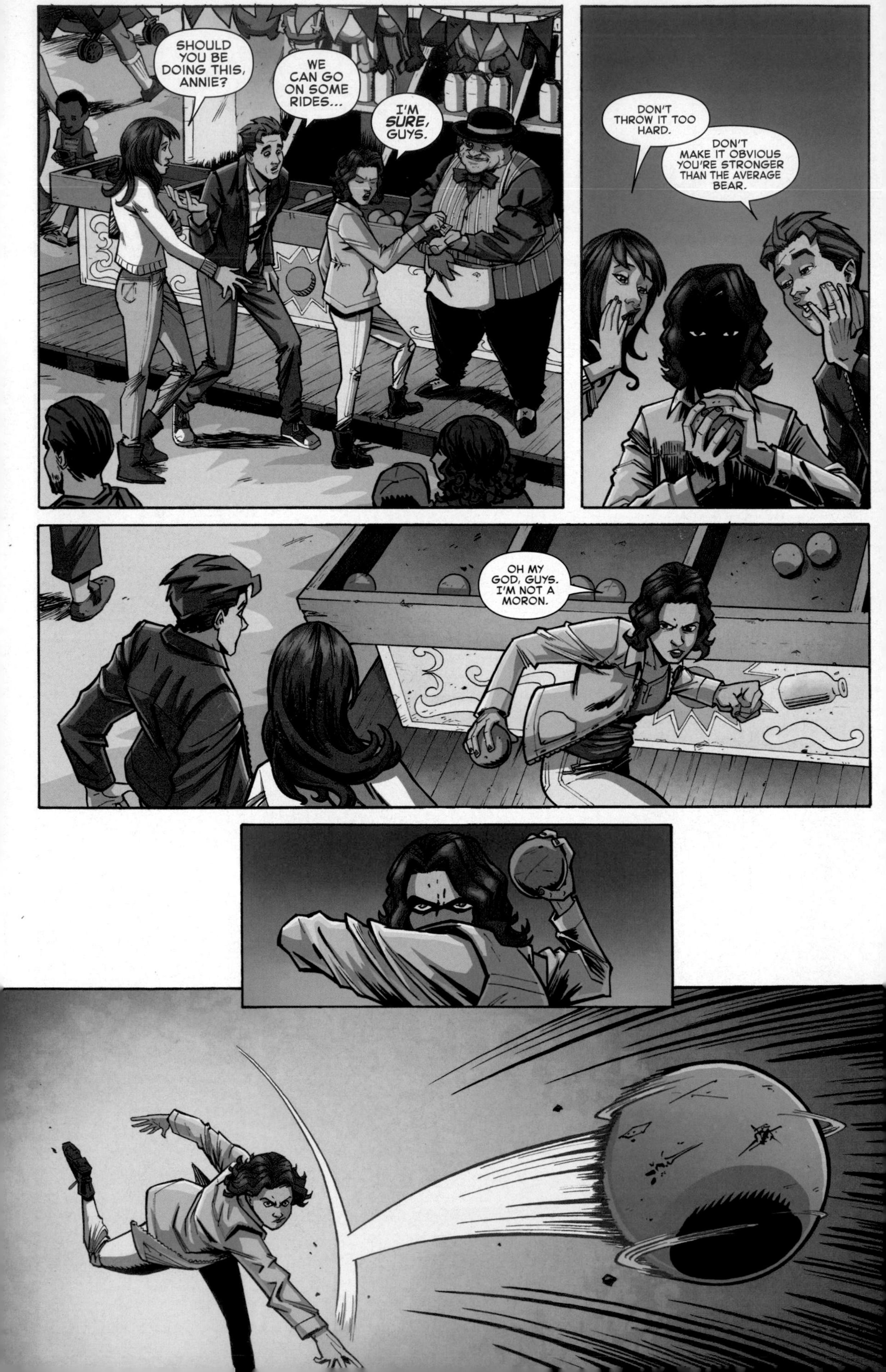
SHOULD YOU BE DOING THIS, ANNIE?
WE CAN GO ON SOME RIDES...
I'M SURE, GUYS.
DON'T THROW IT TOO HARD.
DON'T MAKE IT OBVIOUS YOU'RE STRONGER THAN THE AVERAGE BEAR.
OH MY GOD, GUYS. I'M NOT A MORON.

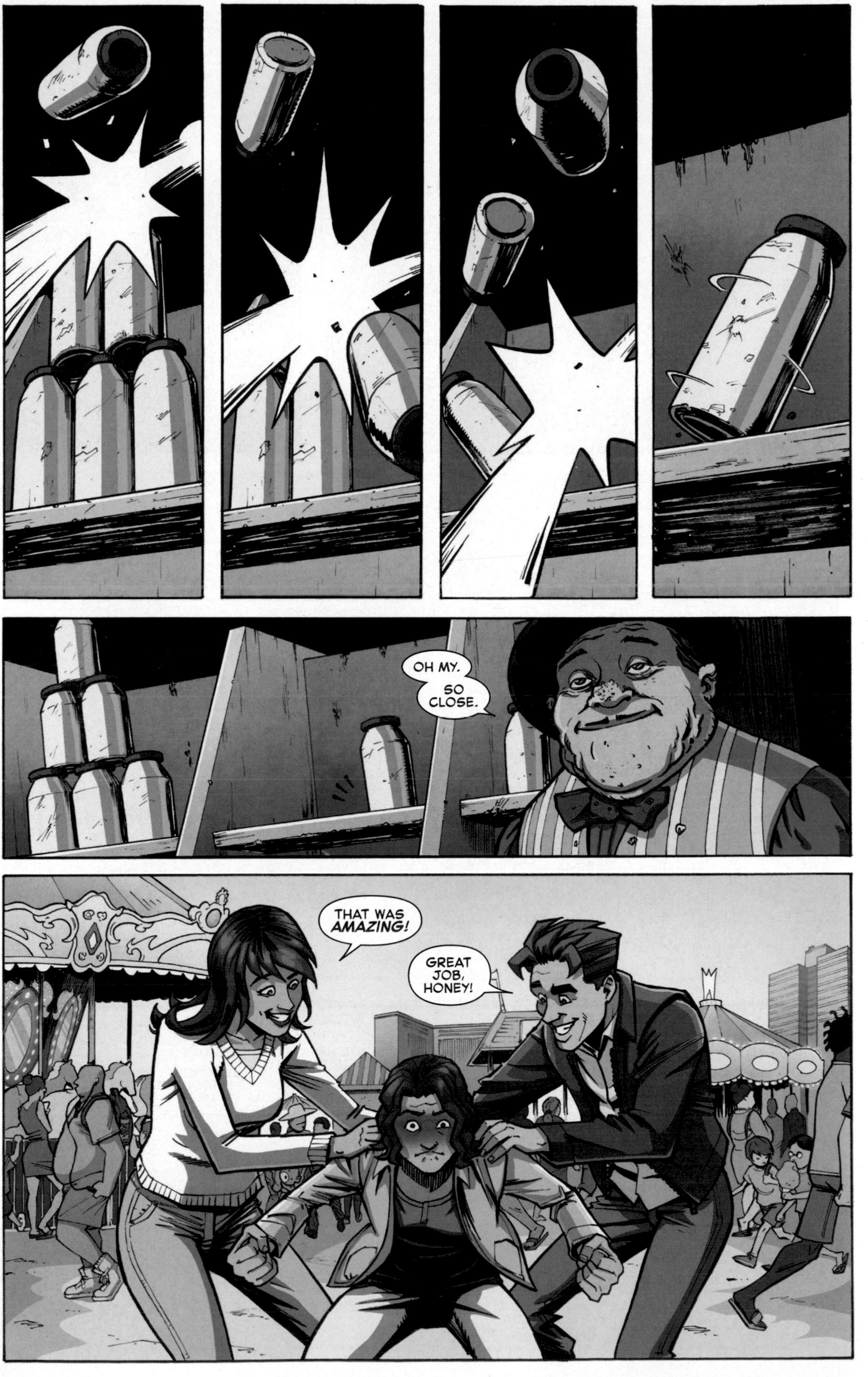
OH MY.
SO CLOSE.
THAT WAS AMAZING!
GREAT JOB, HONEY!

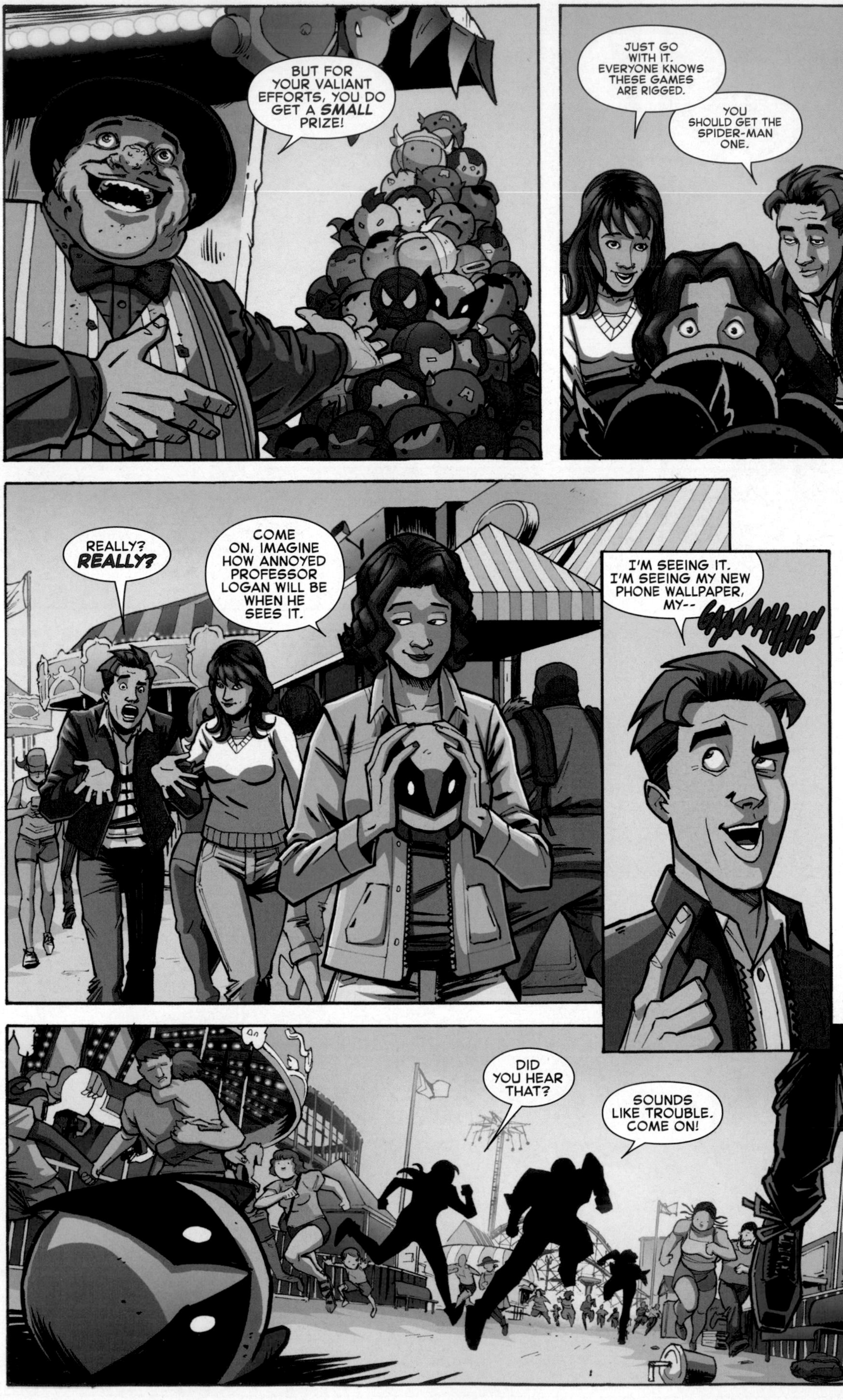

BUT FOR YOUR VALIANT EFFORTS, YOU DO GET A SMALL PRIZE!
JUST GO WITH IT. EVERYONE KNOWS THESE GAMES ARE RIGGED.
YOU SHOULD GET THE SPIDER-MAN ONE.
REALLY? REALLY?
COME ON, IMAGINE HOW ANNOYED PROFESSOR LOGAN WILL BE WHEN HE SEES IT.
I'M SEEING IT. I'M SEEING MY NEW PHONE WALLPAPER, MY--
DID YOU HEAR THAT?
SOUNDS LIKE TROUBLE. COME ON!

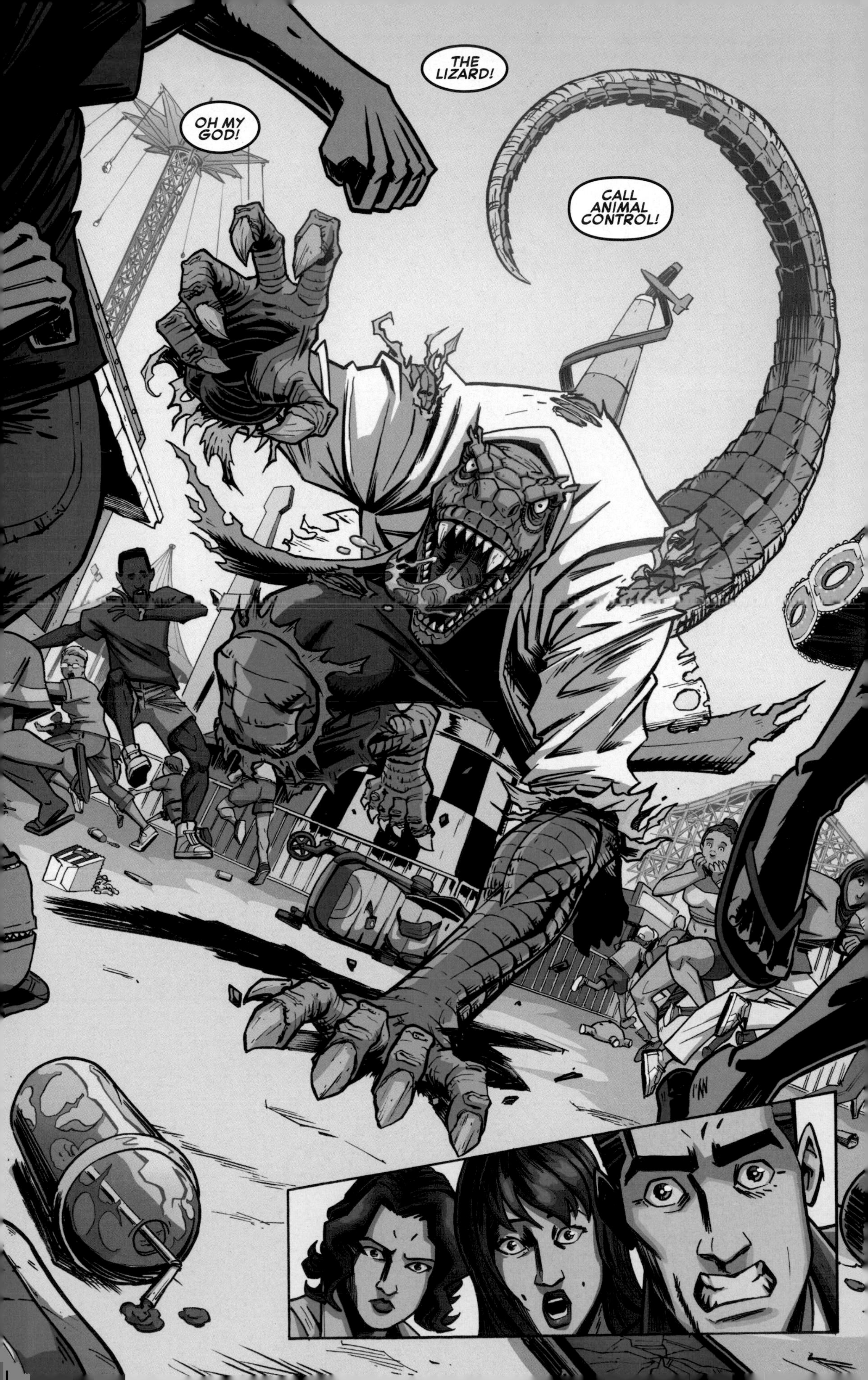
OH MY GOD!
THE LIZARD!
CALL ANIMAL CONTROL!

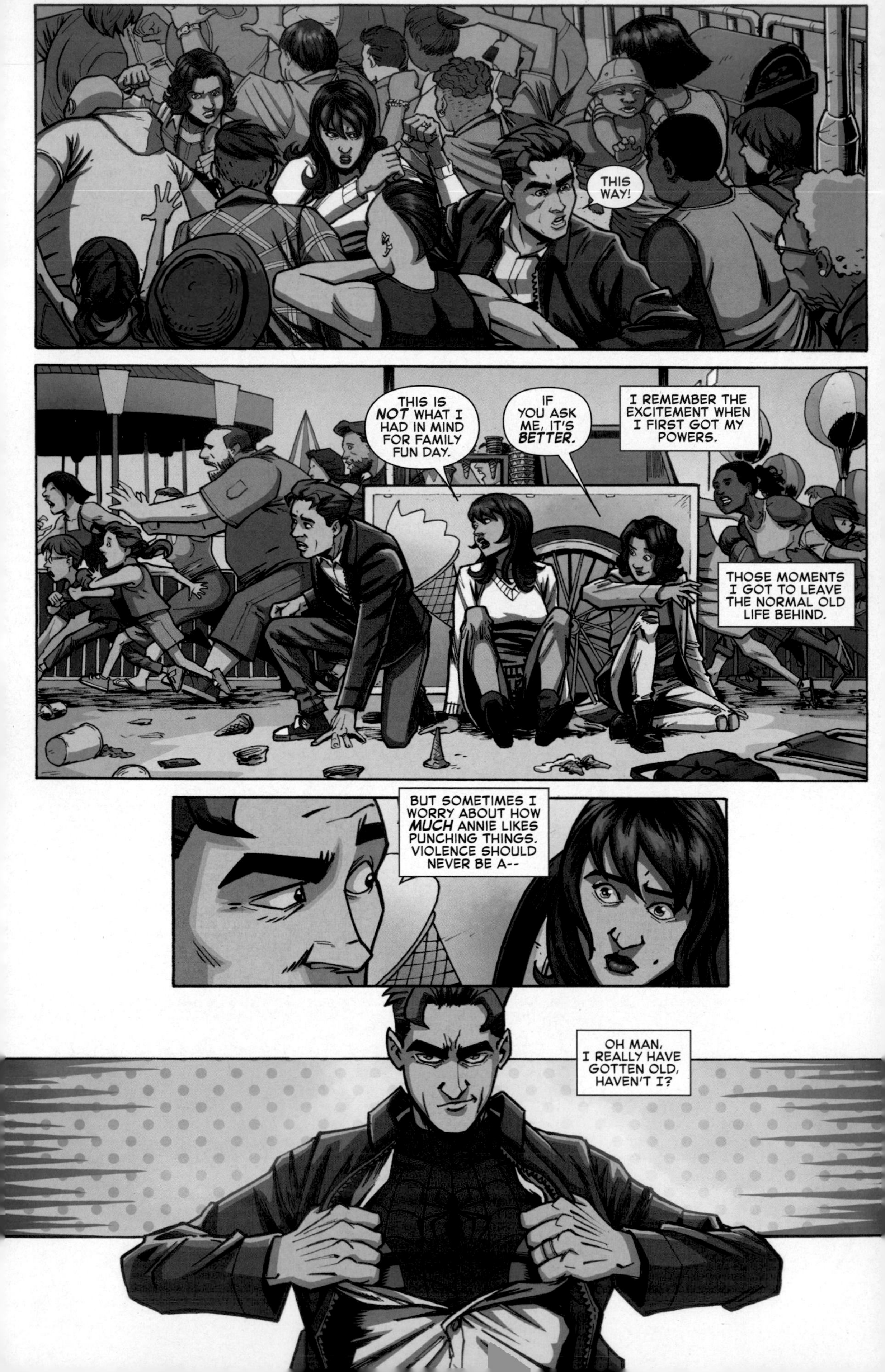
THIS WAY!
THIS IS NOT WHAT I HAD IN MIND FOR FAMILY FUN DAY.
IF YOU ASK ME, IT'S BETTER.
I REMEMBER THE EXCITEMENT WHEN I FIRST GOT MY POWERS.
THOSE MOMENTS I GOT TO LEAVE THE NORMAL OLD LIFE BEHIND.
BUT SOMETIMES I WORRY ABOUT HOW MUCH ANNIE LIKES PUNCHING THINGS. VIOLENCE SHOULD NEVER BE A--
OH MAN, I REALLY HAVE GOTTEN OLD, HAVEN'T I?

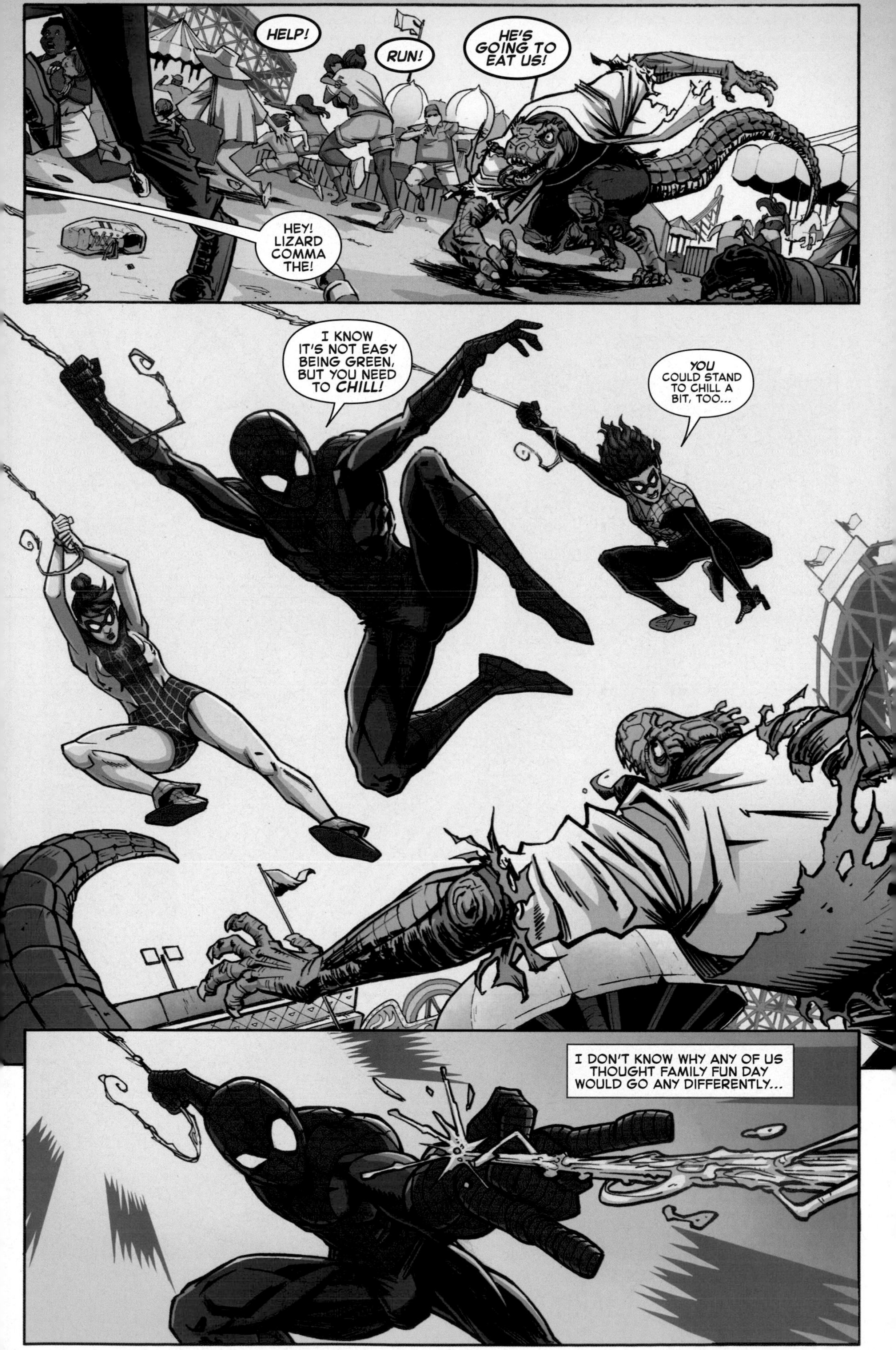
HELP!
RUN!
HE'S GOING TO EAT US!
HEY! LIZARD COMMA THE!
I KNOW IT'S NOT EASY BEING GREEN, BUT YOU NEED TO CHILL!
YOU COULD STAND TO CHILL A BIT, TOO...
I DON'T KNOW WHY ANY OF US THOUGHT FAMILY FUN DAY WOULD GO ANY DIFFERENTLY...

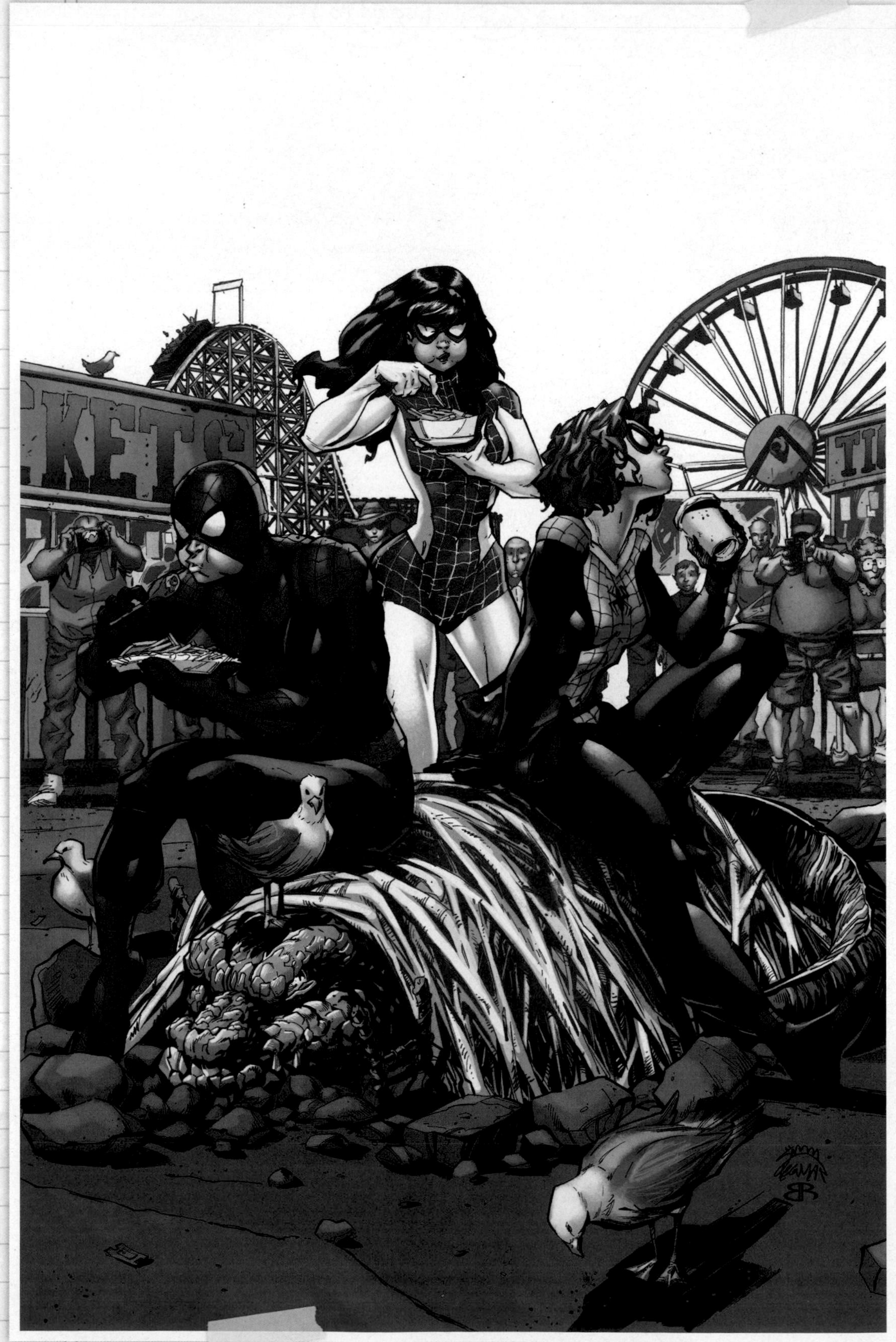

14: EIGHT YEARS LATER — PART 2

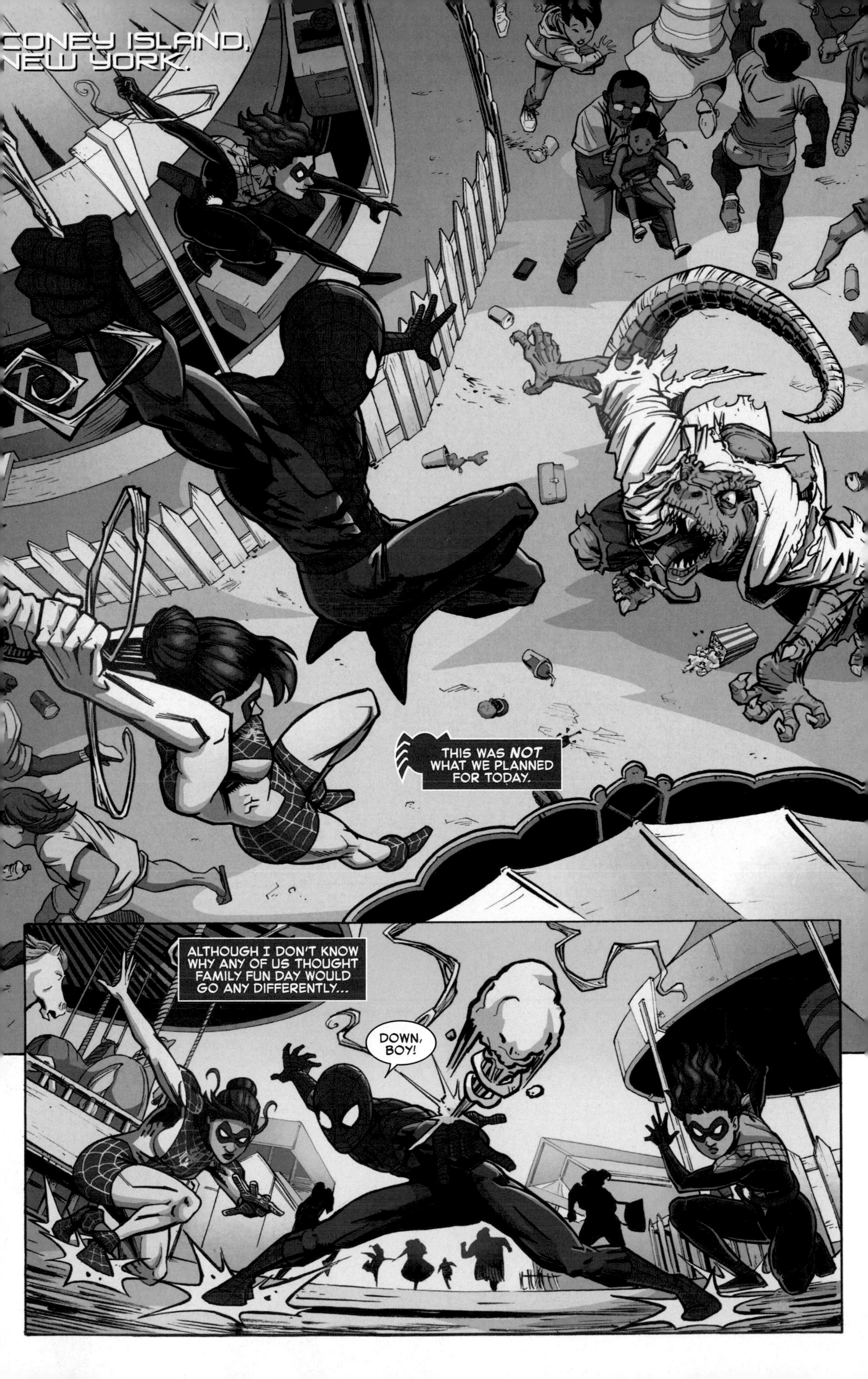
CONEY ISLAND,
NEW YORK.
THIS WAS NOT WHAT WE PLANNED FOR TODAY.
ALTHOUGH I DON'T KNOW WHY ANY OF US THOUGHT FAMILY FUN DAY WOULD GO ANY DIFFERENTLY...
DOWN, BOY!

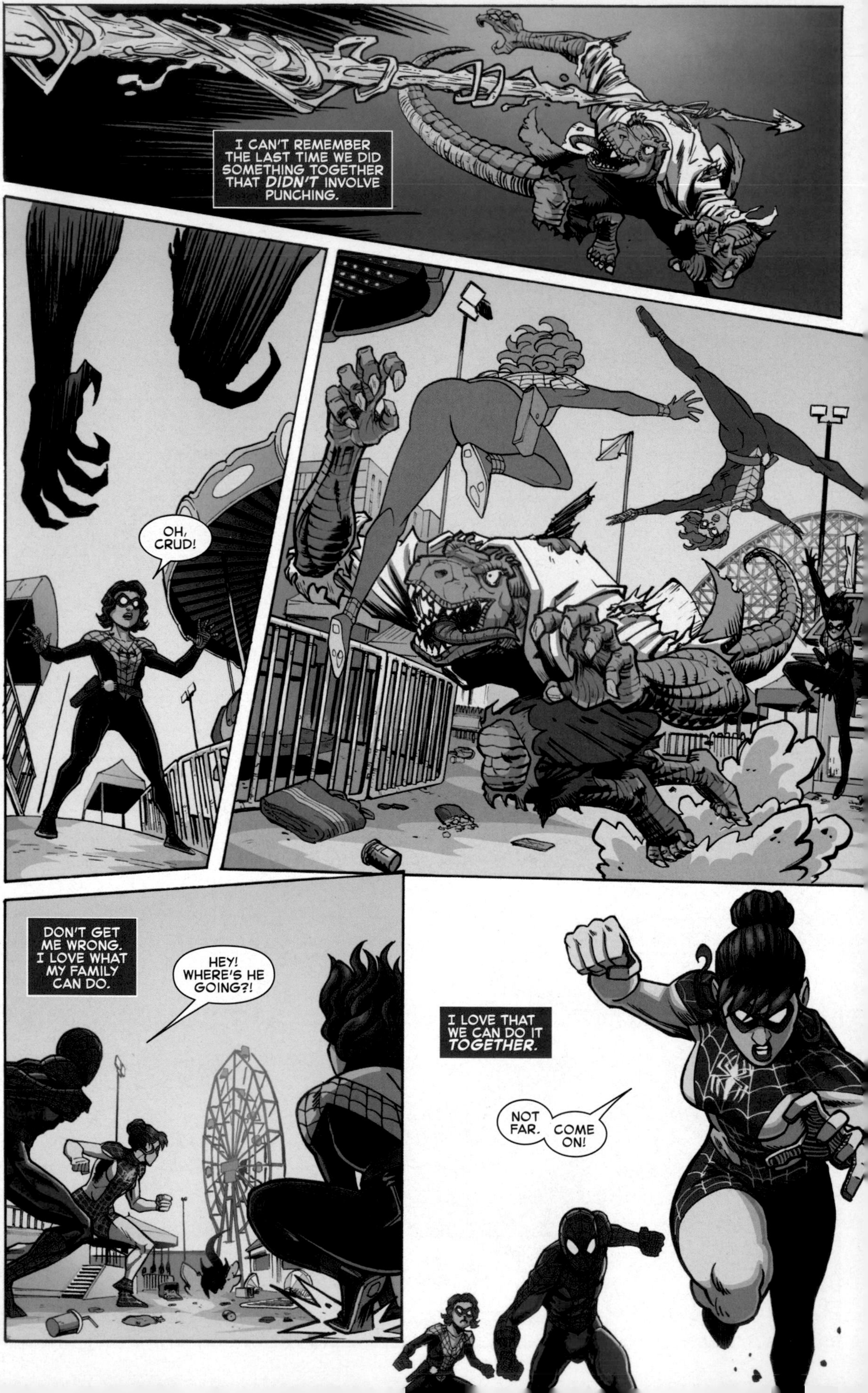
I CAN'T REMEMBER THE LAST TIME WE DID SOMETHING TOGETHER THAT *DIDN'T* INVOLVE PUNCHING.
OH, CRUD!
DON'T GET ME WRONG. I LOVE WHAT MY FAMILY CAN DO.
HEY! WHERE'S HE GOING?!
I LOVE THAT WE CAN DO IT *TOGETHER*.
NOT FAR.
COME ON!

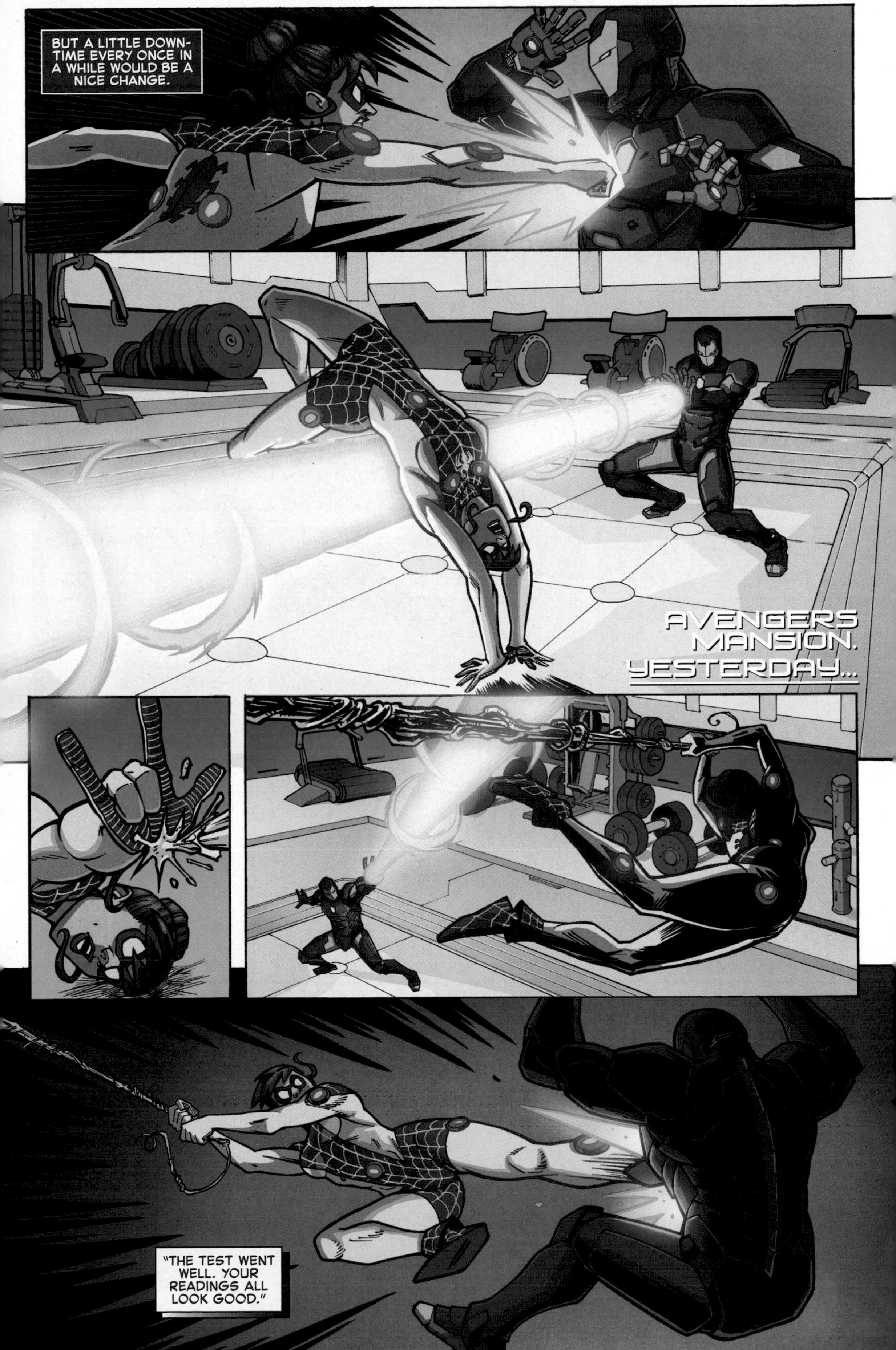
BUT A LITTLE DOWN-TIME EVERY ONCE IN A WHILE WOULD BE A NICE CHANGE.
AVENGERS MANSION. YESTERDAY...
"THE TEST WENT WELL. YOUR READINGS ALL LOOK GOOD."

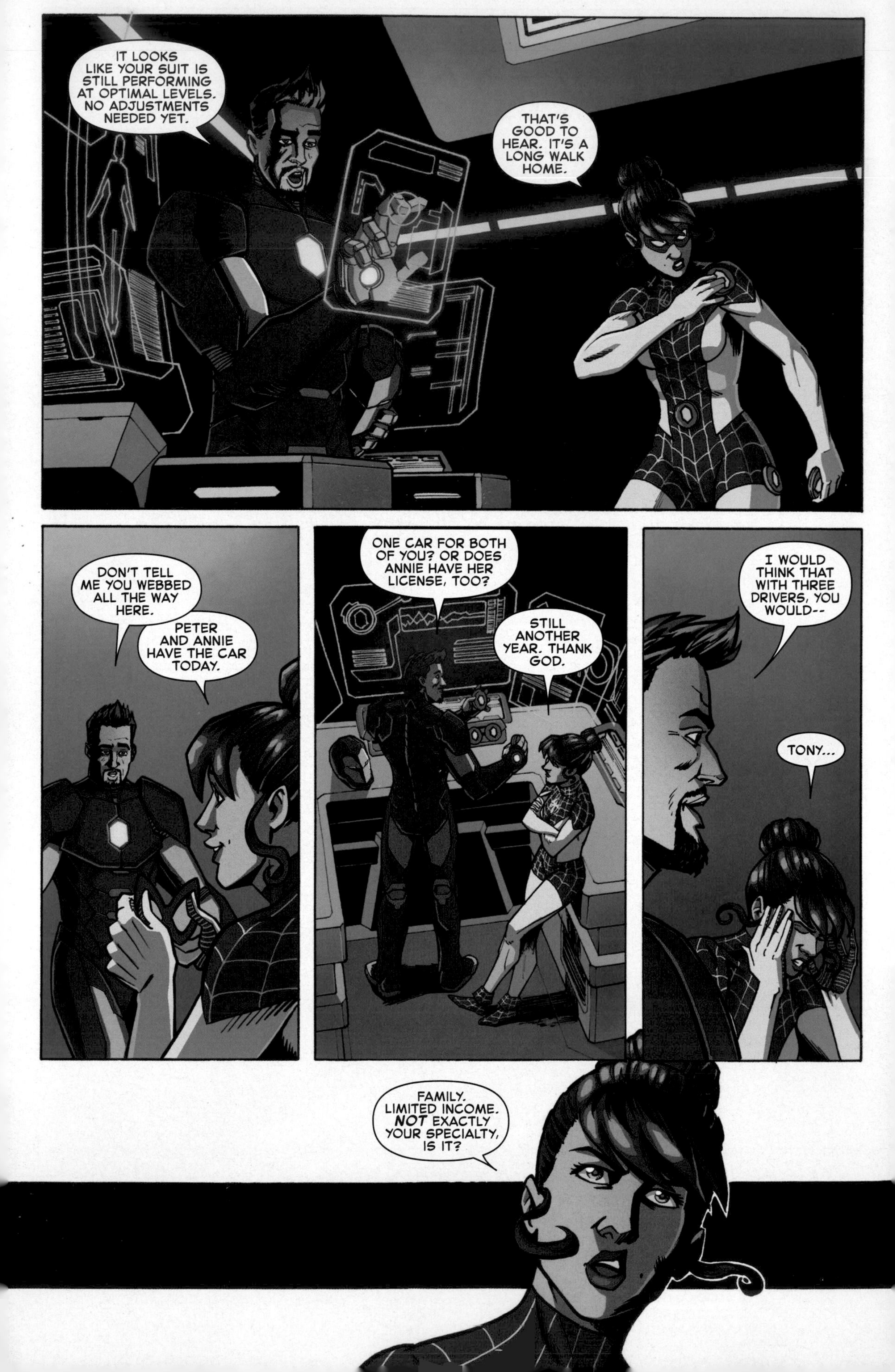
IT LOOKS LIKE YOUR SUIT IS STILL PERFORMING AT OPTIMAL LEVELS. NO ADJUSTMENTS NEEDED YET.
THAT'S GOOD TO HEAR. IT'S A LONG WALK HOME.
DON'T TELL ME YOU WEBBED ALL THE WAY HERE.
PETER AND ANNIE HAVE THE CAR TODAY.
ONE CAR FOR BOTH OF YOU? OR DOES ANNIE HAVE HER LICENSE, TOO?
STILL ANOTHER YEAR. THANK GOD.
I WOULD THINK THAT WITH THREE DRIVERS, YOU WOULD--
TONY...
FAMILY. LIMITED INCOME. *NOT* EXACTLY YOUR SPECIALTY, IS IT?

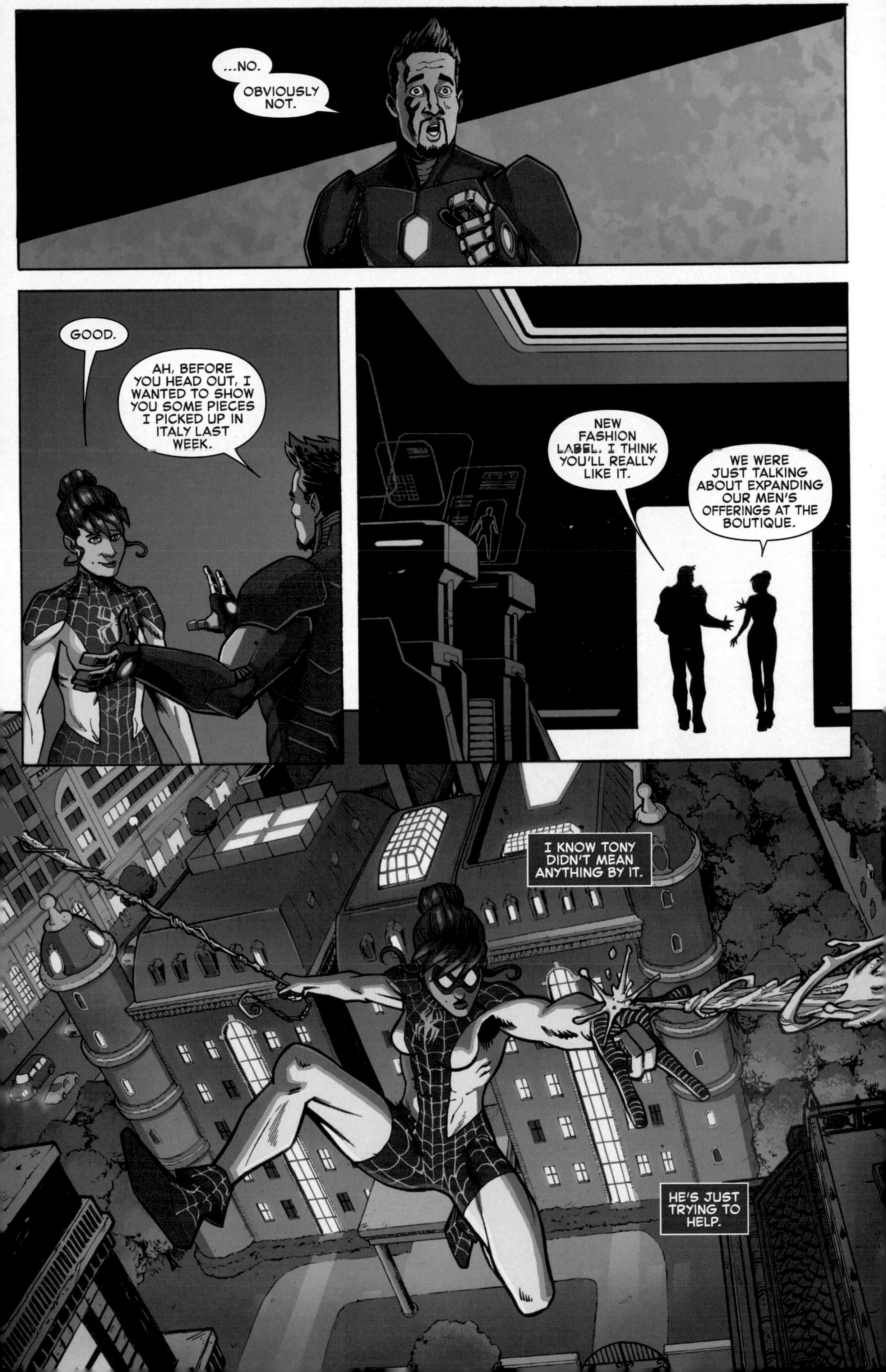
...NO.
OBVIOUSLY NOT.
GOOD.
AH, BEFORE YOU HEAD OUT, I WANTED TO SHOW YOU SOME PIECES I PICKED UP IN ITALY LAST WEEK.
NEW FASHION LABEL. I THINK YOU'LL REALLY LIKE IT.
WE WERE JUST TALKING ABOUT EXPANDING OUR MEN'S OFFERINGS AT THE BOUTIQUE.
I KNOW TONY DIDN'T MEAN ANYTHING BY IT.
HE'S JUST TRYING TO HELP.

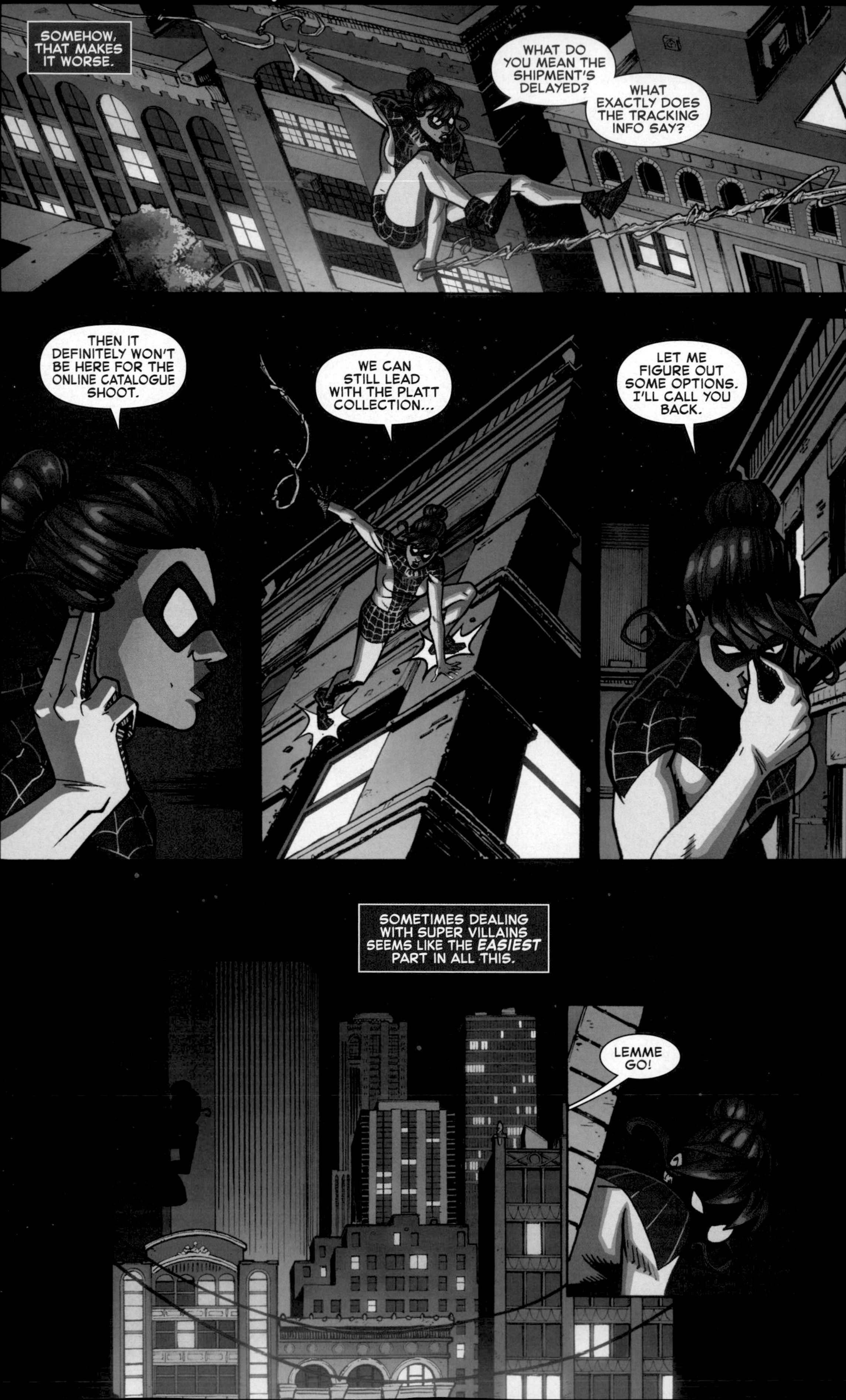
SOMEHOW, THAT MAKES IT WORSE.
WHAT DO YOU MEAN THE SHIPMENT'S DELAYED?
WHAT EXACTLY DOES THE TRACKING INFO SAY?
THEN IT DEFINITELY WON'T BE HERE FOR THE ONLINE CATALOGUE SHOOT.
WE CAN STILL LEAD WITH THE PLATT COLLECTION...
LET ME FIGURE OUT SOME OPTIONS. I'LL CALL YOU BACK.
SOMETIMES DEALING WITH SUPER VILLAINS SEEMS LIKE THE EASIEST PART IN ALL THIS.
LEMME GO!

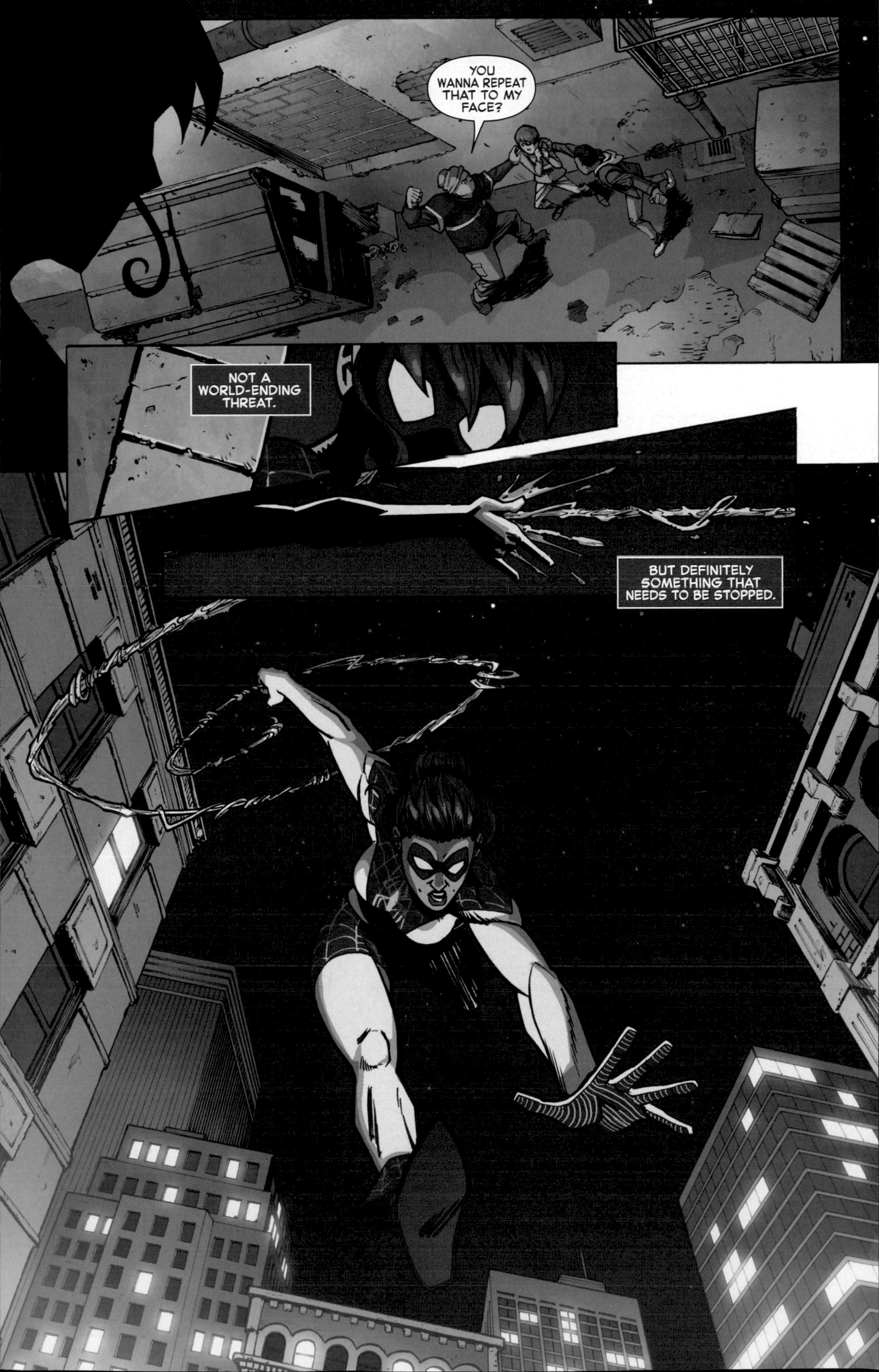
YOU WANNA REPEAT THAT TO MY FACE?
NOT A WORLD-ENDING THREAT.
BUT DEFINITELY SOMETHING THAT NEEDS TO BE STOPPED.

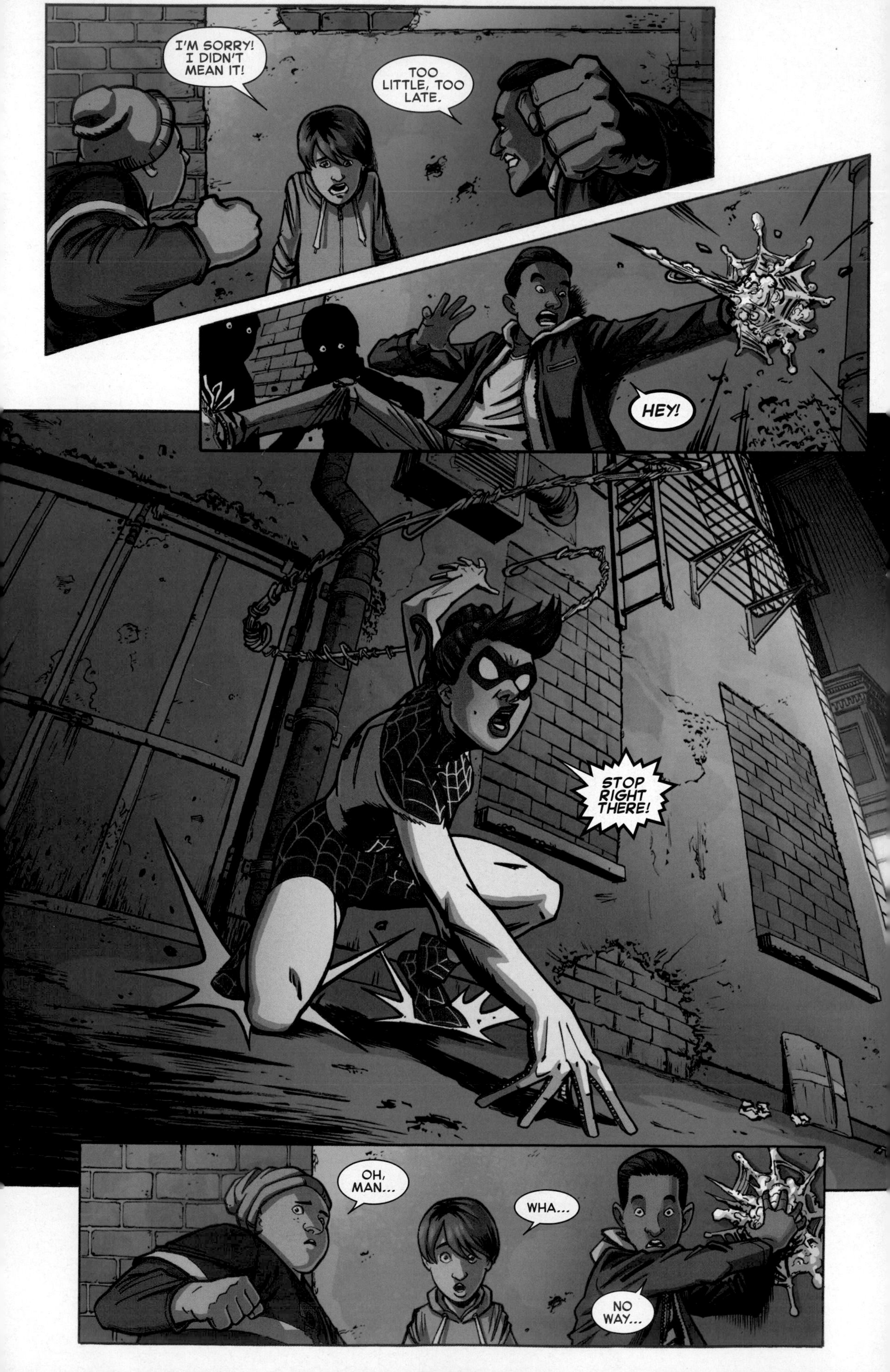

I'M SORRY! I DIDN'T MEAN IT!
TOO LITTLE, TOO LATE.
HEY!
STOP RIGHT THERE!
OH, MAN...
WHA...
NO WAY...

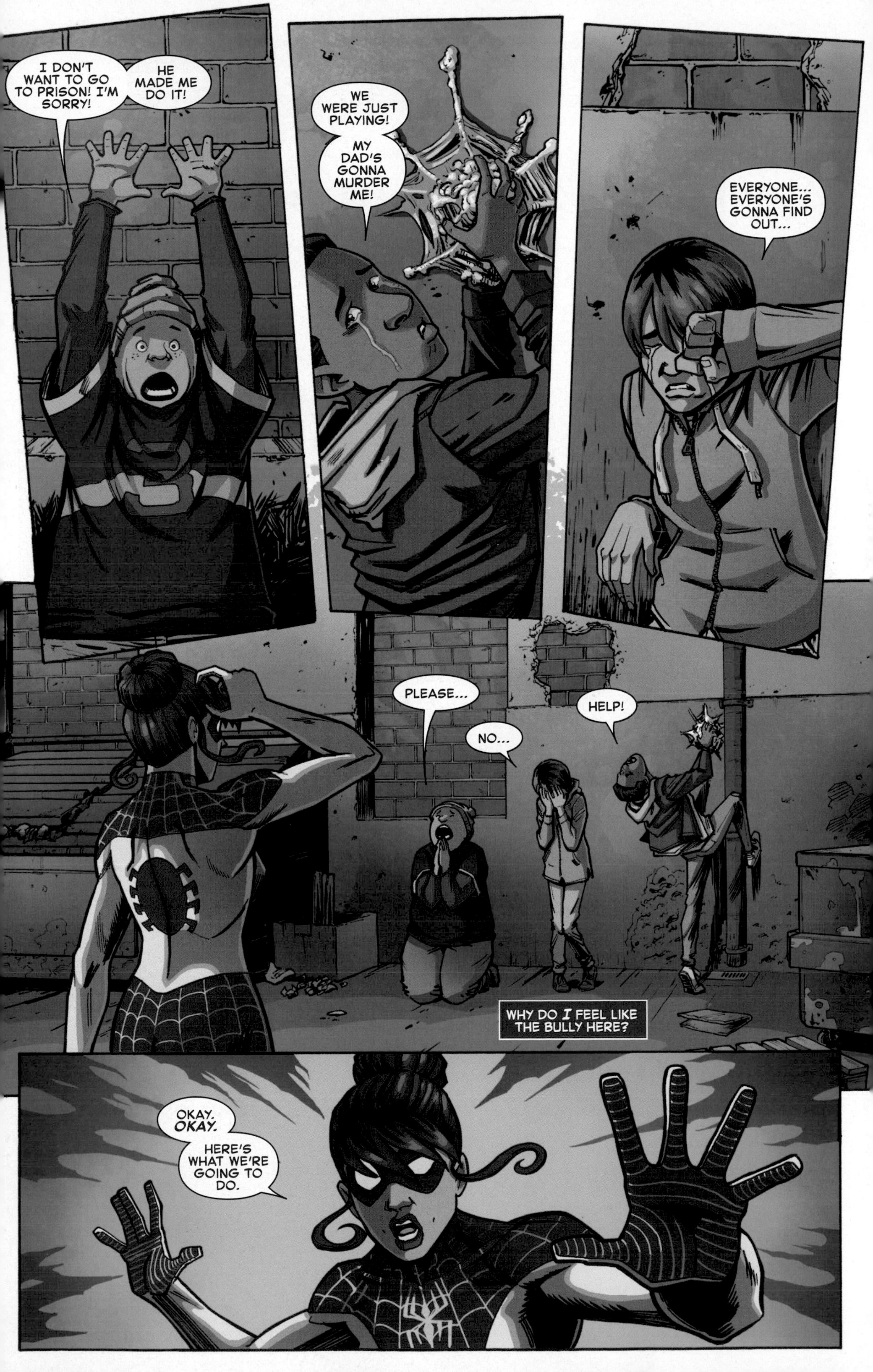
I DON'T WANT TO GO TO PRISON! I'M SORRY!
HE MADE ME DO IT!
WE WERE JUST PLAYING!
MY DAD'S GONNA MURDER ME!
EVERYONE... EVERYONE'S GONNA FIND OUT...
PLEASE...
NO...
HELP!
WHY DO *I* FEEL LIKE THE BULLY HERE?
OKAY. ***OKAY.***
HERE'S WHAT WE'RE GOING TO DO.

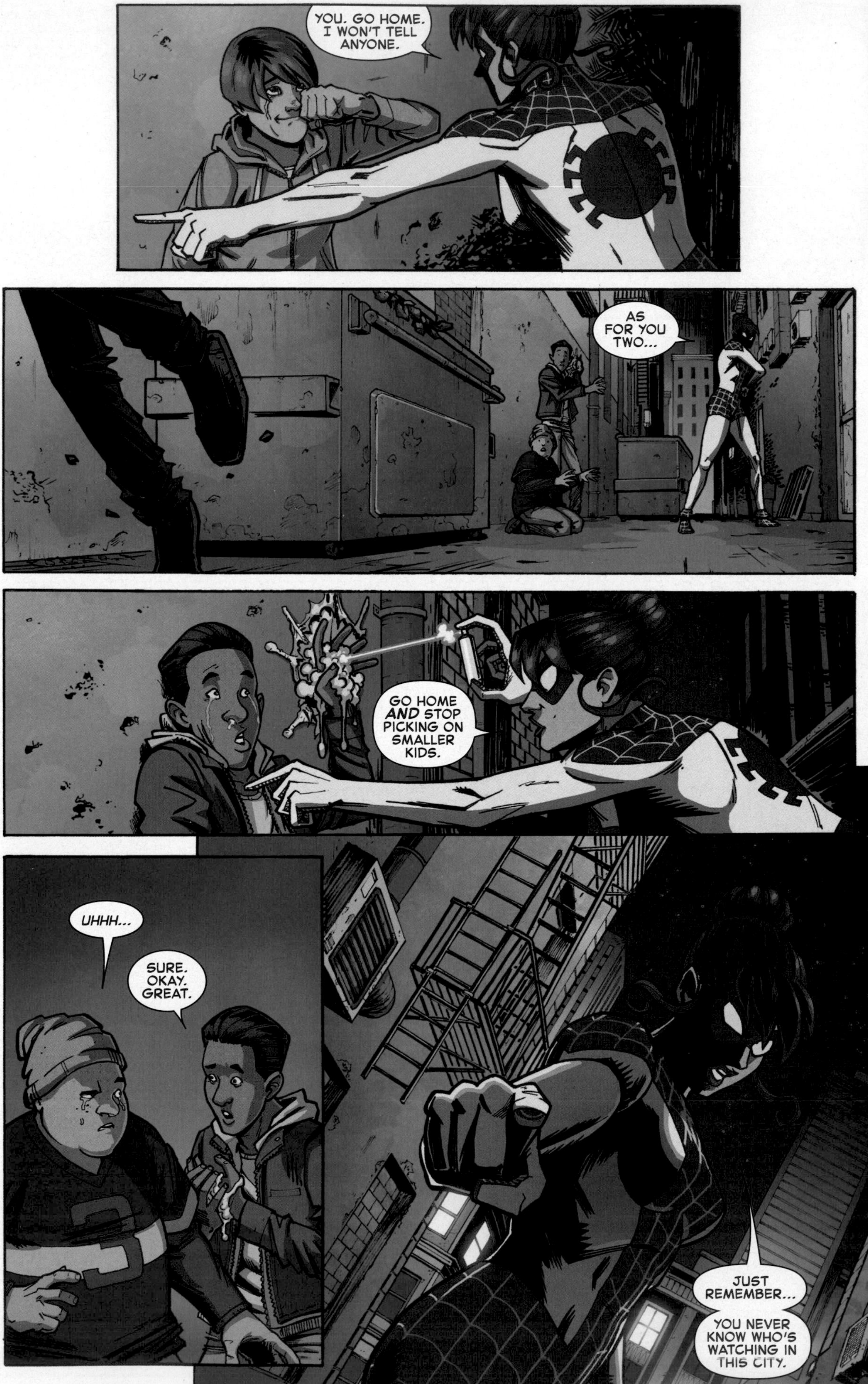
YOU. GO HOME. I WON'T TELL ANYONE.
AS FOR YOU TWO...
GO HOME AND STOP PICKING ON SMALLER KIDS.
UHHH...
SURE. OKAY. GREAT.
JUST REMEMBER...
YOU NEVER KNOW WHO'S WATCHING IN THIS CITY.

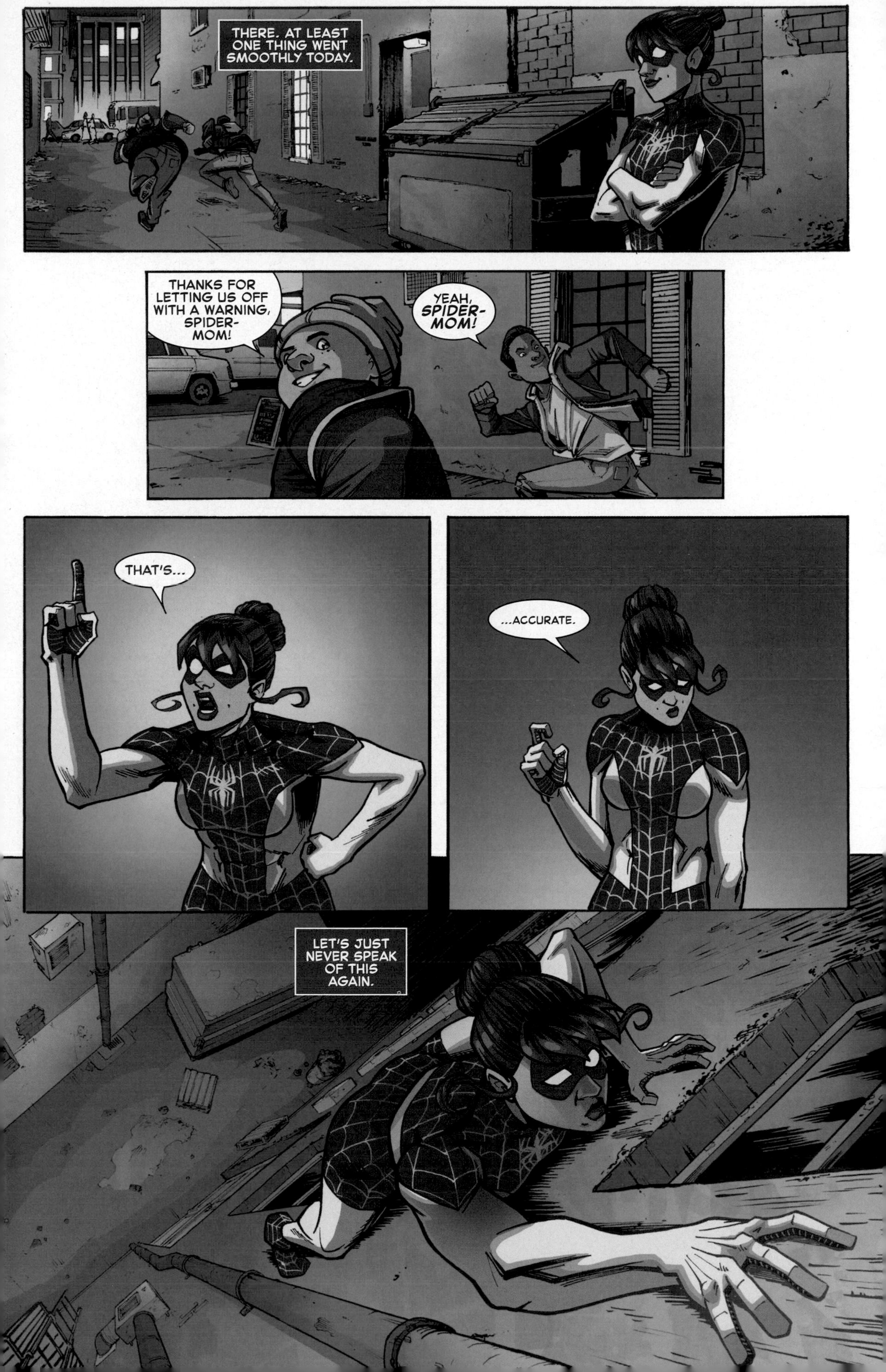

THERE. AT LEAST ONE THING WENT SMOOTHLY TODAY.
THANKS FOR LETTING US OFF WITH A WARNING, SPIDER-MOM!
YEAH, *SPIDER-MOM!*
THAT'S...
...ACCURATE.
LET'S JUST NEVER SPEAK OF THIS AGAIN.

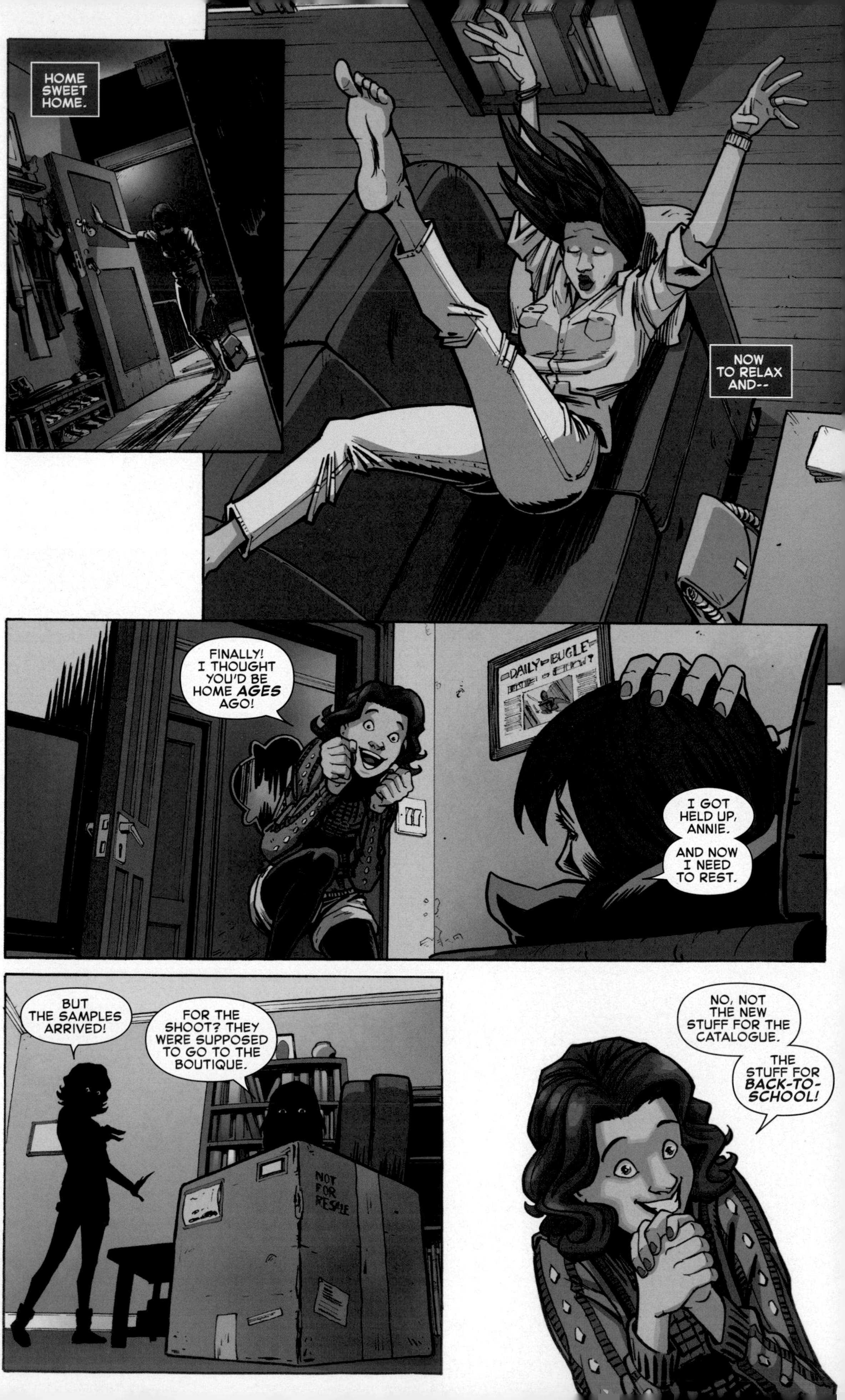
HOME SWEET HOME.
NOW TO RELAX AND--
FINALLY! I THOUGHT YOU'D BE HOME AGES AGO!
DAILY BUGLE
I GOT HELD UP, ANNIE.
AND NOW I NEED TO REST.
BUT THE SAMPLES ARRIVED!
FOR THE SHOOT? THEY WERE SUPPOSED TO GO TO THE BOUTIQUE.
NOT FOR RESALE
NO, NOT THE NEW STUFF FOR THE CATALOGUE.
THE STUFF FOR BACK-TO-SCHOOL!

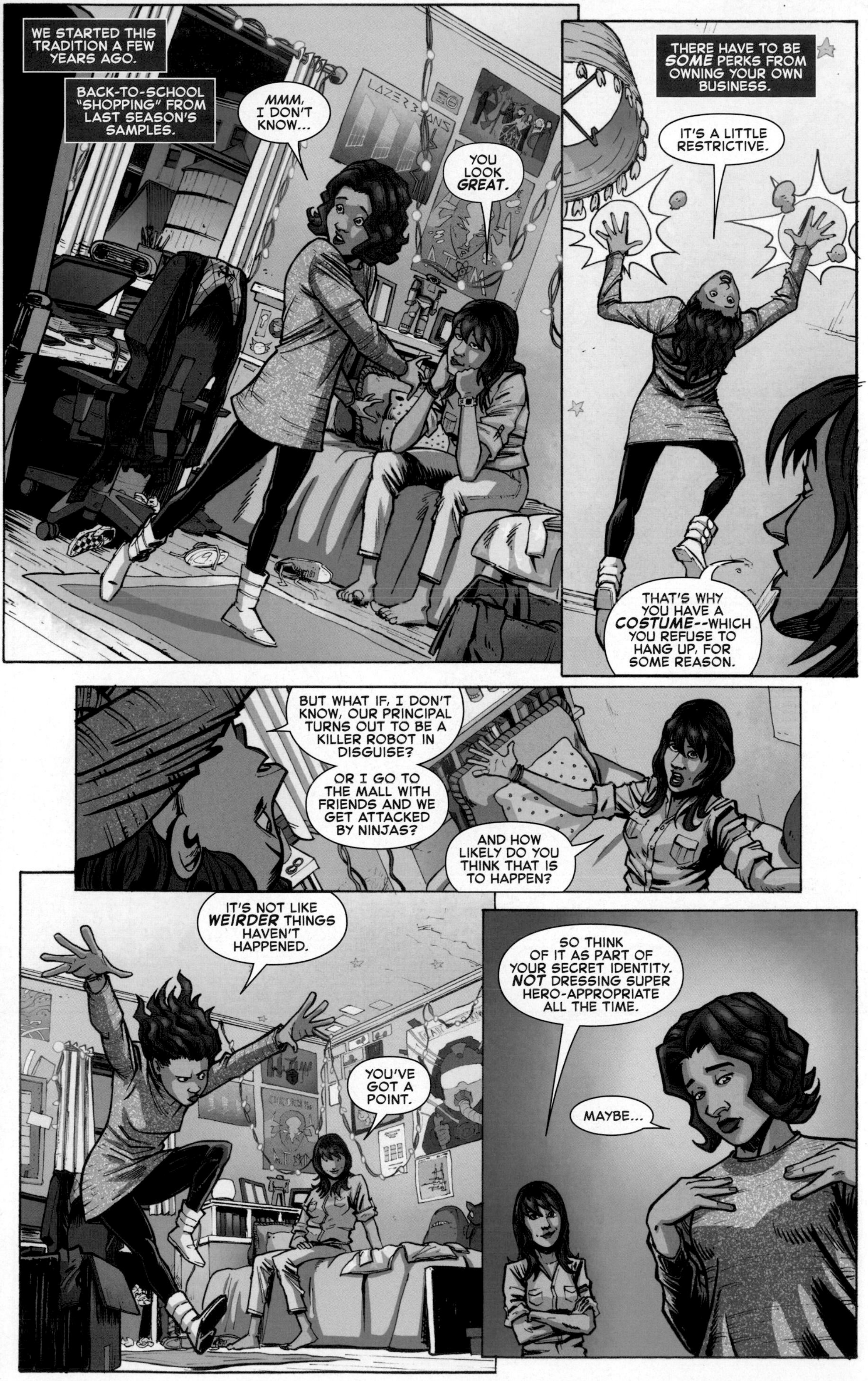
WE STARTED THIS TRADITION A FEW YEARS AGO.
BACK-TO-SCHOOL "SHOPPING" FROM LAST SEASON'S SAMPLES.
MMM, I DON'T KNOW...
YOU LOOK GREAT.
THERE HAVE TO BE SOME PERKS FROM OWNING YOUR OWN BUSINESS.
IT'S A LITTLE RESTRICTIVE.
THAT'S WHY YOU HAVE A COSTUME--WHICH YOU REFUSE TO HANG UP, FOR SOME REASON.
BUT WHAT IF, I DON'T KNOW, OUR PRINCIPAL TURNS OUT TO BE A KILLER ROBOT IN DISGUISE?
OR I GO TO THE MALL WITH FRIENDS AND WE GET ATTACKED BY NINJAS?
AND HOW LIKELY DO YOU THINK THAT IS TO HAPPEN?
IT'S NOT LIKE WEIRDER THINGS HAVEN'T HAPPENED.
YOU'VE GOT A POINT.
SO THINK OF IT AS PART OF YOUR SECRET IDENTITY. NOT DRESSING SUPER HERO-APPROPRIATE ALL THE TIME.
MAYBE...

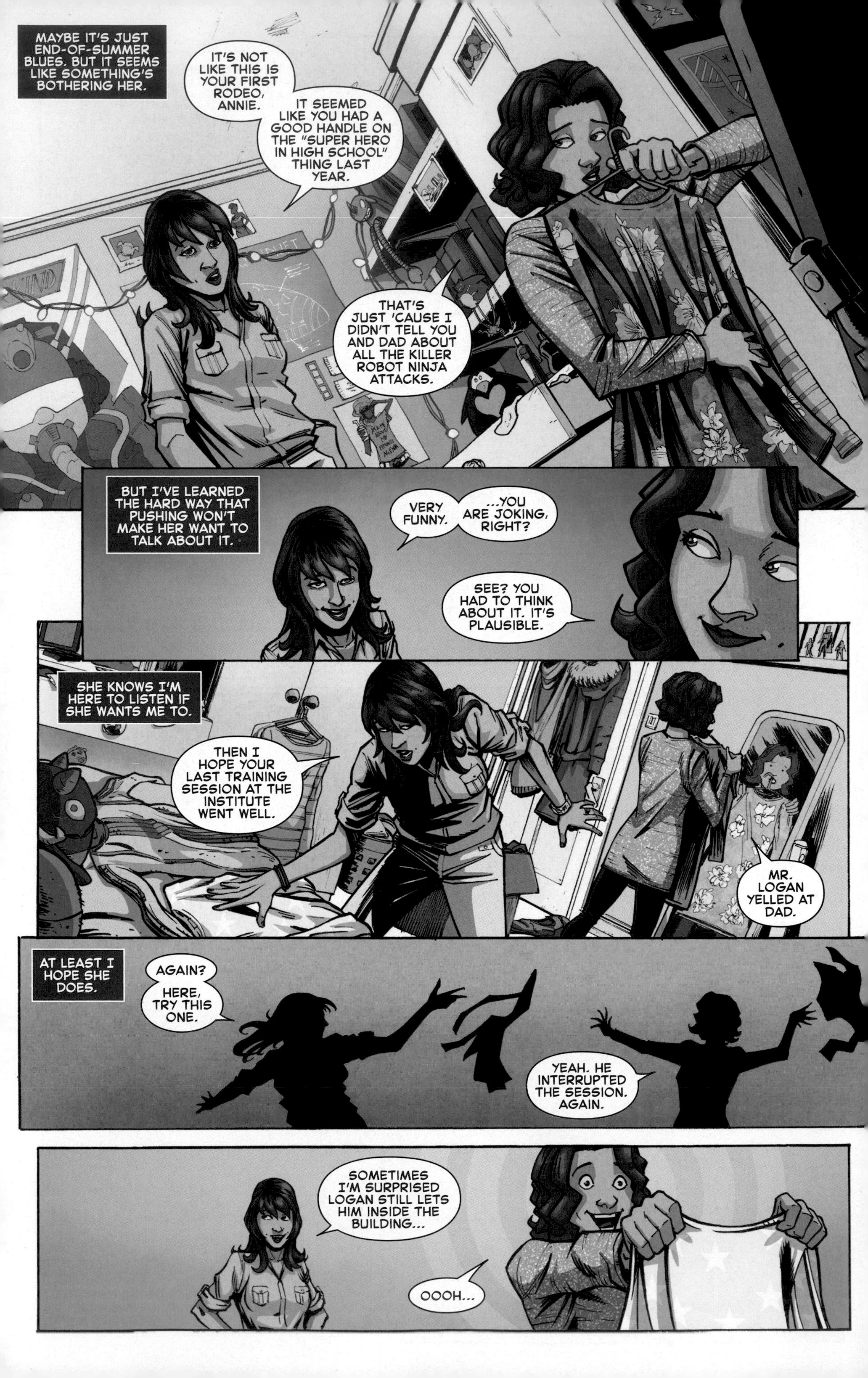
MAYBE IT'S JUST END-OF-SUMMER BLUES. BUT IT SEEMS LIKE SOMETHING'S BOTHERING HER.
IT'S NOT LIKE THIS IS YOUR FIRST RODEO, ANNIE.
IT SEEMED LIKE YOU HAD A GOOD HANDLE ON THE "SUPER HERO IN HIGH SCHOOL" THING LAST YEAR.
THAT'S JUST 'CAUSE I DIDN'T TELL YOU AND DAD ABOUT ALL THE KILLER ROBOT NINJA ATTACKS.
BUT I'VE LEARNED THE HARD WAY THAT PUSHING WON'T MAKE HER WANT TO TALK ABOUT IT.
VERY FUNNY.
...YOU ARE JOKING, RIGHT?
SEE? YOU HAD TO THINK ABOUT IT. IT'S PLAUSIBLE.
SHE KNOWS I'M HERE TO LISTEN IF SHE WANTS ME TO.
THEN I HOPE YOUR LAST TRAINING SESSION AT THE INSTITUTE WENT WELL.
MR. LOGAN YELLED AT DAD.
AT LEAST I HOPE SHE DOES.
AGAIN?
HERE, TRY THIS ONE.
YEAH. HE INTERRUPTED THE SESSION. AGAIN.
SOMETIMES I'M SURPRISED LOGAN STILL LETS HIM INSIDE THE BUILDING...
OOOH...

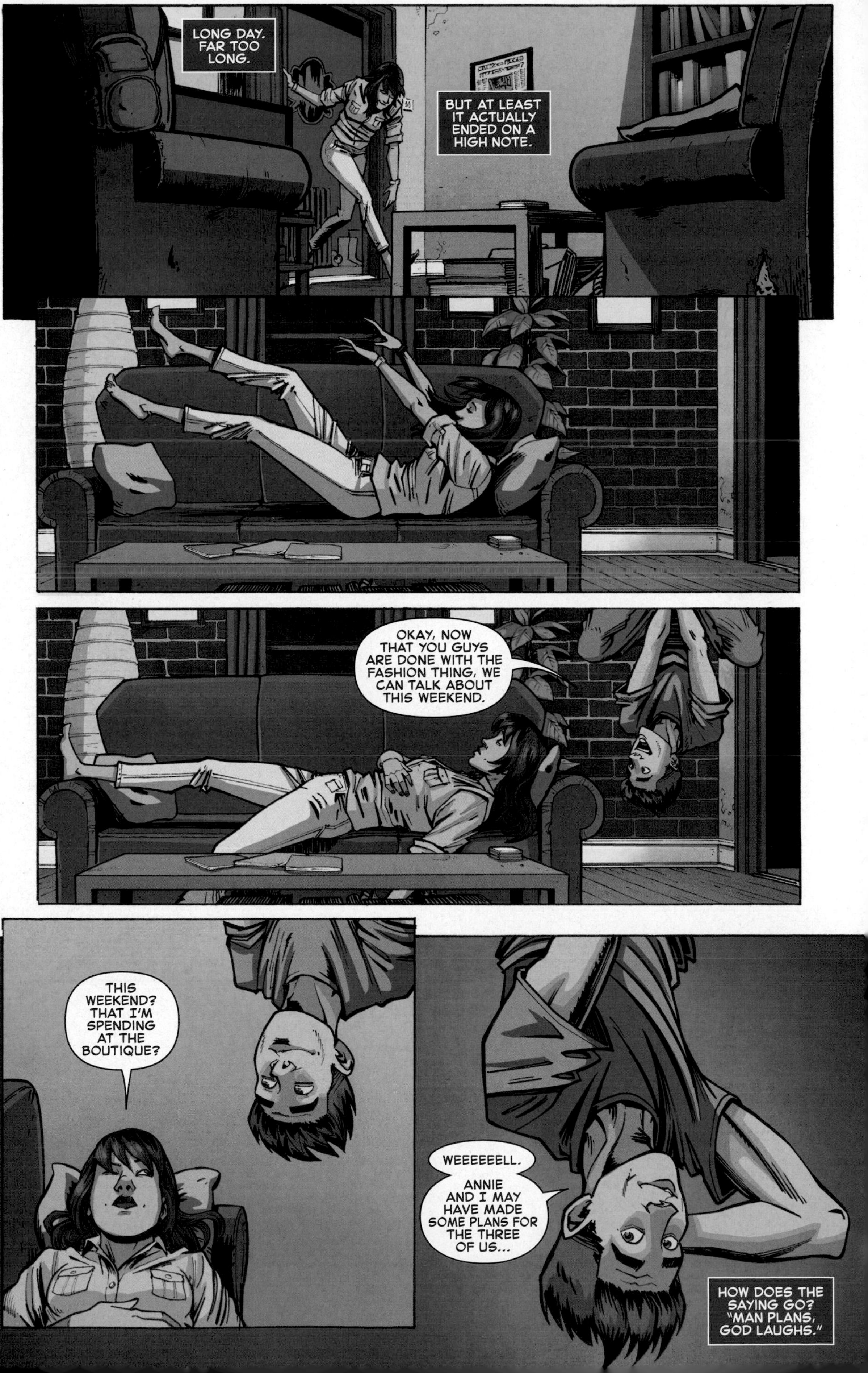
LONG DAY. FAR TOO LONG.
BUT AT LEAST IT ACTUALLY ENDED ON A HIGH NOTE.
OKAY, NOW THAT YOU GUYS ARE DONE WITH THE FASHION THING, WE CAN TALK ABOUT THIS WEEKEND.
THIS WEEKEND? THAT I'M SPENDING AT THE BOUTIQUE?
WEEEEEELL.
ANNIE AND I MAY HAVE MADE SOME PLANS FOR THE THREE OF US...
HOW DOES THE SAYING GO? "MAN PLANS, GOD LAUGHS."

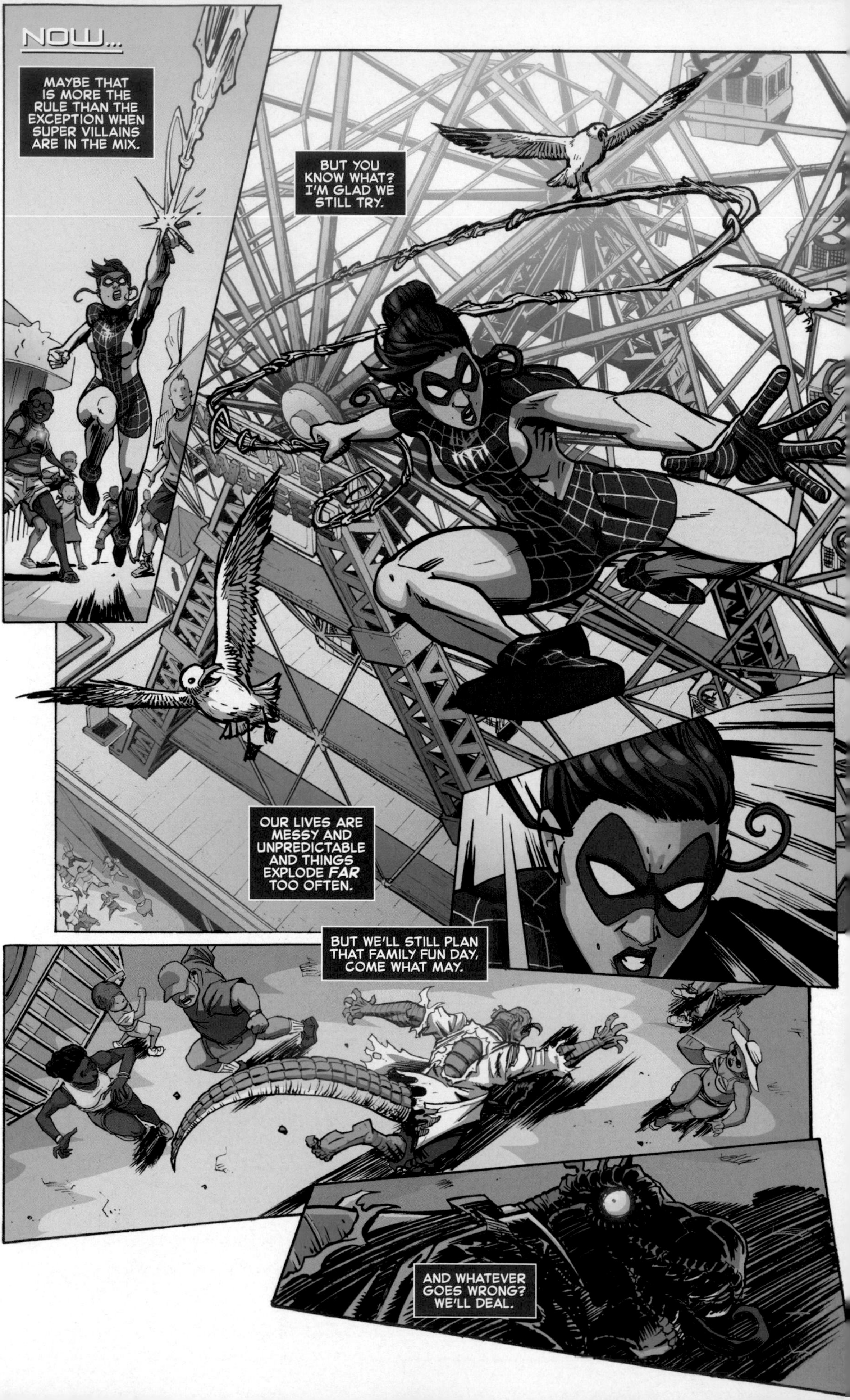
NOW...
MAYBE THAT IS MORE THE RULE THAN THE EXCEPTION WHEN SUPER VILLAINS ARE IN THE MIX.
BUT YOU KNOW WHAT? I'M GLAD WE STILL TRY.
OUR LIVES ARE MESSY AND UNPREDICTABLE AND THINGS EXPLODE FAR TOO OFTEN.
BUT WE'LL STILL PLAN THAT FAMILY FUN DAY, COME WHAT MAY.
AND WHATEVER GOES WRONG? WE'LL DEAL.

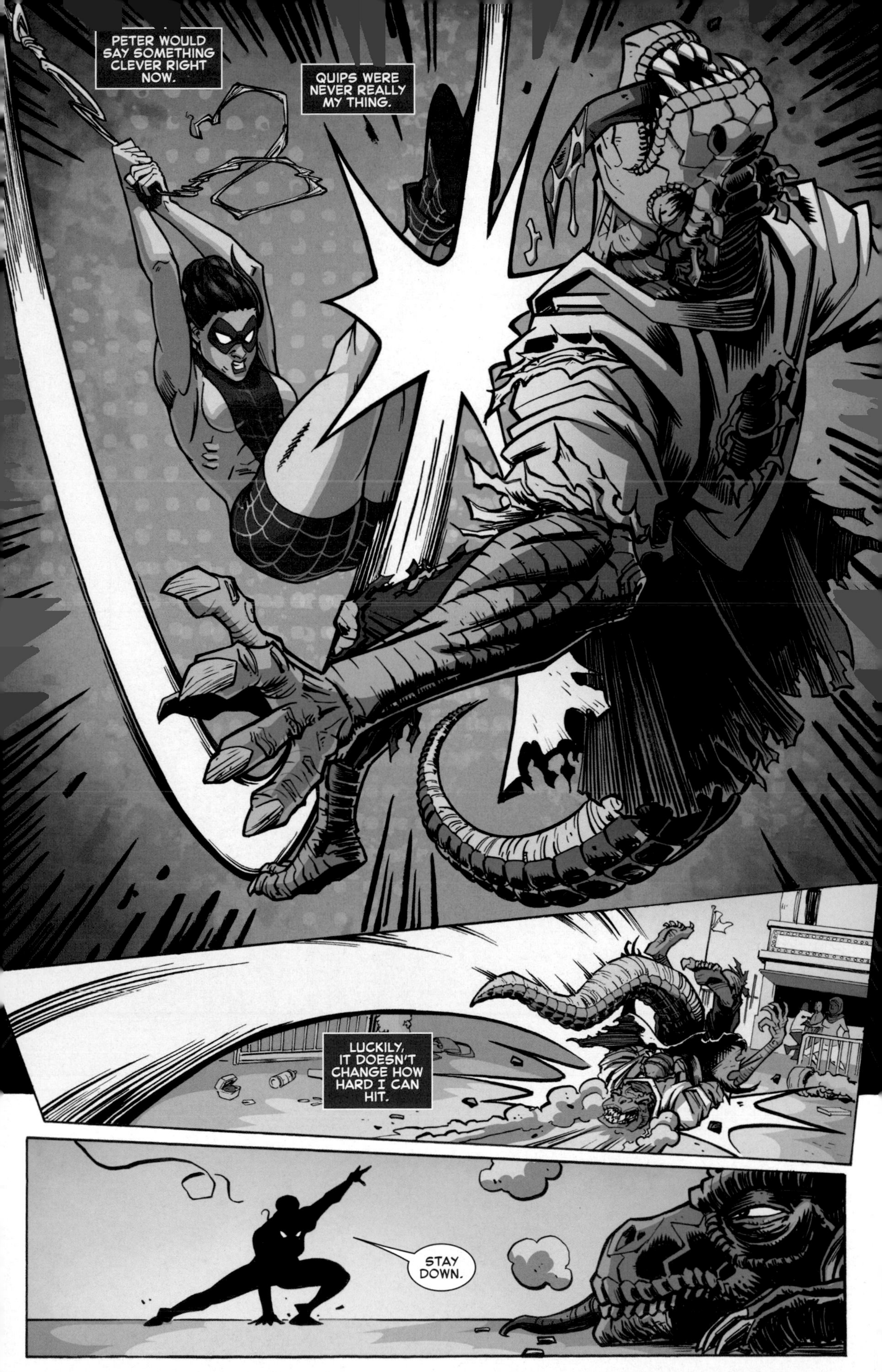
PETER WOULD SAY SOMETHING CLEVER RIGHT NOW.
QUIPS WERE NEVER REALLY MY THING.
LUCKILY, IT DOESN'T CHANGE HOW HARD I CAN HIT.
STAY DOWN.

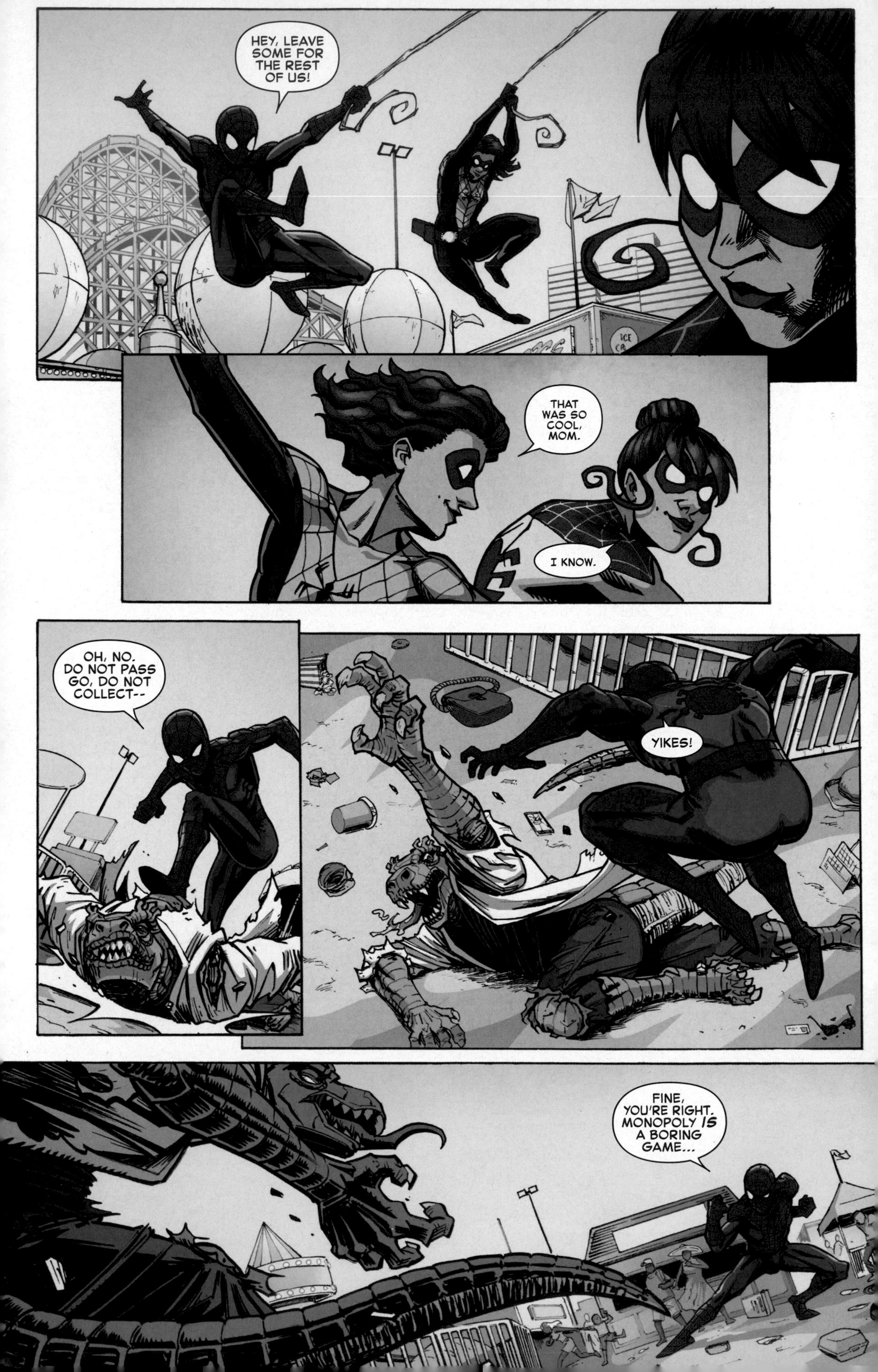
HEY, LEAVE SOME FOR THE REST OF US!
THAT WAS SO COOL, MOM.
I KNOW.
OH, NO. DO NOT PASS GO, DO NOT COLLECT--
YIKES!
FINE, YOU'RE RIGHT. MONOPOLY *IS* A BORING GAME...

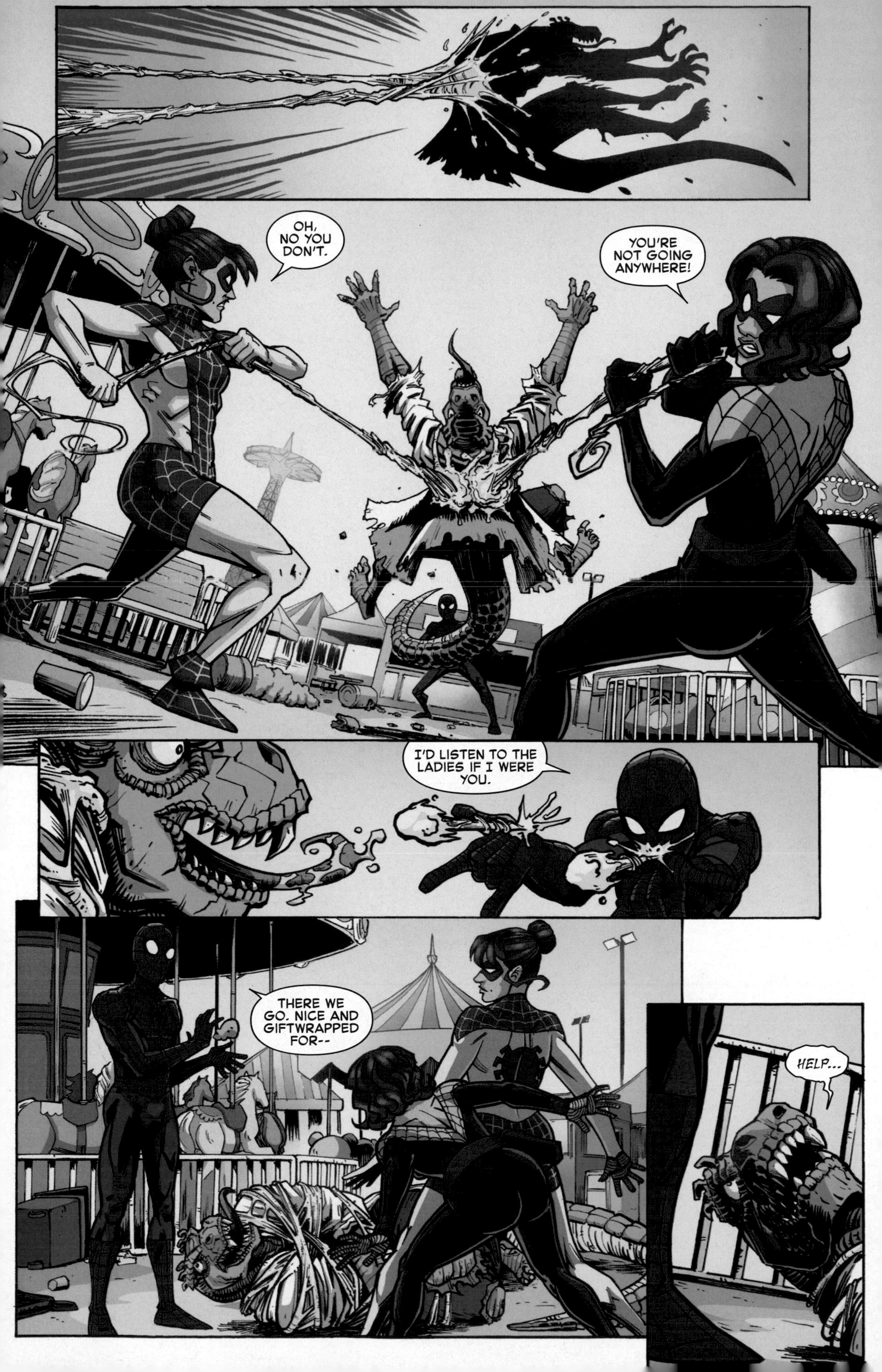

OH, NO YOU DON'T.
YOU'RE NOT GOING ANYWHERE!
I'D LISTEN TO THE LADIES IF I WERE YOU.
THERE WE GO. NICE AND GIFTWRAPPED FOR--
HELP...

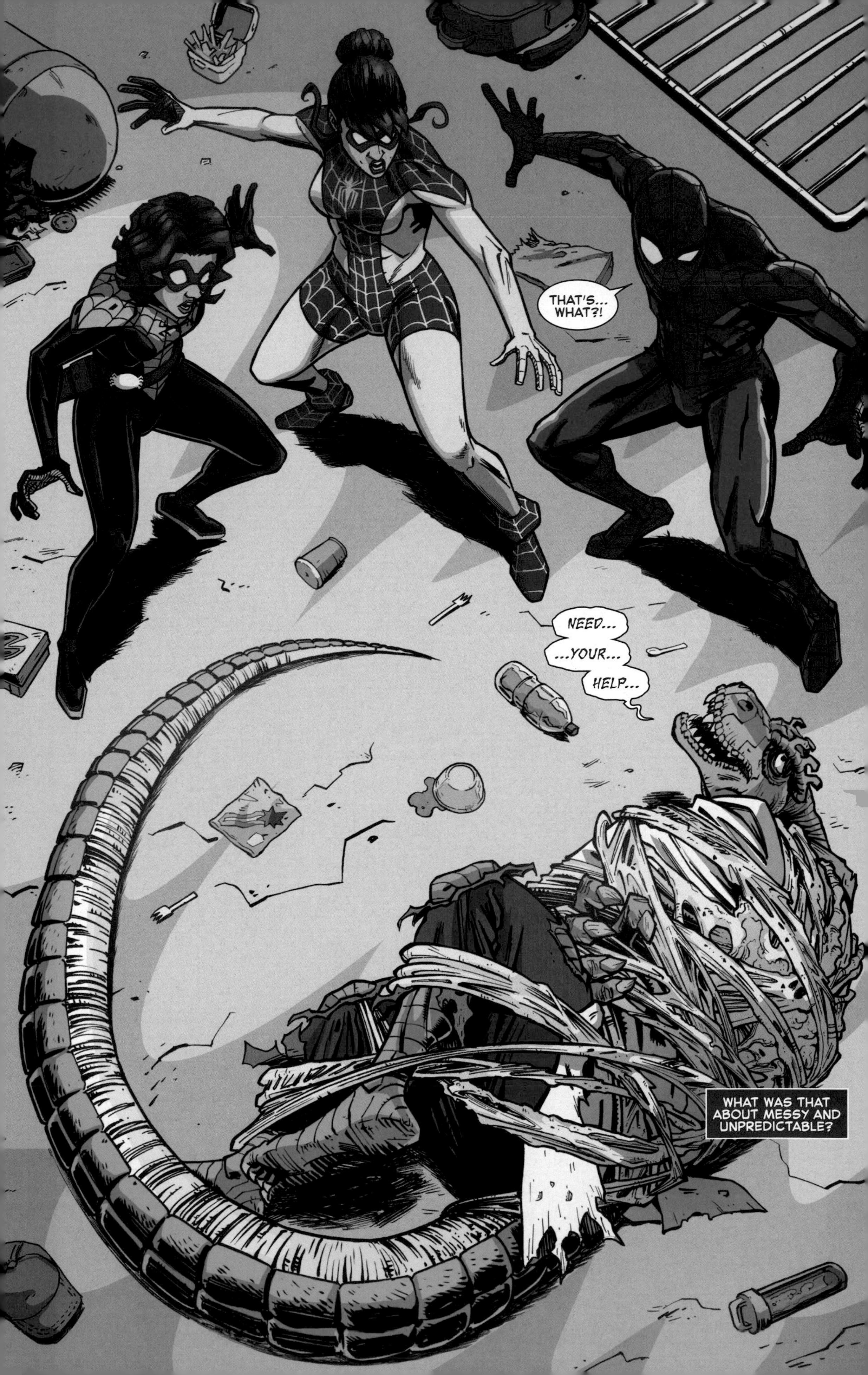
THAT'S... WHAT?!
NEED...
...YOUR...
HELP...
WHAT WAS THAT ABOUT MESSY AND UNPREDICTABLE?

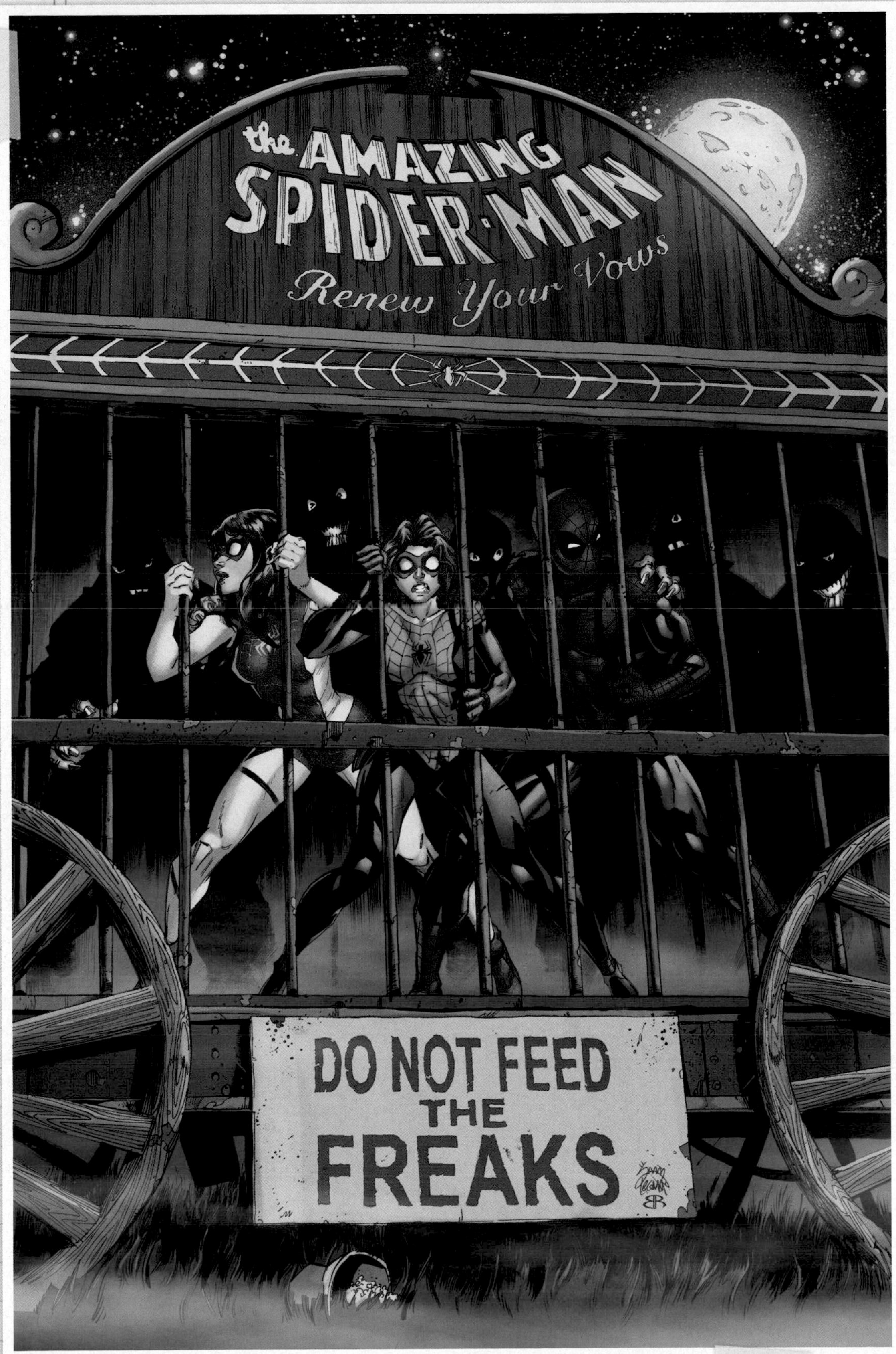
the AMAZING SPIDER-MAN
Renew Your Vows
DO NOT FEED THE FREAKS

15: EIGHT YEARS LATER — PART 3

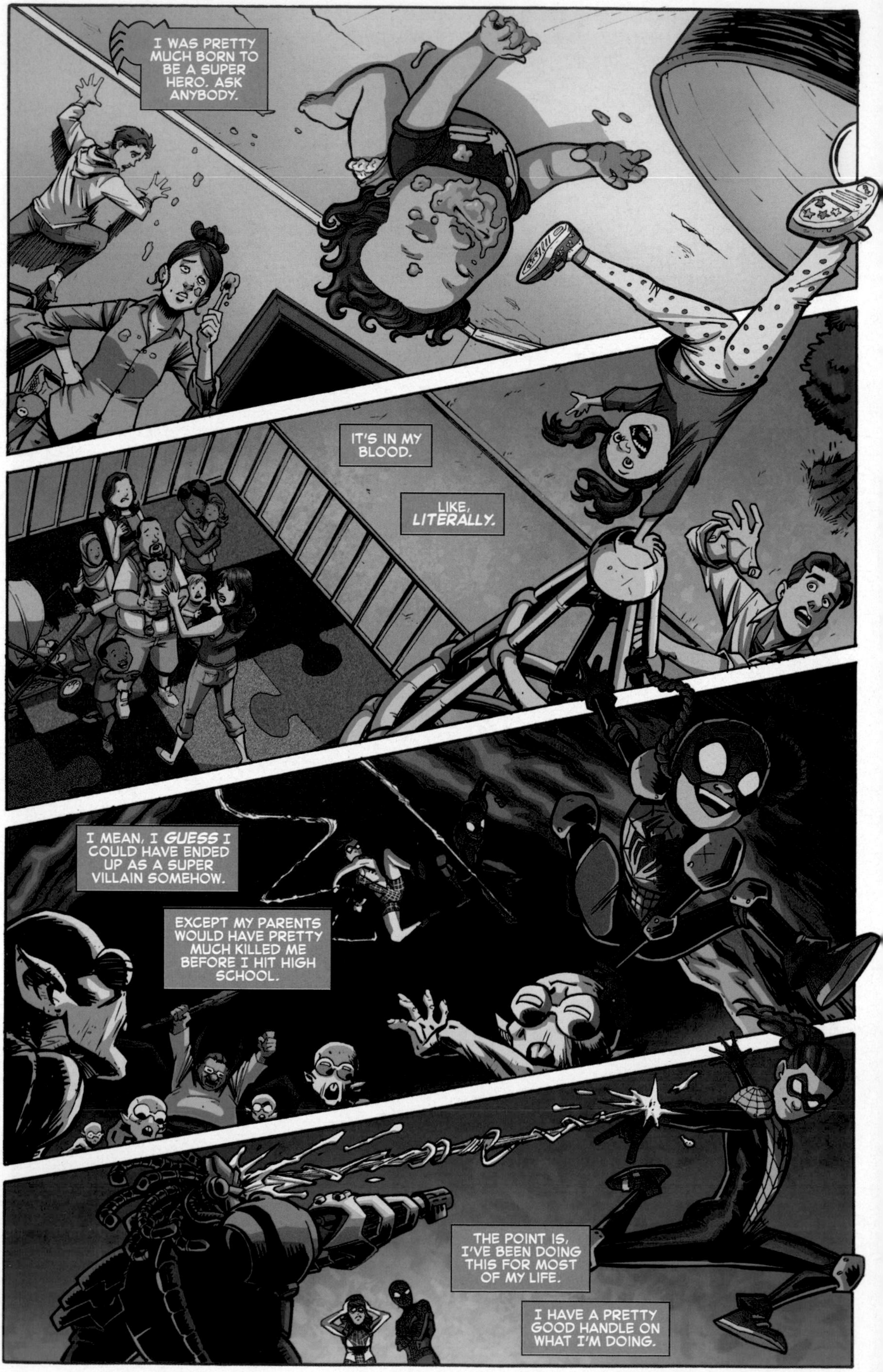
I WAS PRETTY MUCH BORN TO BE A SUPER HERO. ASK ANYBODY.
IT'S IN MY BLOOD.
LIKE, *LITERALLY.*
I MEAN, I *GUESS* I COULD HAVE ENDED UP AS A SUPER VILLAIN SOMEHOW.
EXCEPT MY PARENTS WOULD HAVE PRETTY MUCH KILLED ME BEFORE I HIT HIGH SCHOOL.
THE POINT IS, I'VE BEEN DOING THIS FOR MOST OF MY LIFE.
I HAVE A PRETTY GOOD HANDLE ON WHAT I'M DOING.

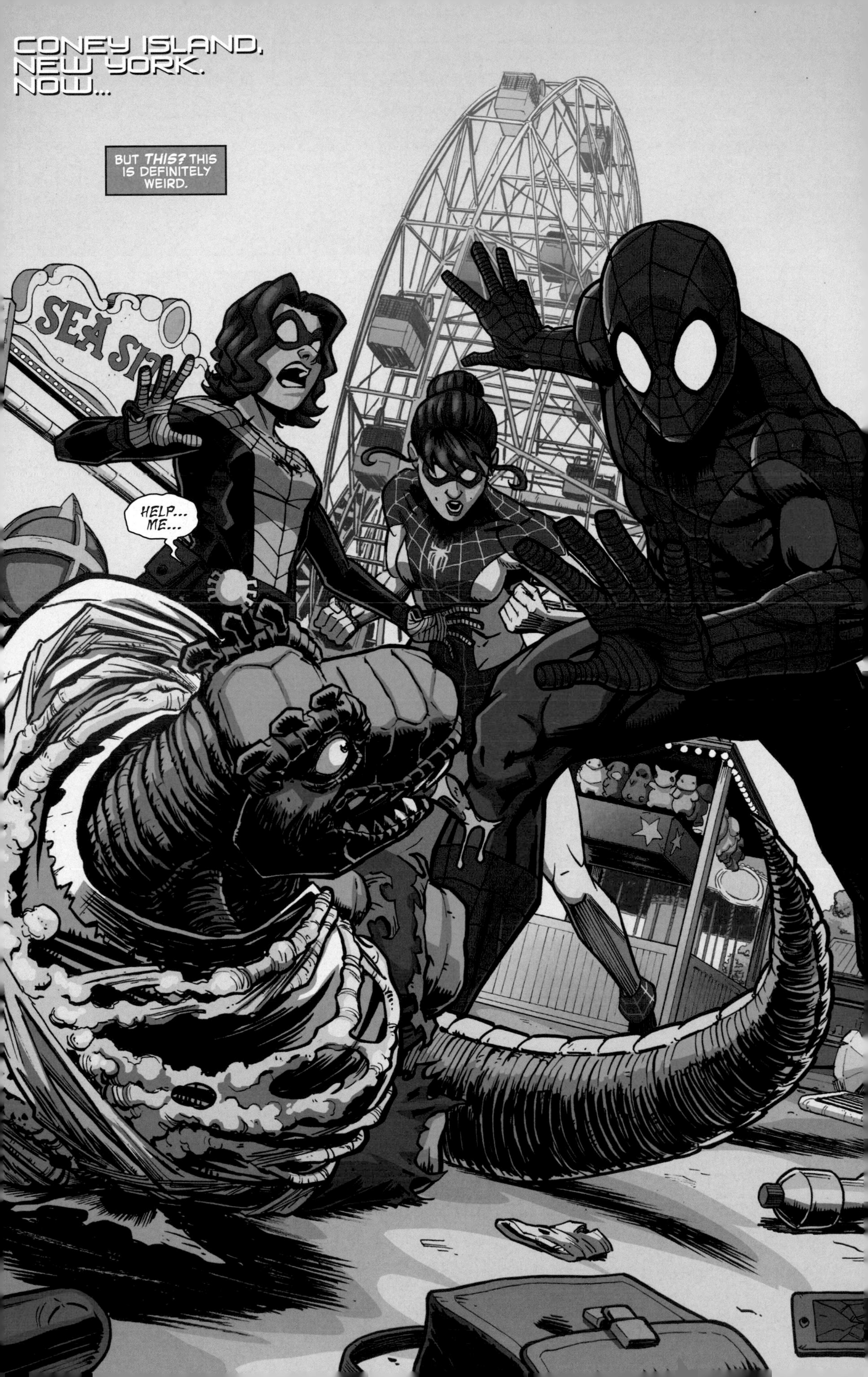
CONEY ISLAND, NEW YORK. NOW...
BUT *THIS?* THIS IS DEFINITELY WEIRD.
SEA SI
HELP... ME...

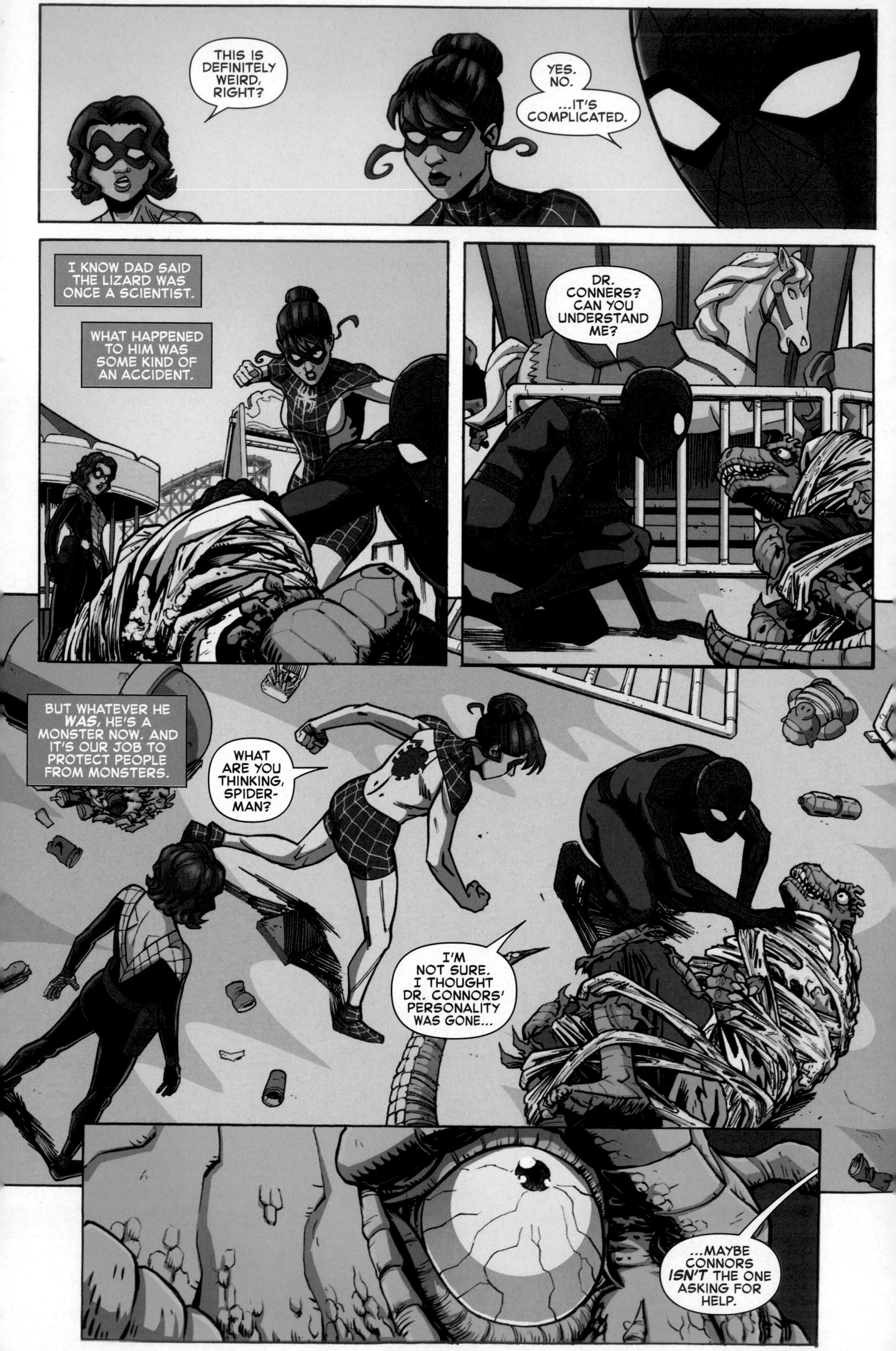
THIS IS DEFINITELY WEIRD, RIGHT?
YES. NO.
...IT'S COMPLICATED.
I KNOW DAD SAID THE LIZARD WAS ONCE A SCIENTIST.
WHAT HAPPENED TO HIM WAS SOME KIND OF AN ACCIDENT.
DR. CONNERS? CAN YOU UNDERSTAND ME?
BUT WHATEVER HE WAS, HE'S A MONSTER NOW. AND IT'S OUR JOB TO PROTECT PEOPLE FROM MONSTERS.
WHAT ARE YOU THINKING, SPIDER-MAN?
I'M NOT SURE. I THOUGHT DR. CONNORS' PERSONALITY WAS GONE...
...MAYBE CONNORS ISN'T THE ONE ASKING FOR HELP.

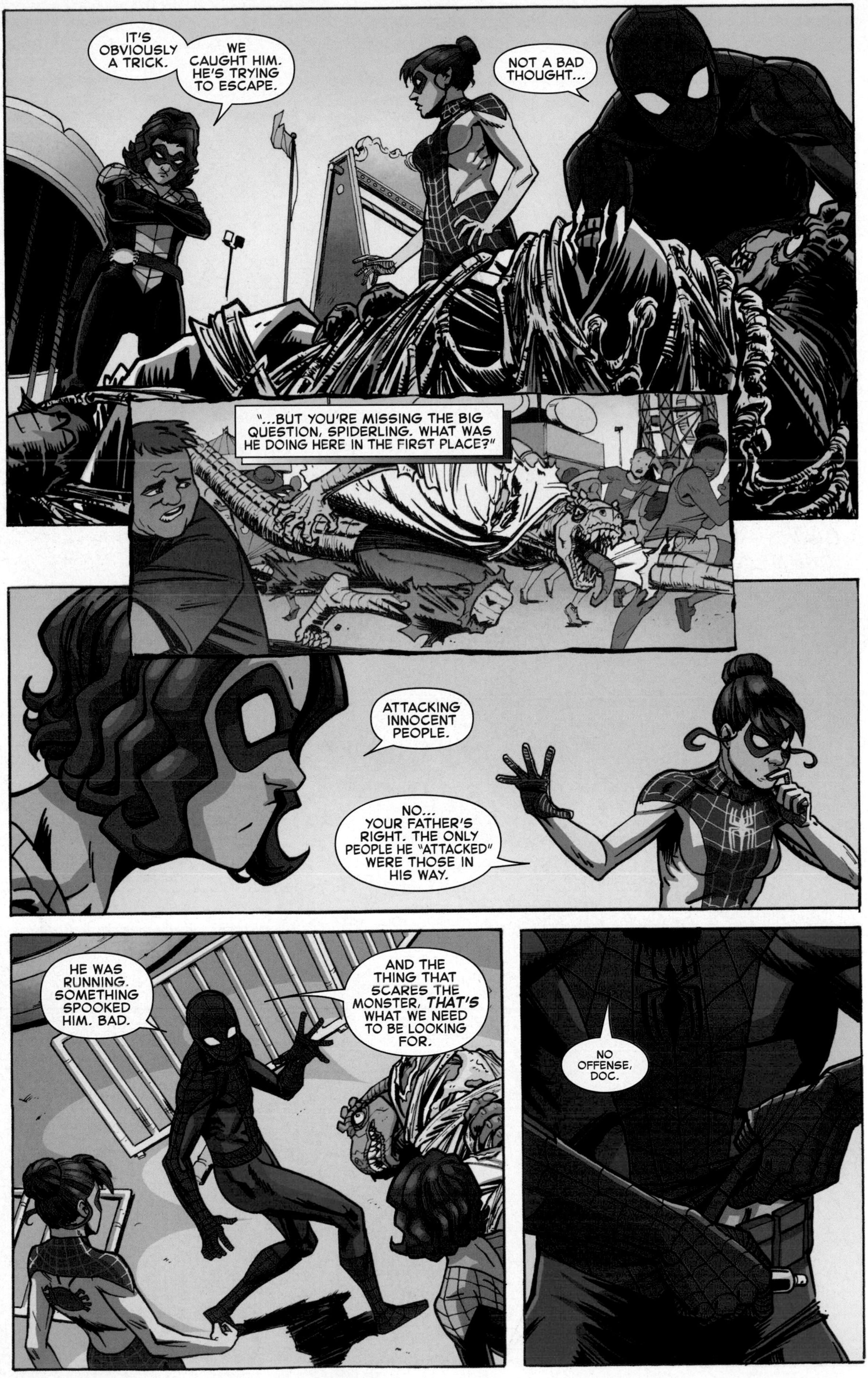
IT'S OBVIOUSLY A TRICK.
WE CAUGHT HIM. HE'S TRYING TO ESCAPE.
NOT A BAD THOUGHT...
"...BUT YOU'RE MISSING THE BIG QUESTION, SPIDERLING. WHAT WAS HE DOING HERE IN THE FIRST PLACE?"
ATTACKING INNOCENT PEOPLE.
NO... YOUR FATHER'S RIGHT. THE ONLY PEOPLE HE "ATTACKED" WERE THOSE IN HIS WAY.
HE WAS RUNNING. SOMETHING SPOOKED HIM. BAD.
AND THE THING THAT SCARES THE MONSTER, *THAT'S* WHAT WE NEED TO BE LOOKING FOR.
NO OFFENSE, DOC.

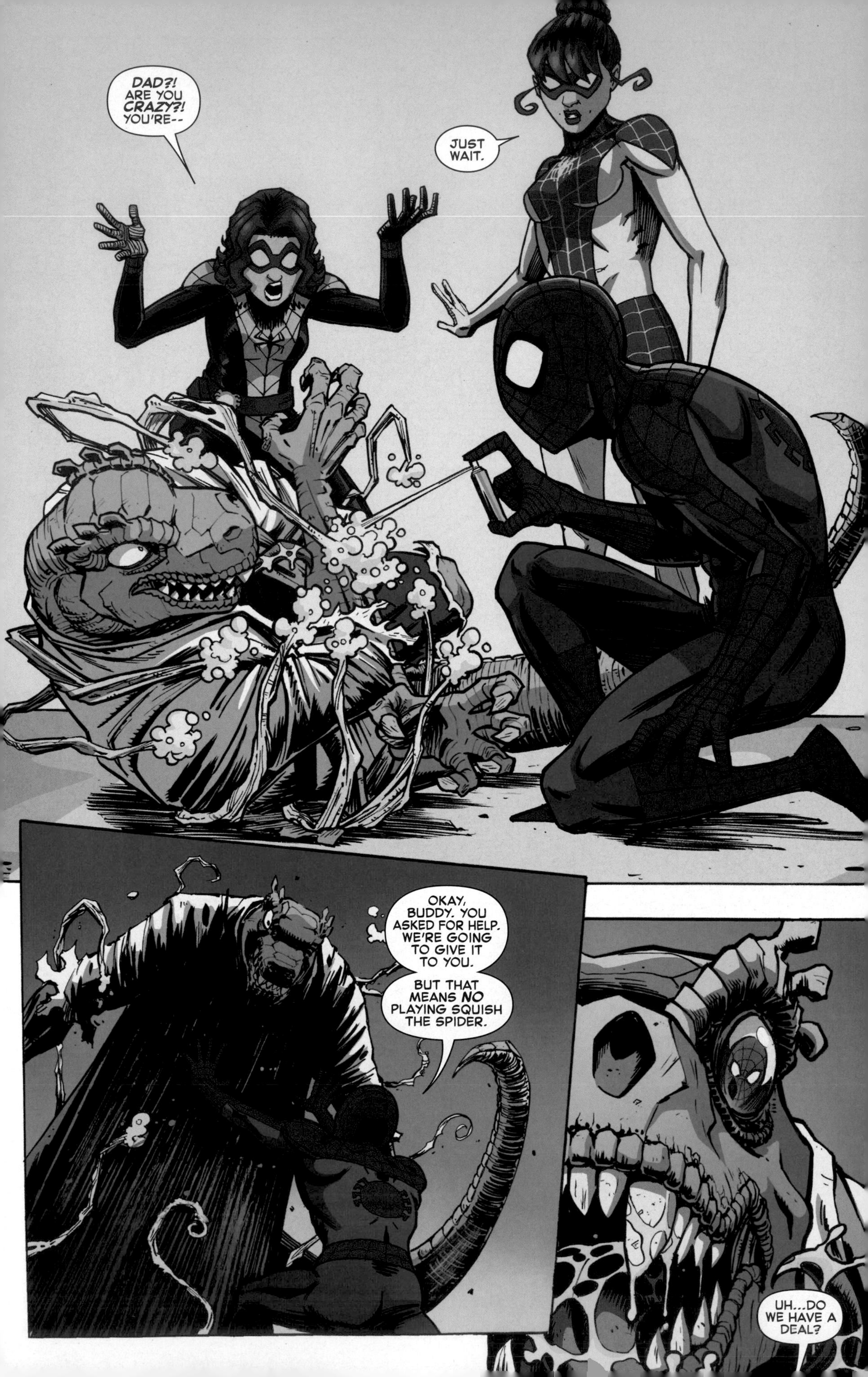
DAD?! ARE YOU CRAZY?! YOU'RE--
JUST WAIT.
OKAY, BUDDY. YOU ASKED FOR HELP. WE'RE GOING TO GIVE IT TO YOU.
BUT THAT MEANS NO PLAYING SQUISH THE SPIDER.
UH...DO WE HAVE A DEAL?

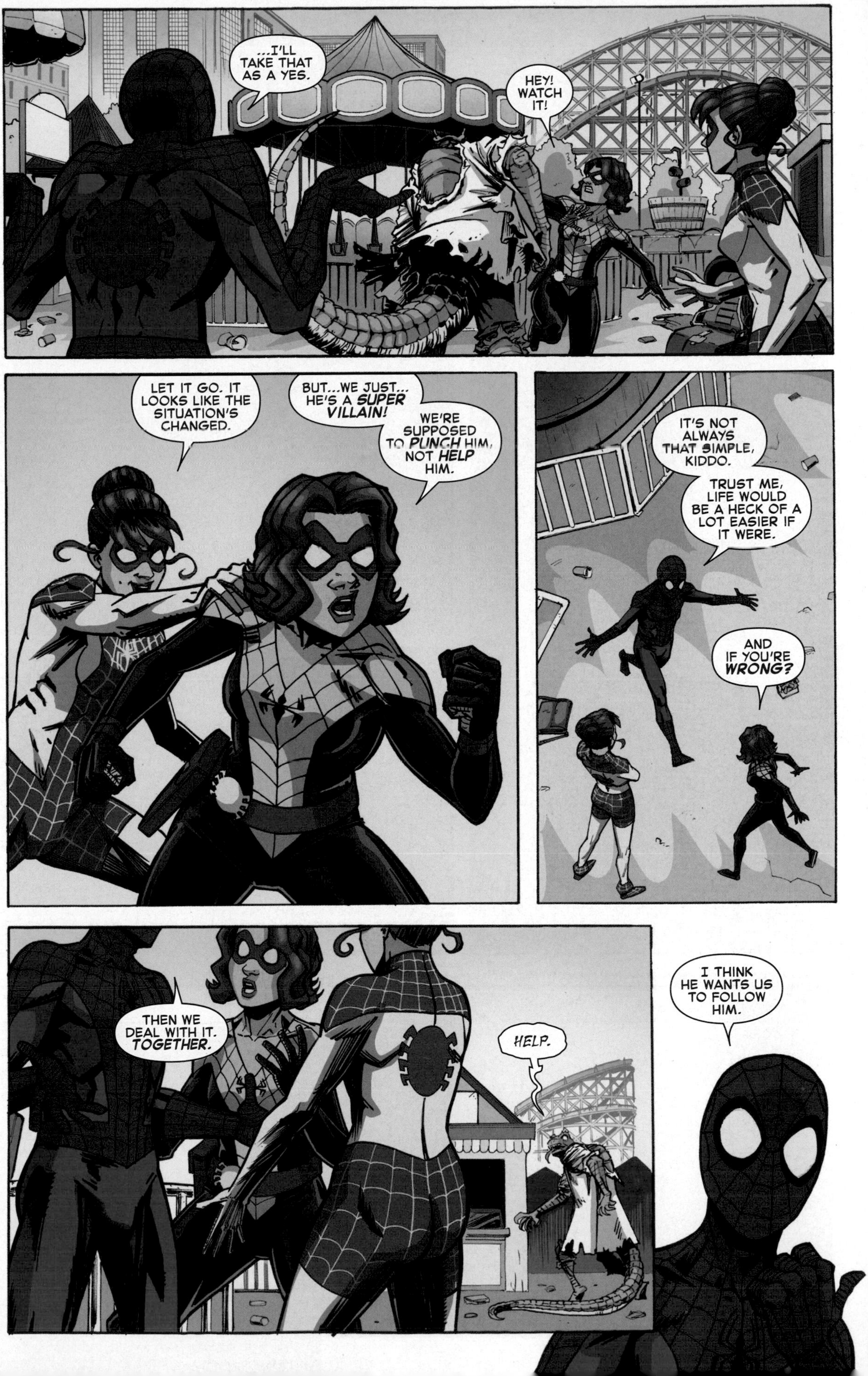

...I'LL TAKE THAT AS A YES.
HEY! WATCH IT!
LET IT GO. IT LOOKS LIKE THE SITUATION'S CHANGED.
BUT...WE JUST... HE'S A SUPER VILLAIN!
WE'RE SUPPOSED TO PUNCH HIM, NOT HELP HIM.
IT'S NOT ALWAYS THAT SIMPLE, KIDDO.
TRUST ME, LIFE WOULD BE A HECK OF A LOT EASIER IF IT WERE.
AND IF YOU'RE WRONG?
THEN WE DEAL WITH IT. TOGETHER.
HELP.
I THINK HE WANTS US TO FOLLOW HIM.

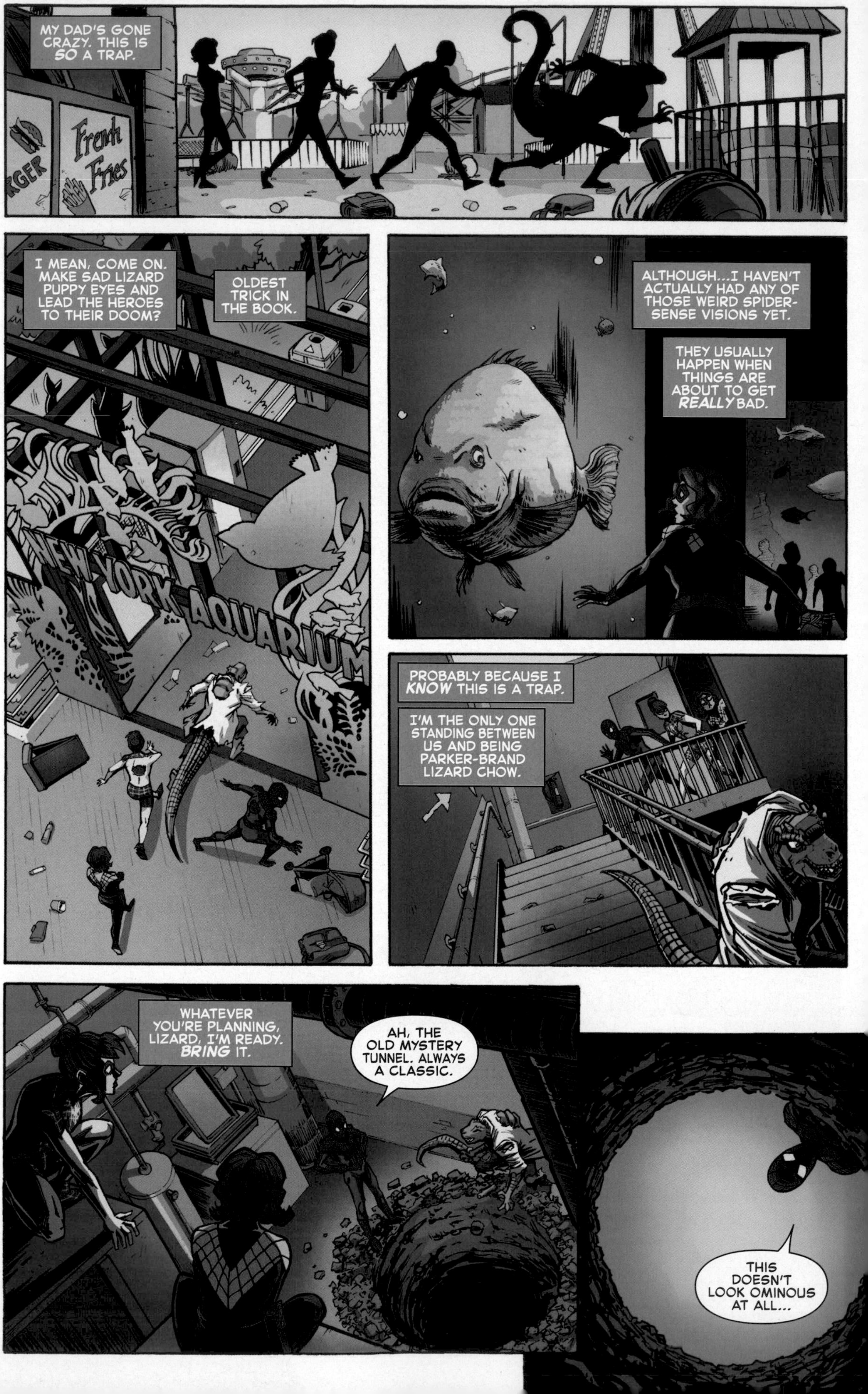
MY DAD'S GONE CRAZY. THIS IS SO A TRAP.
RGER
French Fries
I MEAN, COME ON. MAKE SAD LIZARD PUPPY EYES AND LEAD THE HEROES TO THEIR DOOM?
OLDEST TRICK IN THE BOOK.
NEW YORK AQUARIUM
ALTHOUGH...I HAVEN'T ACTUALLY HAD ANY OF THOSE WEIRD SPIDER-SENSE VISIONS YET.
THEY USUALLY HAPPEN WHEN THINGS ARE ABOUT TO GET REALLY BAD.
PROBABLY BECAUSE I KNOW THIS IS A TRAP.
I'M THE ONLY ONE STANDING BETWEEN US AND BEING PARKER-BRAND LIZARD CHOW.
WHATEVER YOU'RE PLANNING, LIZARD, I'M READY. BRING IT.
AH, THE OLD MYSTERY TUNNEL. ALWAYS A CLASSIC.
THIS DOESN'T LOOK OMINOUS AT ALL...

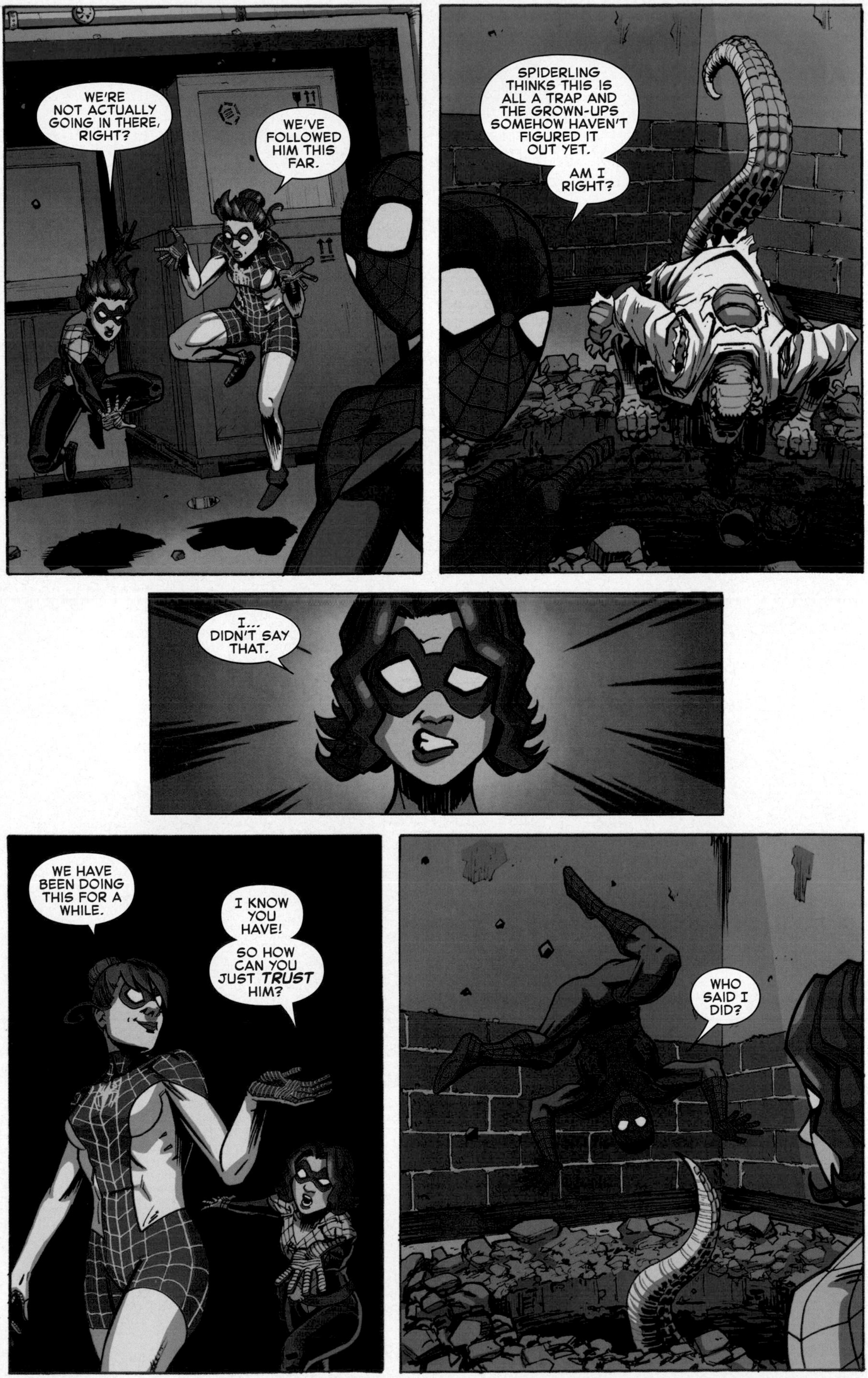
WE'RE NOT ACTUALLY GOING IN THERE, RIGHT?
WE'VE FOLLOWED HIM THIS FAR.
SPIDERLING THINKS THIS IS ALL A TRAP AND THE GROWN-UPS SOMEHOW HAVEN'T FIGURED IT OUT YET.
AM I RIGHT?
I... DIDN'T SAY THAT.
WE HAVE BEEN DOING THIS FOR A WHILE.
I KNOW YOU HAVE!
SO HOW CAN YOU JUST *TRUST* HIM?
WHO SAID I DID?

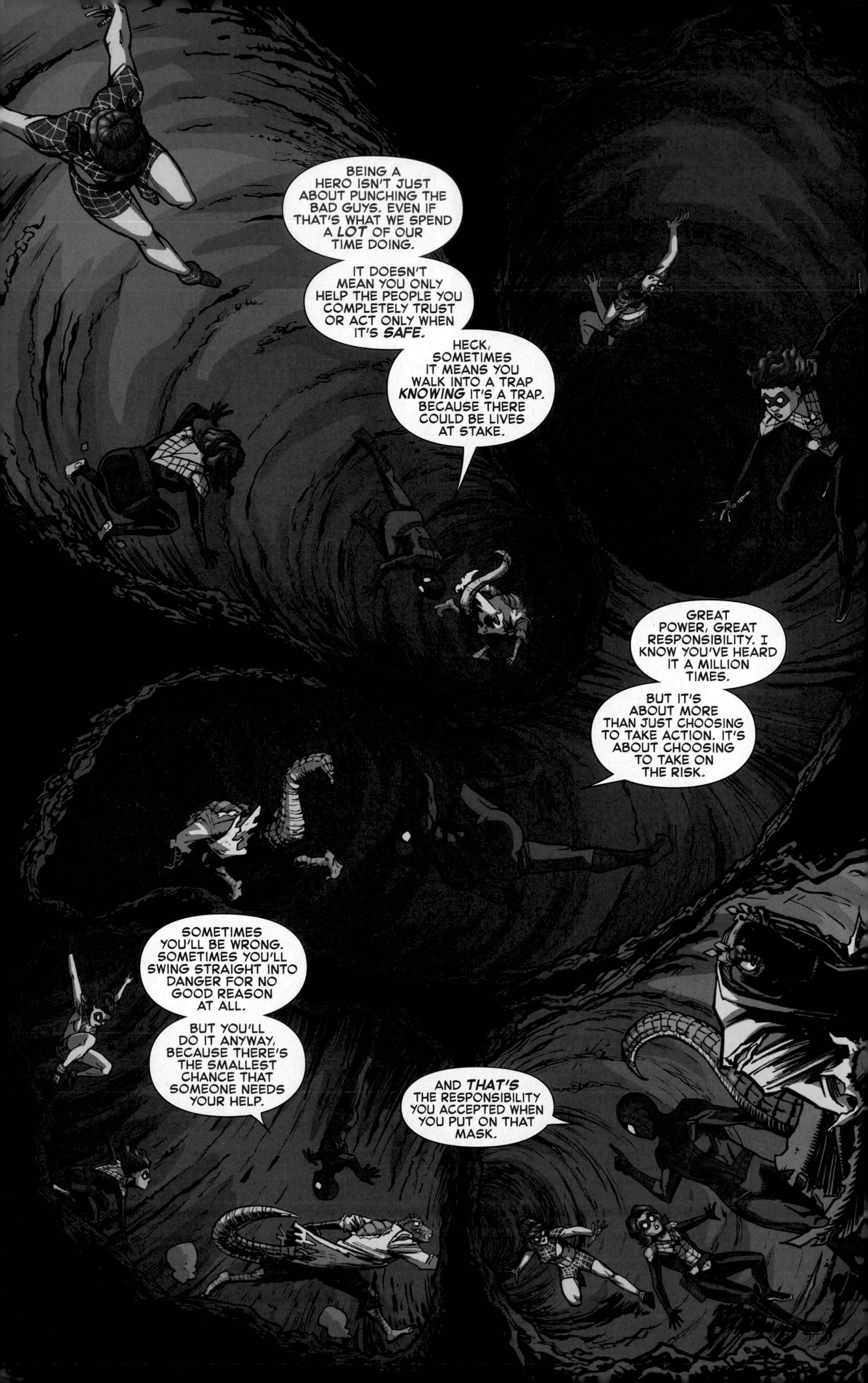
BEING A HERO ISN'T JUST ABOUT PUNCHING THE BAD GUYS. EVEN IF THAT'S WHAT WE SPEND A *LOT* OF OUR TIME DOING.
IT DOESN'T MEAN YOU ONLY HELP THE PEOPLE YOU COMPLETELY TRUST OR ACT ONLY WHEN IT'S *SAFE.*
HECK, SOMETIMES IT MEANS YOU WALK INTO A TRAP *KNOWING* IT'S A TRAP. BECAUSE THERE COULD BE LIVES AT STAKE.
GREAT POWER, GREAT RESPONSIBILITY. I KNOW YOU'VE HEARD IT A MILLION TIMES.
BUT IT'S ABOUT MORE THAN JUST CHOOSING TO TAKE ACTION. IT'S ABOUT CHOOSING TO TAKE ON THE RISK.
SOMETIMES YOU'LL BE WRONG. SOMETIMES YOU'LL SWING STRAIGHT INTO DANGER FOR NO GOOD REASON AT ALL.
BUT YOU'LL DO IT ANYWAY, BECAUSE THERE'S THE SMALLEST CHANCE THAT SOMEONE NEEDS YOUR HELP.
AND *THAT'S* THE RESPONSIBILITY YOU ACCEPTED WHEN YOU PUT ON THAT MASK.

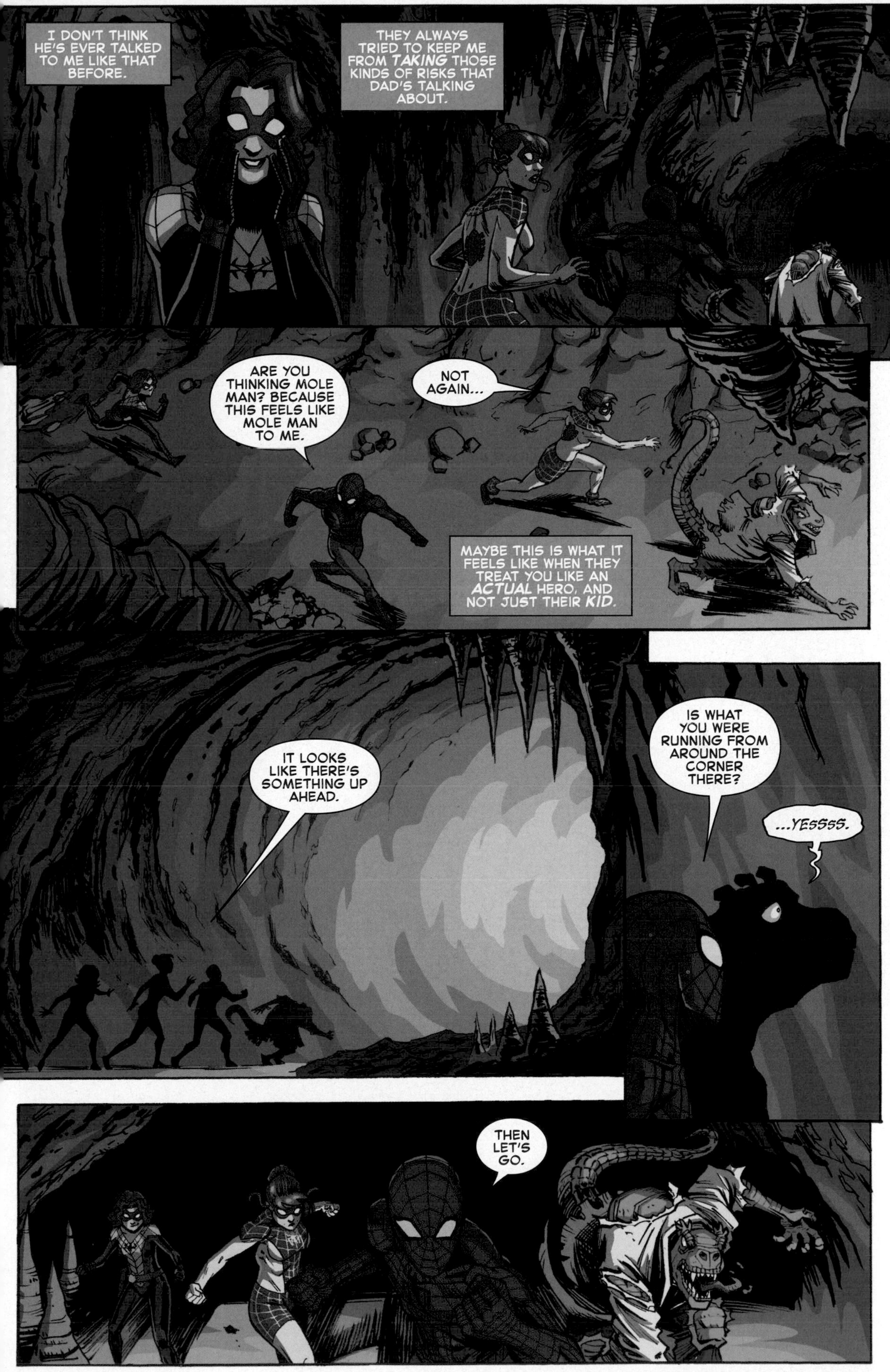
I DON'T THINK HE'S EVER TALKED TO ME LIKE THAT BEFORE.
THEY ALWAYS TRIED TO KEEP ME FROM *TAKING* THOSE KINDS OF RISKS THAT DAD'S TALKING ABOUT.
ARE YOU THINKING MOLE MAN? BECAUSE THIS FEELS LIKE MOLE MAN TO ME.
NOT AGAIN...
MAYBE THIS IS WHAT IT FEELS LIKE WHEN THEY TREAT YOU LIKE AN *ACTUAL* HERO, AND NOT JUST THEIR *KID*.
IT LOOKS LIKE THERE'S SOMETHING UP AHEAD.
IS WHAT YOU WERE RUNNING FROM AROUND THE CORNER THERE?
...YESSSS.
THEN LET'S GO.

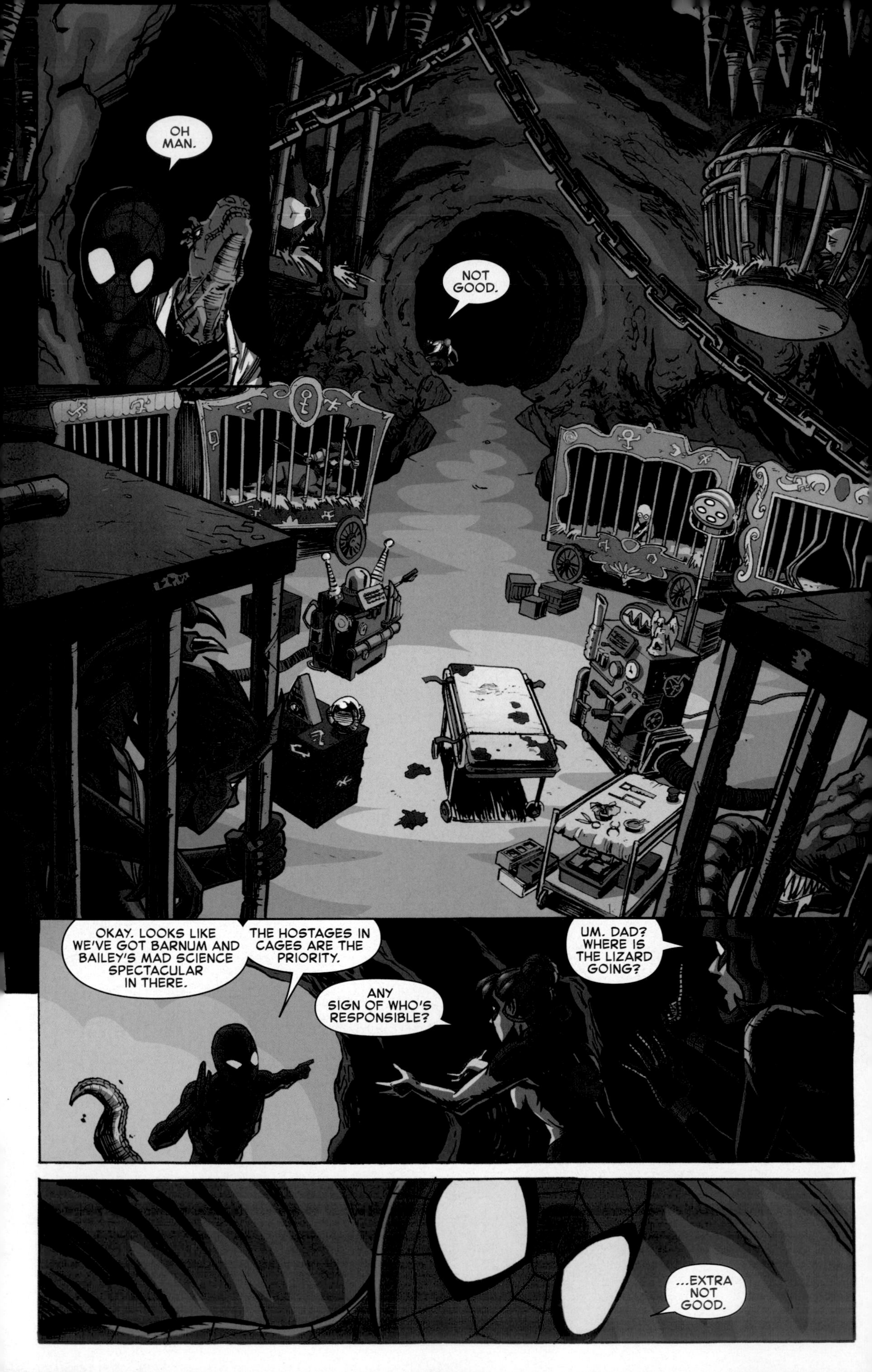
OH MAN.
NOT GOOD.
OKAY. LOOKS LIKE WE'VE GOT BARNUM AND BAILEY'S MAD SCIENCE SPECTACULAR IN THERE.
THE HOSTAGES IN CAGES ARE THE PRIORITY.
ANY SIGN OF WHO'S RESPONSIBLE?
UM. DAD? WHERE IS THE LIZARD GOING?
...EXTRA NOT GOOD.

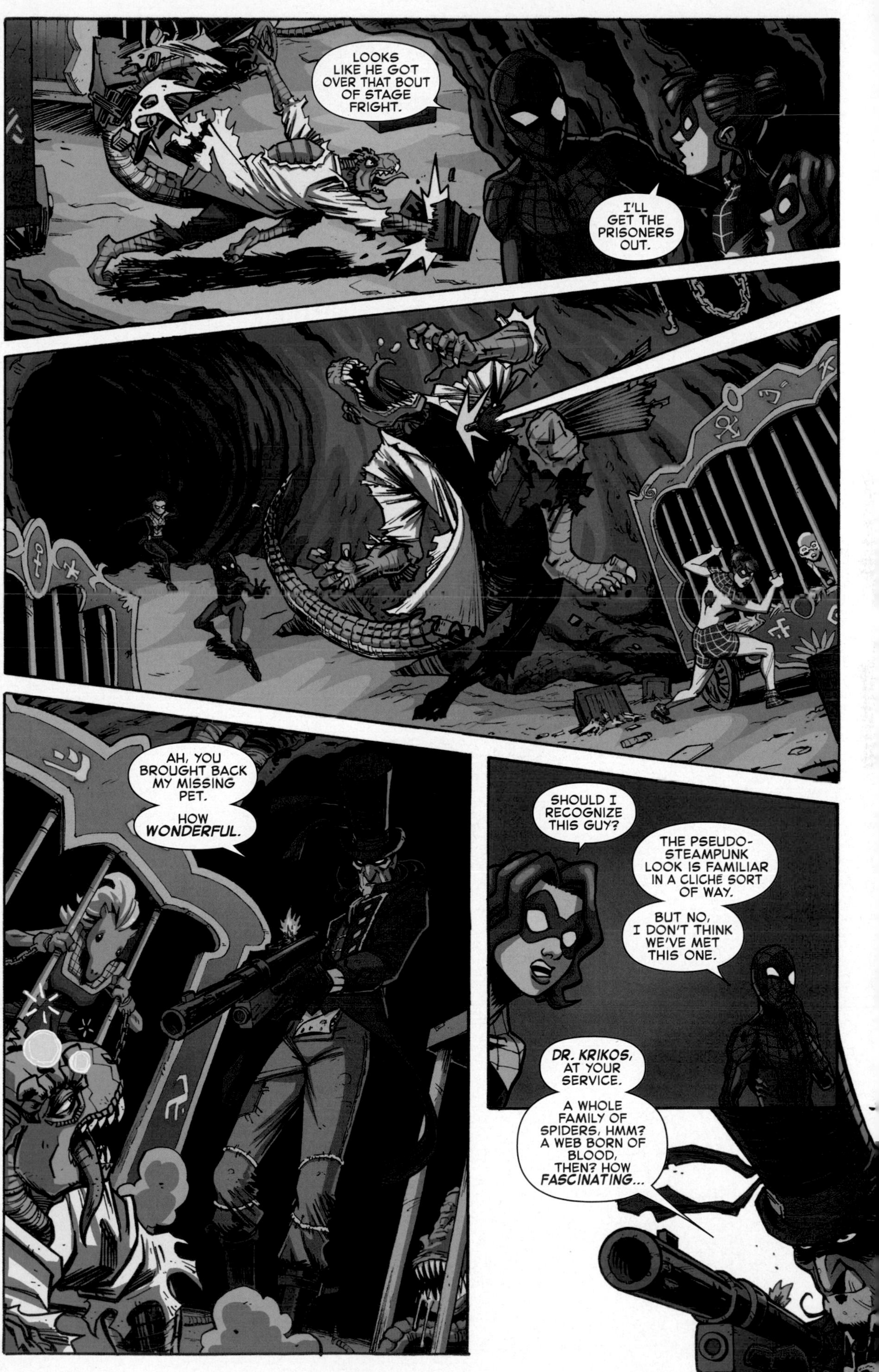
LOOKS LIKE HE GOT OVER THAT BOUT OF STAGE FRIGHT.
I'LL GET THE PRISONERS OUT.
AH, YOU BROUGHT BACK MY MISSING PET.
HOW *WONDERFUL*.
SHOULD I RECOGNIZE THIS GUY?
THE PSEUDO-STEAMPUNK LOOK IS FAMILIAR IN A CLICHÉ SORT OF WAY.
BUT NO, I DON'T THINK WE'VE MET THIS ONE.
DR. KRIKOS, AT YOUR SERVICE.
A WHOLE FAMILY OF SPIDERS, HMM? A WEB BORN OF BLOOD, THEN? HOW *FASCINATING*...

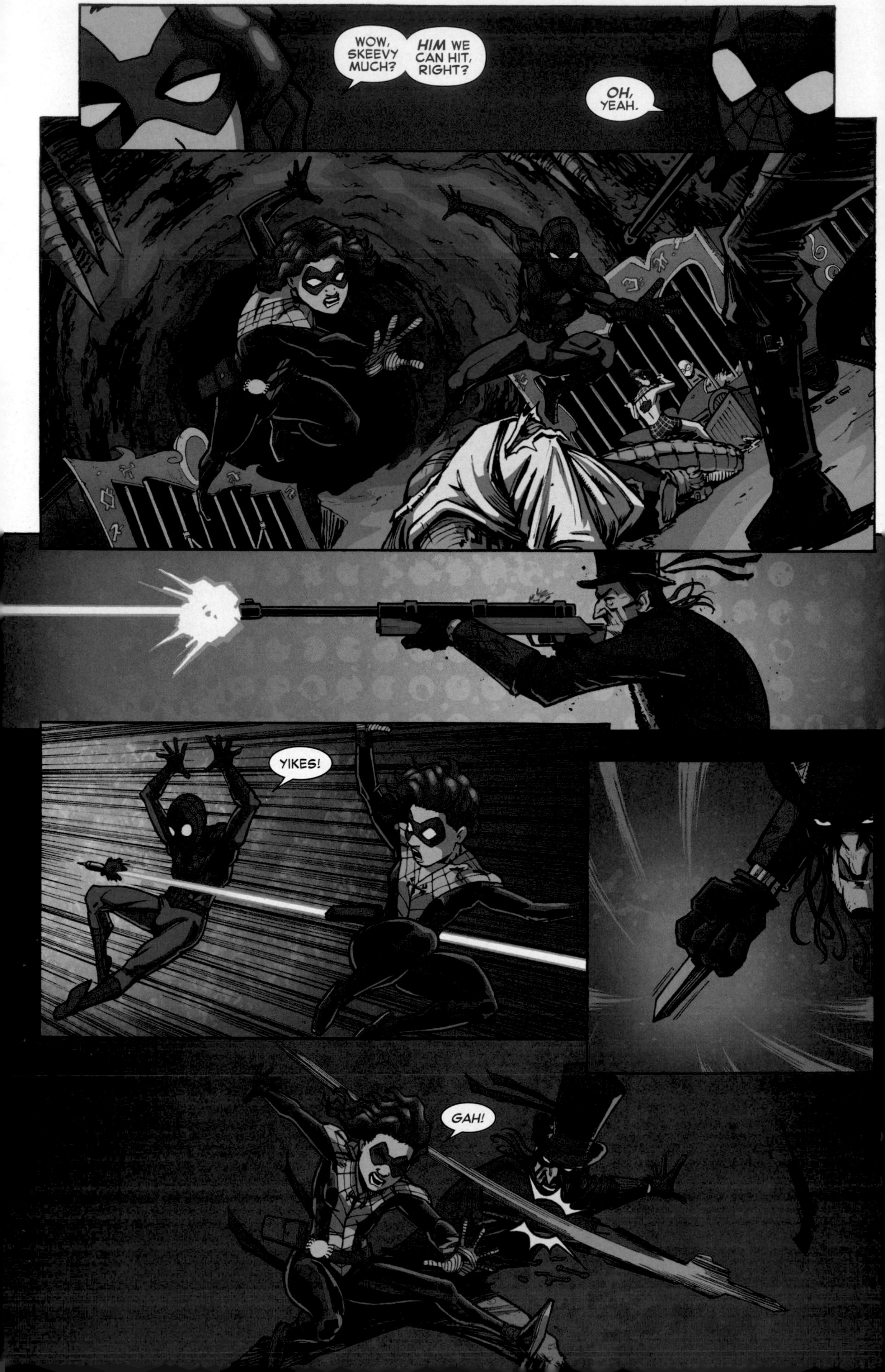
WOW, SKEEVY MUCH?
HIM WE CAN HIT, RIGHT?
OH, YEAH.
YIKES!
GAH!

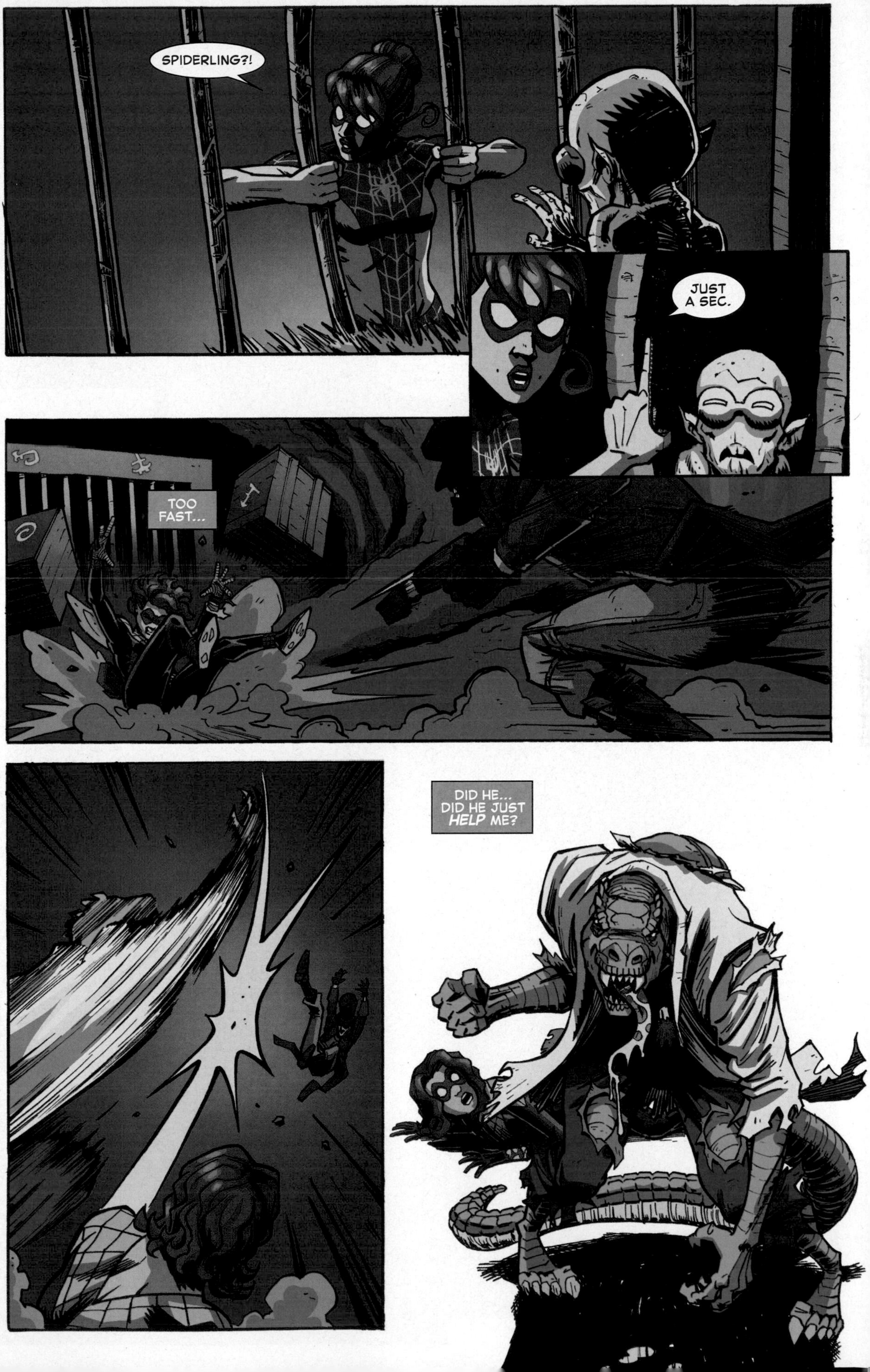SPIDERLING?!
JUST A SEC.
TOO FAST...
DID HE... DID HE JUST HELP ME?

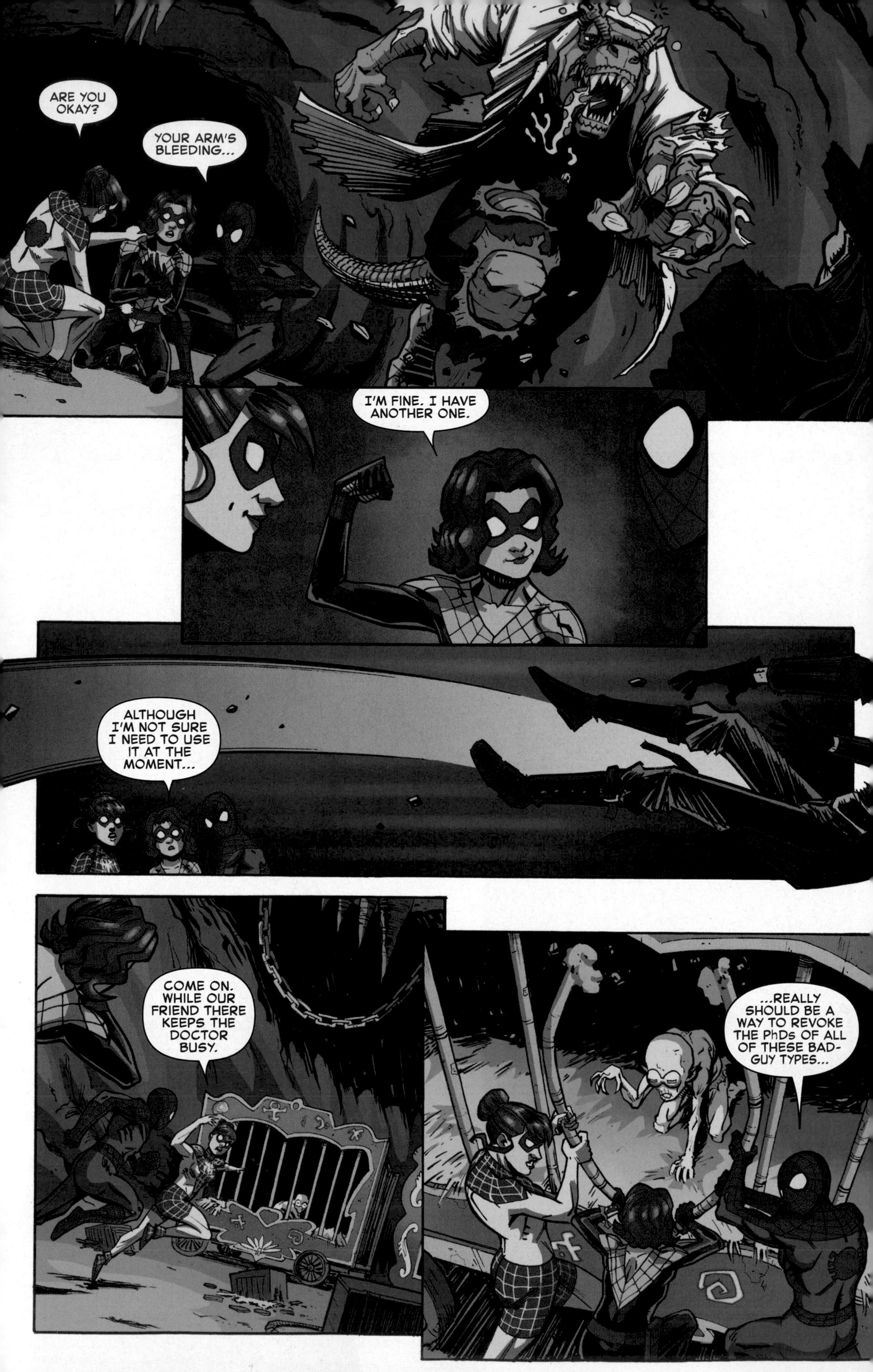
ARE YOU OKAY?
YOUR ARM'S BLEEDING...
I'M FINE. I HAVE ANOTHER ONE.
ALTHOUGH I'M NOT SURE I NEED TO USE IT AT THE MOMENT...
COME ON. WHILE OUR FRIEND THERE KEEPS THE DOCTOR BUSY.
...REALLY SHOULD BE A WAY TO REVOKE THE PhDs OF ALL OF THESE BAD-GUY TYPES...

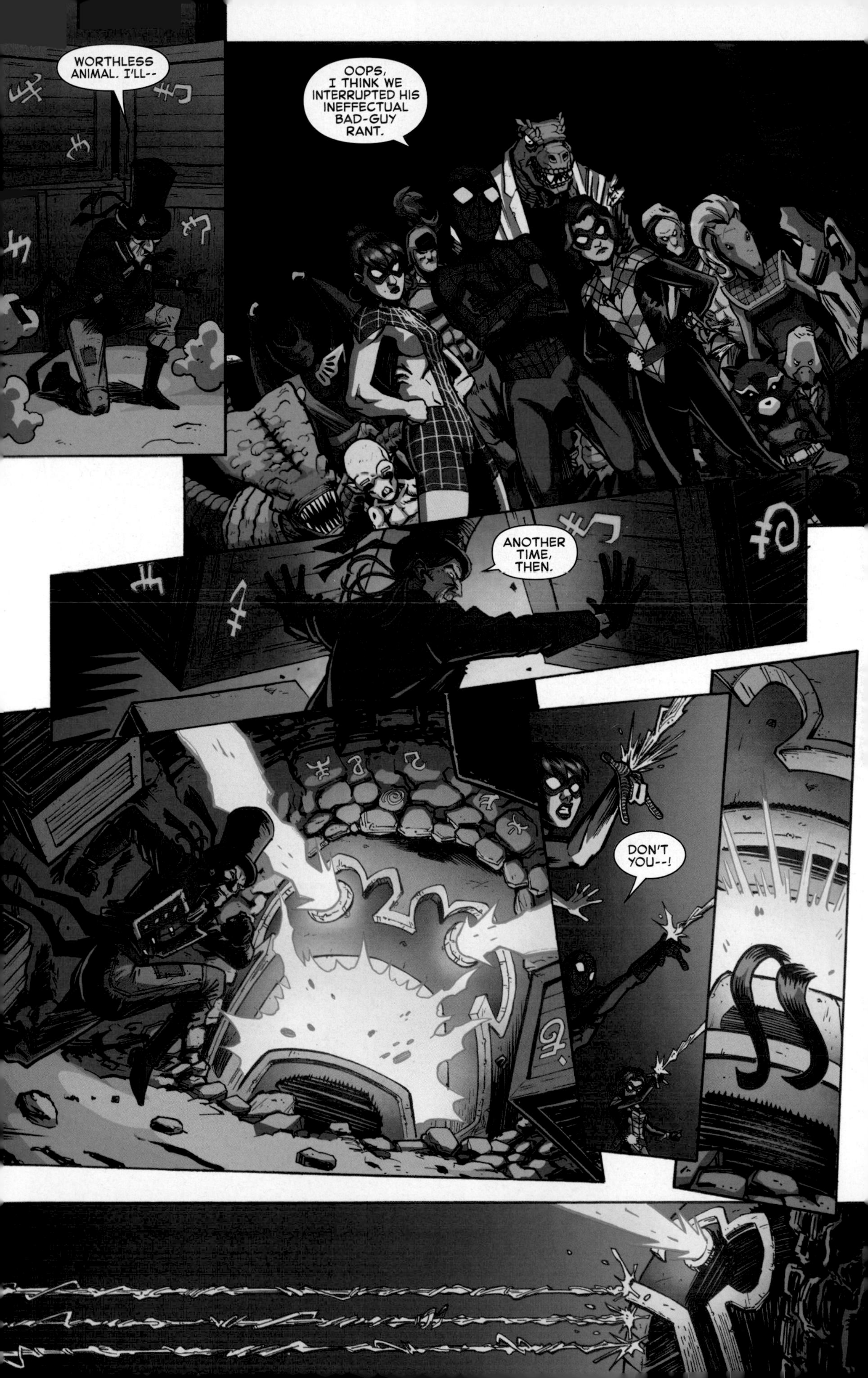
WORTHLESS ANIMAL. I'LL--
OOPS, I THINK WE INTERRUPTED HIS INEFFECTUAL BAD-GUY RANT.
ANOTHER TIME, THEN.
DON'T YOU--!

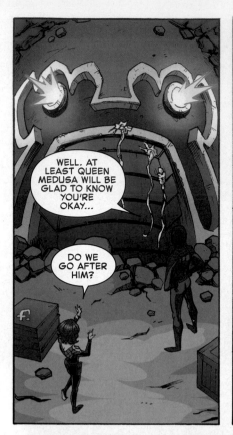

WELL. AT LEAST QUEEN MEDUSA WILL BE GLAD TO KNOW YOU'RE OKAY...

DO WE GO AFTER HIM?

NO. WE DON'T KNOW WHERE HE'S TELEPORTING TO.

BESIDES, FREEING HIS PRISONERS IS THE MOST IMPORTANT THING HERE.

WHAT WAS HE *DOING* DOWN HERE?

INHUMANS. ALIENS. MAD SCIENCE GONE WRONG. WHATEVER THAT PURPLE THING IS.

NO OFFENSE, BUDDY.

SO HE WAS RUNNING EXPERIMENTS ON A BUNCH OF NOT-QUITE-HUMANS?

LOOKS LIKE. TRYING TO REPLICATE THEIR POWERS? OR SOMETHING ELSE?

ALTHOUGH, IT LOOKS LIKE HE MISSED THE MUTANT AISLE ON HIS KIDNAPPERS 'R' US SPREE.

MAYBE THOSE WERE HIS NEXT TARGETS BEFORE WE SHOWED UP.

UH. ARE YOU OKAY?

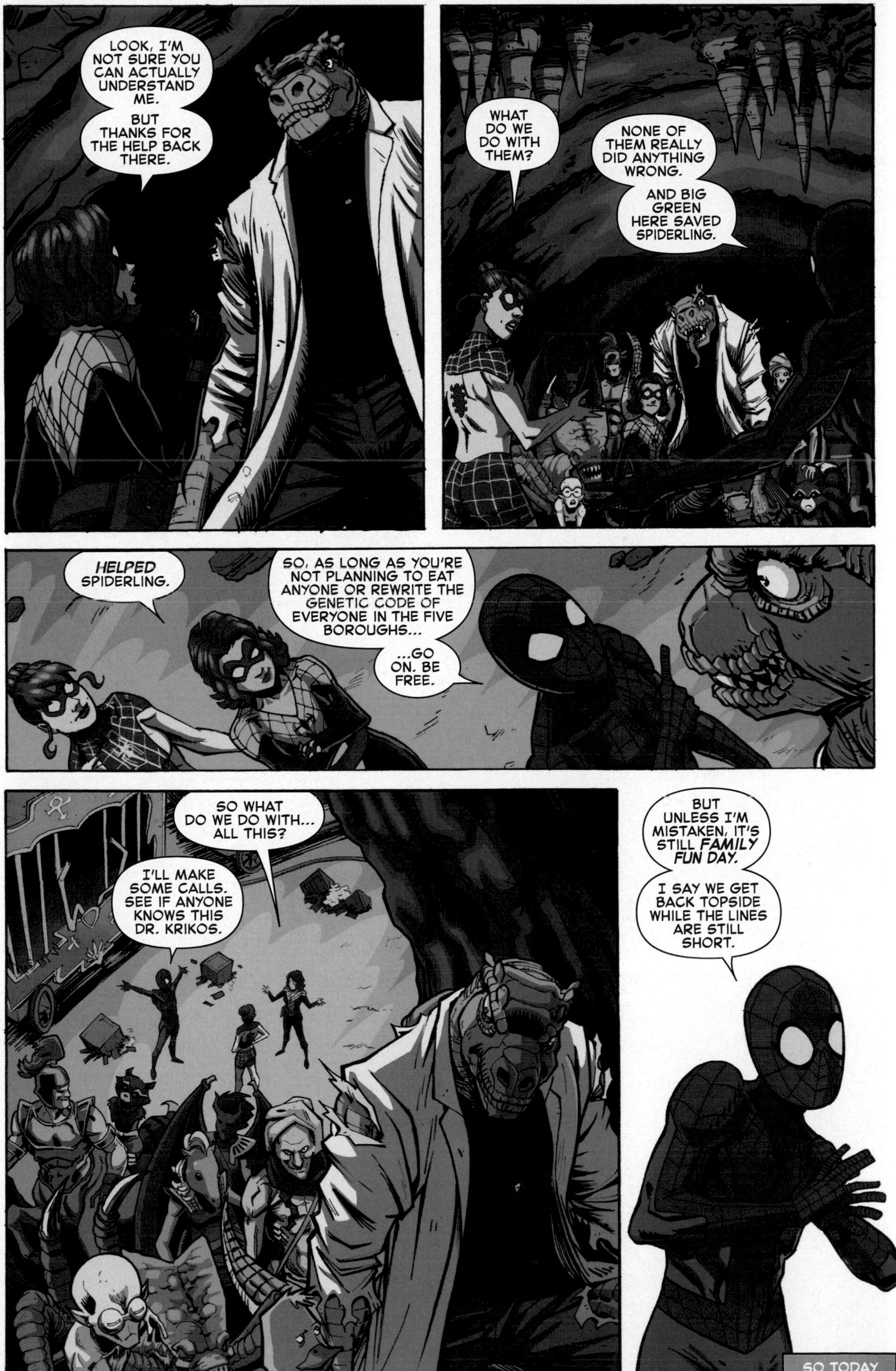
LOOK, I'M NOT SURE YOU CAN ACTUALLY UNDERSTAND ME.
BUT THANKS FOR THE HELP BACK THERE.
WHAT DO WE DO WITH THEM?
NONE OF THEM REALLY DID ANYTHING WRONG.
AND BIG GREEN HERE SAVED SPIDERLING.
HELPED SPIDERLING.
SO, AS LONG AS YOU'RE NOT PLANNING TO EAT ANYONE OR REWRITE THE GENETIC CODE OF EVERYONE IN THE FIVE BOROUGHS...
...GO ON. BE FREE.
SO WHAT DO WE DO WITH... ALL THIS?
I'LL MAKE SOME CALLS. SEE IF ANYONE KNOWS THIS DR. KRIKOS.
BUT UNLESS I'M MISTAKEN, IT'S STILL *FAMILY FUN DAY.*
I SAY WE GET BACK TOPSIDE WHILE THE LINES ARE STILL SHORT.
SO TODAY DIDN'T EXACTLY GO AS PLANNED.

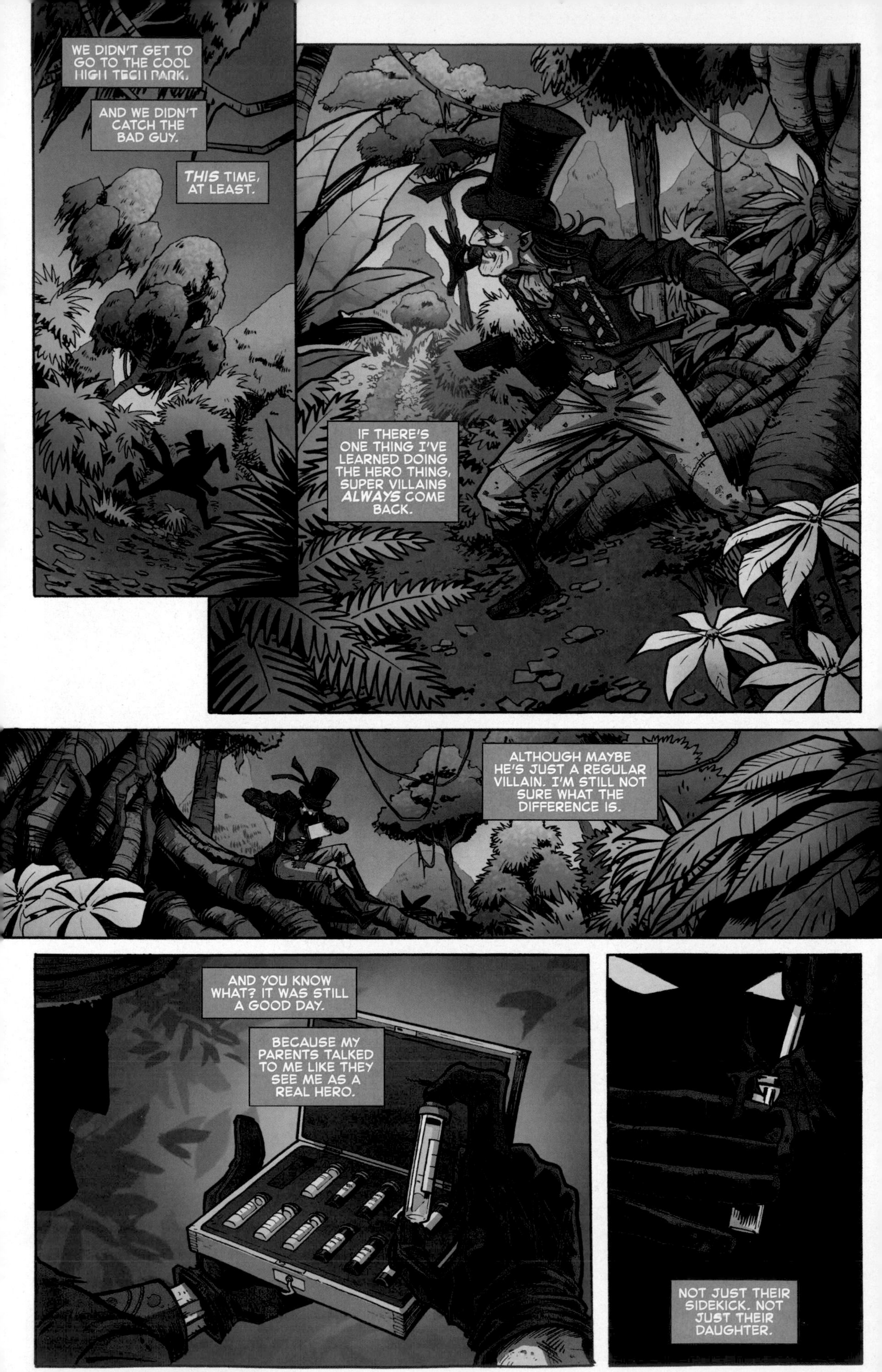
WE DIDN'T GET TO GO TO THE COOL HIGH TECH PARK.
AND WE DIDN'T CATCH THE BAD GUY.
THIS TIME, AT LEAST.
IF THERE'S ONE THING I'VE LEARNED DOING THE HERO THING, SUPER VILLAINS ALWAYS COME BACK.
ALTHOUGH MAYBE HE'S JUST A REGULAR VILLAIN. I'M STILL NOT SURE WHAT THE DIFFERENCE IS.
AND YOU KNOW WHAT? IT WAS STILL A GOOD DAY.
BECAUSE MY PARENTS TALKED TO ME LIKE THEY SEE ME AS A REAL HERO.
NOT JUST THEIR SIDEKICK. NOT JUST THEIR DAUGHTER.

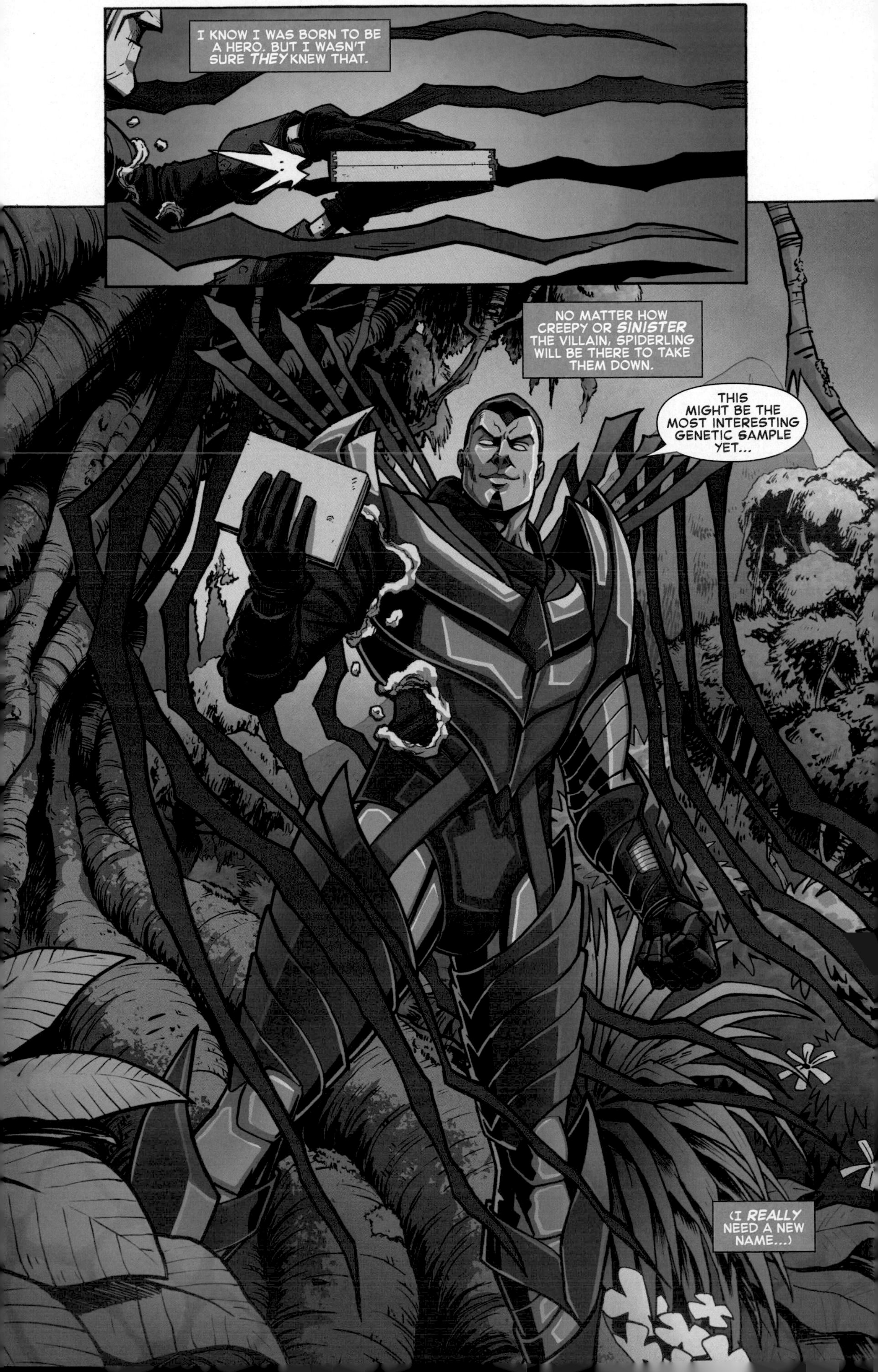
I KNOW I WAS BORN TO BE A HERO. BUT I WASN'T SURE THEY KNEW THAT.
NO MATTER HOW CREEPY OR SINISTER THE VILLAIN, SPIDERLING WILL BE THERE TO TAKE THEM DOWN.
THIS MIGHT BE THE MOST INTERESTING GENETIC SAMPLE YET...
(I REALLY NEED A NEW NAME...)

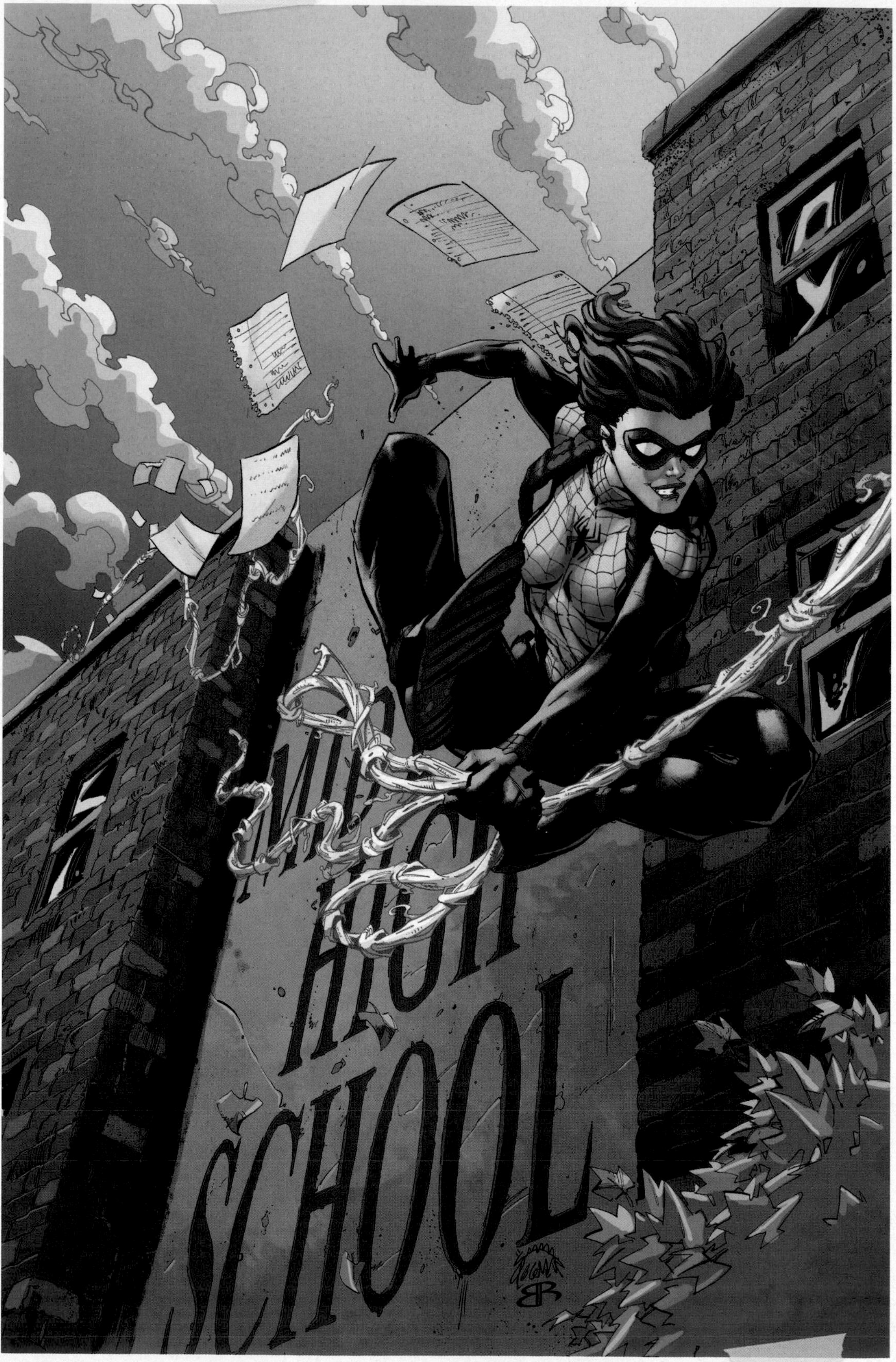
HIGH
SCHOOL

16: FAST TIMES AT MIDTOWN HIGH — PART 1

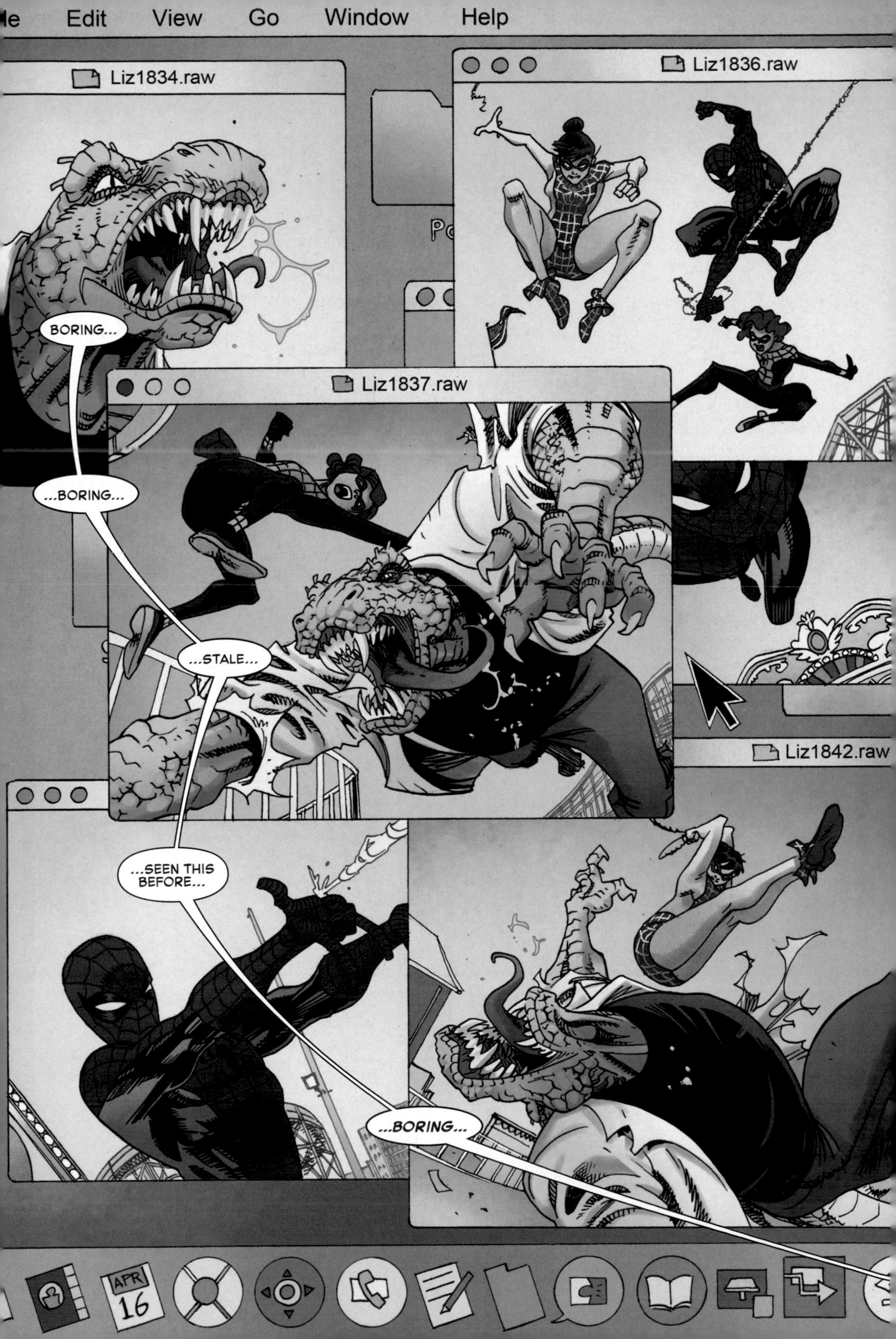
le Edit View Go Window Help
Liz1834.raw
Liz1836.raw
Liz1837.raw
Liz1842.raw
BORING...
...BORING...
...STALE...
...SEEN THIS BEFORE...
...BORING...
APR 16

THE SPIDER-FAMILY IS *OLD NEWS*, PARKER. NO ONE CARES ANYMORE. AND THE LIZARD? *REALLY?*

COULDN'T YOU AT LEAST GET SOME KIND OF FLASHY NEW SUPER VILLAIN?

I DIDN'T ACTUALLY *SEND* THE LIZARD AFTER THEM, SIR.

THERE ACTUALLY WAS A NEW GUY BEHIND IT ALL, *DR. KRIKOS.* BUT HE WAS UNDERGROUND.

NOT PART OF THE LITTLE PHOTO SHOOT.

AND THEN, AFTER ALL THAT, THE LIZARD *ESCAPED?*

THEY STILL STOPPED HIM FROM HURTING ANYONE! THAT'S NEWSWORTHY, ISN'T IT?

BESIDES, DOCUMENTING THE SPIDERS HAS ALWAYS BEEN MY THING.

THREAT OR MENACE?

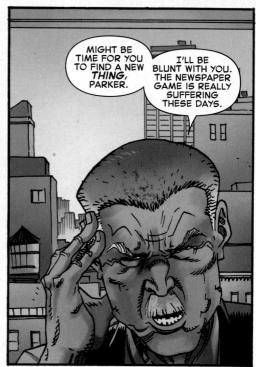

MIGHT BE TIME FOR YOU TO FIND A NEW *THING,* PARKER.

I'LL BE BLUNT WITH YOU. THE NEWSPAPER GAME IS REALLY SUFFERING THESE DAYS.

MAYBE YOU WERE THE FIRST TO USE DRONES TO GET PRESS SHOTS.

BUT NOW EVERY KID WITH TWENTY BUCKS AND A CELL PHONE IS DOING THE SAME. AND POSTING IT ON TWEETER.

I CAN BUY SOME OF THE PHOTOS, PARKER.

BUT IT HAS TO BE AT A LOWER RATE.

SECOND PAY CUT THIS YEAR...

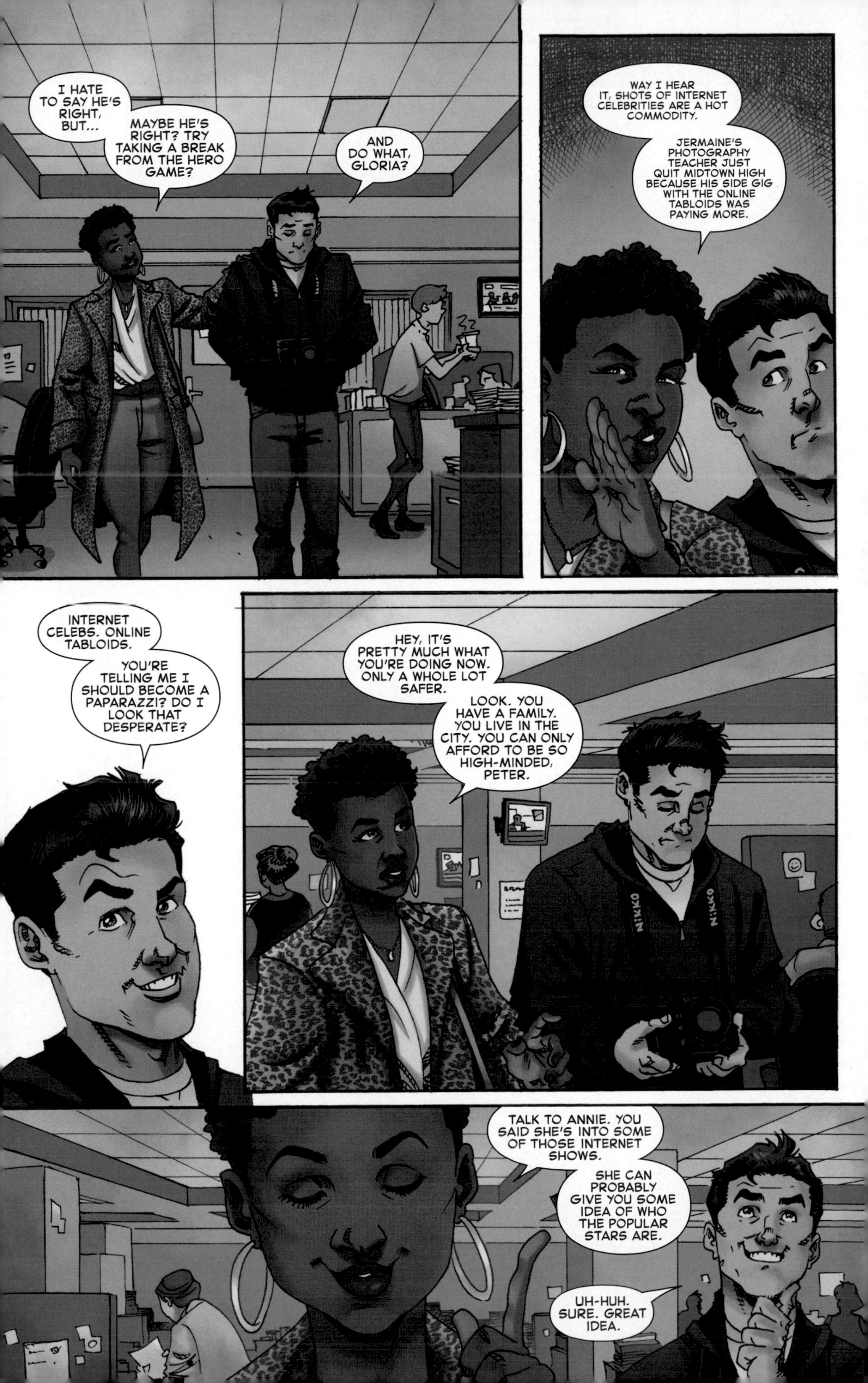
I HATE TO SAY HE'S RIGHT, BUT...
MAYBE HE'S RIGHT? TRY TAKING A BREAK FROM THE HERO GAME?
AND DO WHAT, GLORIA?
WAY I HEAR IT, SHOTS OF INTERNET CELEBRITIES ARE A HOT COMMODITY.
JERMAINE'S PHOTOGRAPHY TEACHER JUST QUIT MIDTOWN HIGH BECAUSE HIS SIDE GIG WITH THE ONLINE TABLOIDS WAS PAYING MORE.
INTERNET CELEBS. ONLINE TABLOIDS.
YOU'RE TELLING ME I SHOULD BECOME A PAPARAZZI? DO I LOOK THAT DESPERATE?
HEY, IT'S PRETTY MUCH WHAT YOU'RE DOING NOW. ONLY A WHOLE LOT SAFER.
LOOK. YOU HAVE A FAMILY. YOU LIVE IN THE CITY. YOU CAN ONLY AFFORD TO BE SO HIGH-MINDED, PETER.
NIKKO
NIKKO
TALK TO ANNIE. YOU SAID SHE'S INTO SOME OF THOSE INTERNET SHOWS.
SHE CAN PROBABLY GIVE YOU SOME IDEA OF WHO THE POPULAR STARS ARE.
UH-HUH. SURE. GREAT IDEA.

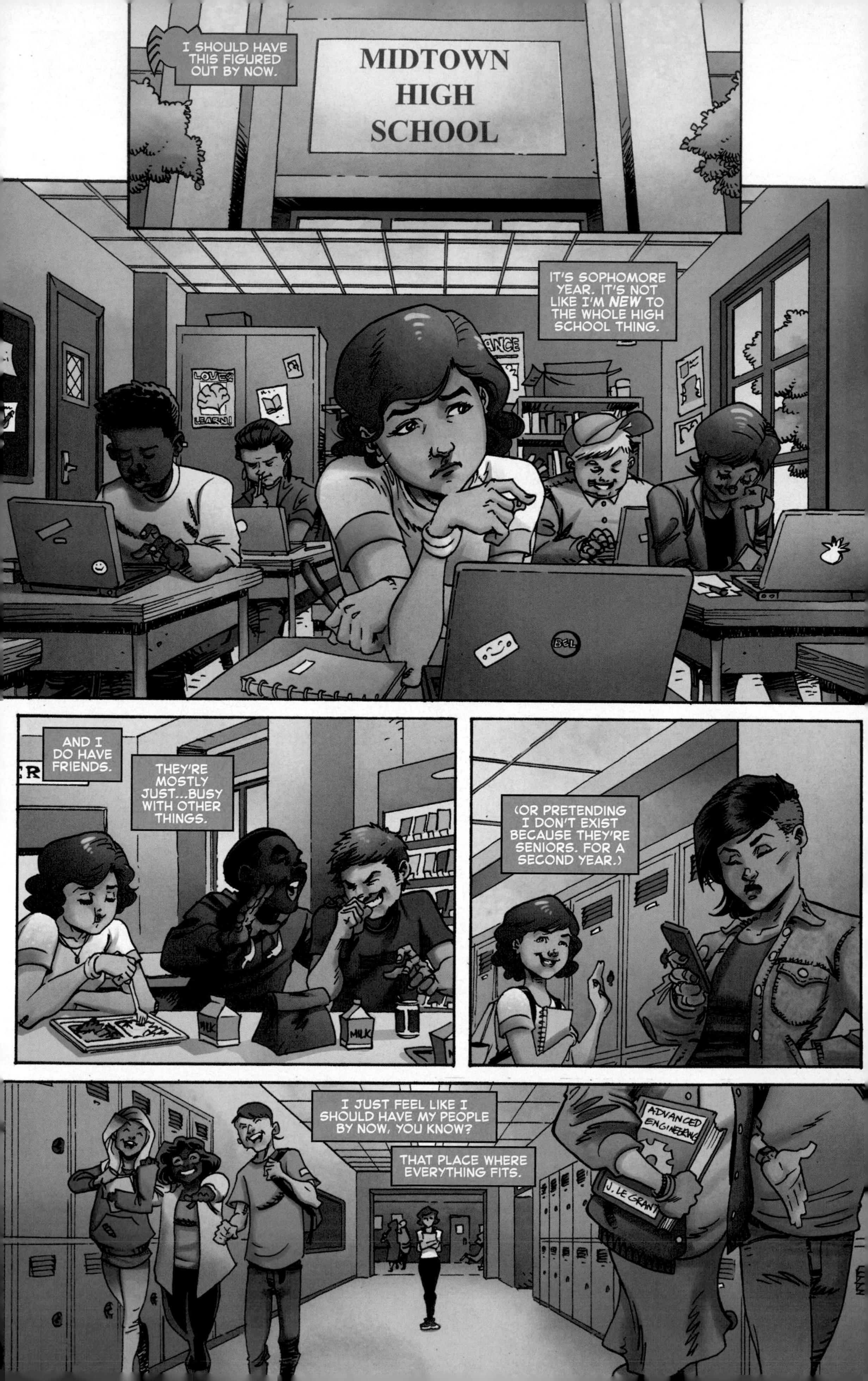

I SHOULD HAVE THIS FIGURED OUT BY NOW.
MIDTOWN HIGH SCHOOL
IT'S SOPHOMORE YEAR. IT'S NOT LIKE I'M *NEW* TO THE WHOLE HIGH SCHOOL THING.
LOVE? LEARN!
AND I DO HAVE FRIENDS.
THEY'RE MOSTLY JUST...BUSY WITH OTHER THINGS.
MILK
MILK
(OR PRETENDING I DON'T EXIST BECAUSE THEY'RE SENIORS. FOR A SECOND YEAR.)
I JUST FEEL LIKE I SHOULD HAVE MY PEOPLE BY NOW, YOU KNOW?
THAT PLACE WHERE EVERYTHING FITS.
ADVANCED ENGINEERING
J. LE GRANT

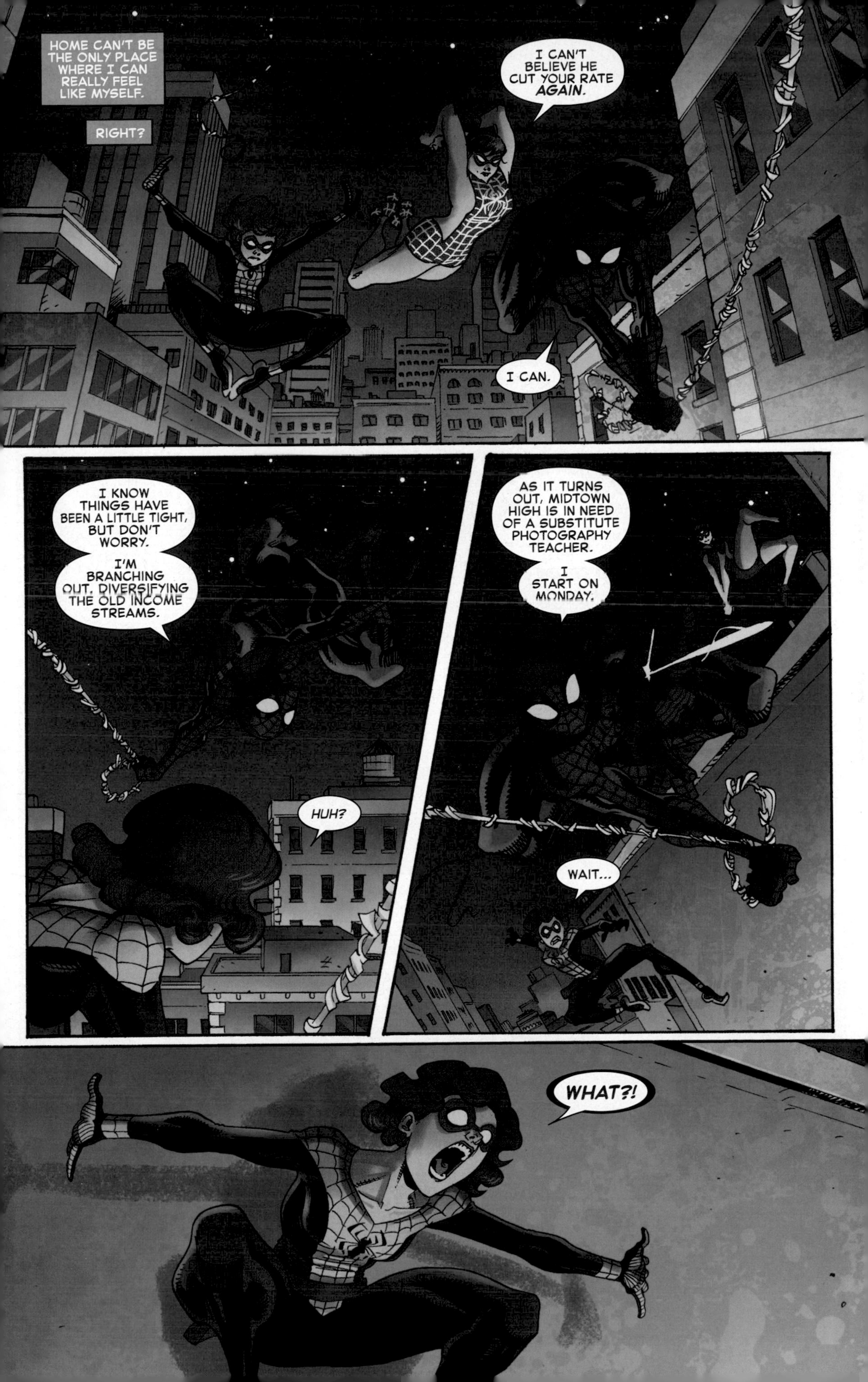
HOME CAN'T BE THE ONLY PLACE WHERE I CAN REALLY FEEL LIKE MYSELF.
RIGHT?
I CAN'T BELIEVE HE CUT YOUR RATE AGAIN.
I CAN.
I KNOW THINGS HAVE BEEN A LITTLE TIGHT, BUT DON'T WORRY.
I'M BRANCHING OUT. DIVERSIFYING THE OLD INCOME STREAMS.
HUH?
AS IT TURNS OUT, MIDTOWN HIGH IS IN NEED OF A SUBSTITUTE PHOTOGRAPHY TEACHER.
I START ON MONDAY.
WAIT...
WHAT?!

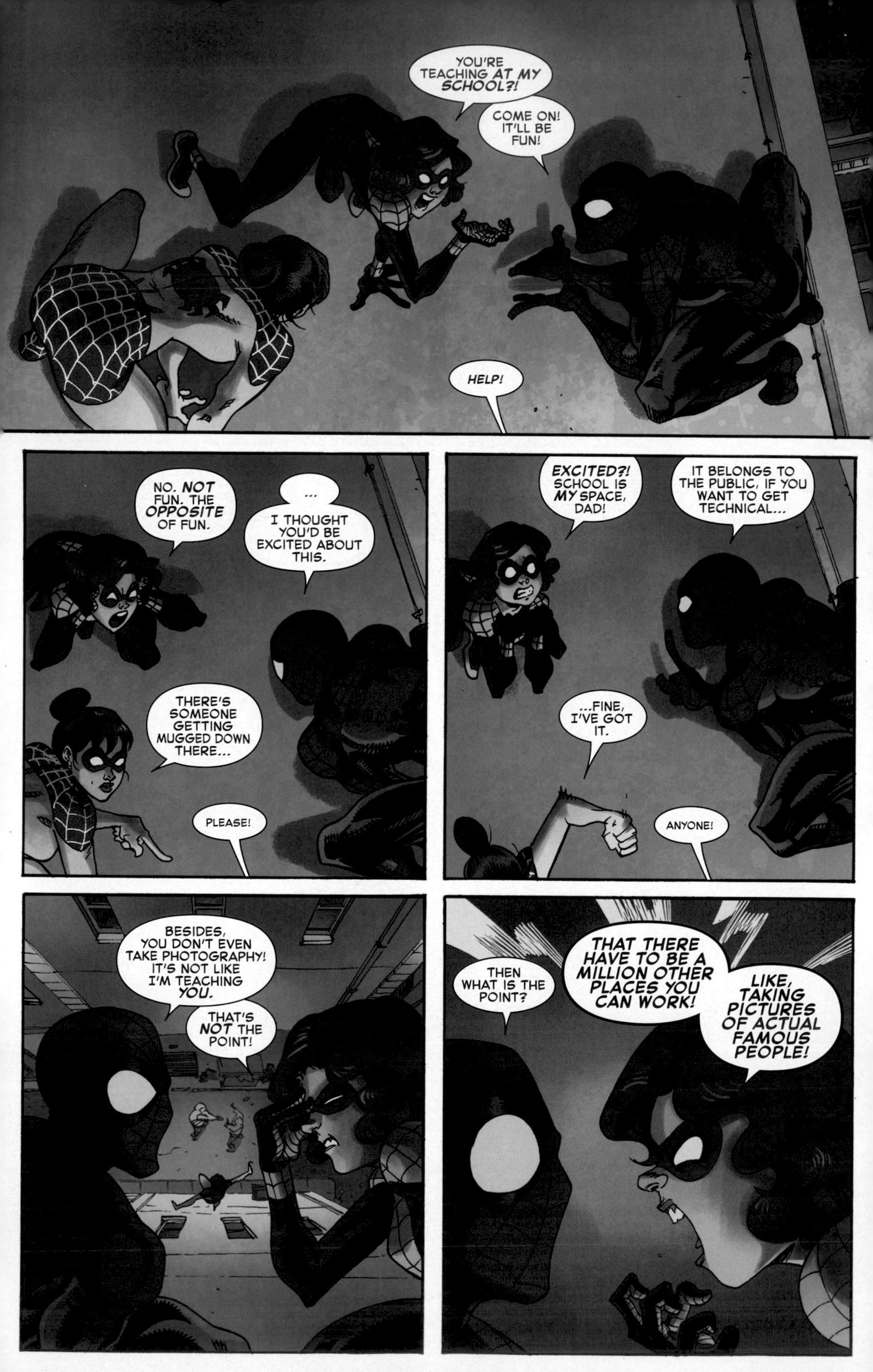
YOU'RE TEACHING AT MY SCHOOL?!
COME ON! IT'LL BE FUN!
HELP!
NO. NOT FUN. THE OPPOSITE OF FUN.
... I THOUGHT YOU'D BE EXCITED ABOUT THIS.
THERE'S SOMEONE GETTING MUGGED DOWN THERE...
PLEASE!
EXCITED?! SCHOOL IS MY SPACE, DAD!
IT BELONGS TO THE PUBLIC, IF YOU WANT TO GET TECHNICAL...
...FINE, I'VE GOT IT.
ANYONE!
BESIDES, YOU DON'T EVEN TAKE PHOTOGRAPHY! IT'S NOT LIKE I'M TEACHING YOU.
THAT'S NOT THE POINT!
THEN WHAT IS THE POINT?
THAT THERE HAVE TO BE A MILLION OTHER PLACES YOU CAN WORK!
LIKE, TAKING PICTURES OF ACTUAL FAMOUS PEOPLE!

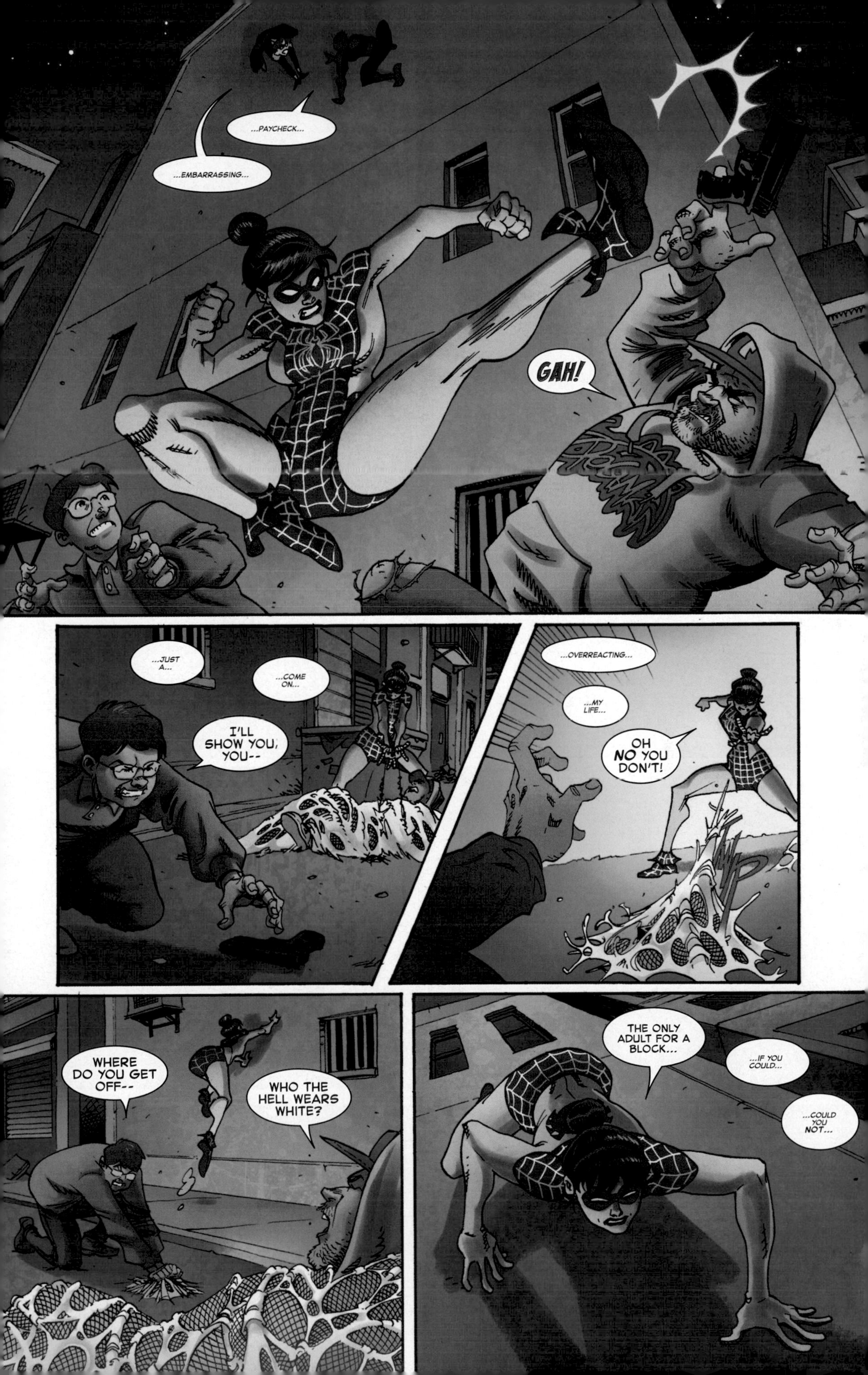

...PAYCHECK...
...EMBARRASSING...
GAH!
...JUST A...
...COME ON...
I'LL SHOW YOU, YOU--
...OVERREACTING...
...MY LIFE...
OH NO YOU DON'T!
WHERE DO YOU GET OFF--
WHO THE HELL WEARS WHITE?
THE ONLY ADULT FOR A BLOCK...
...IF YOU COULD...
...COULD YOU NOT...

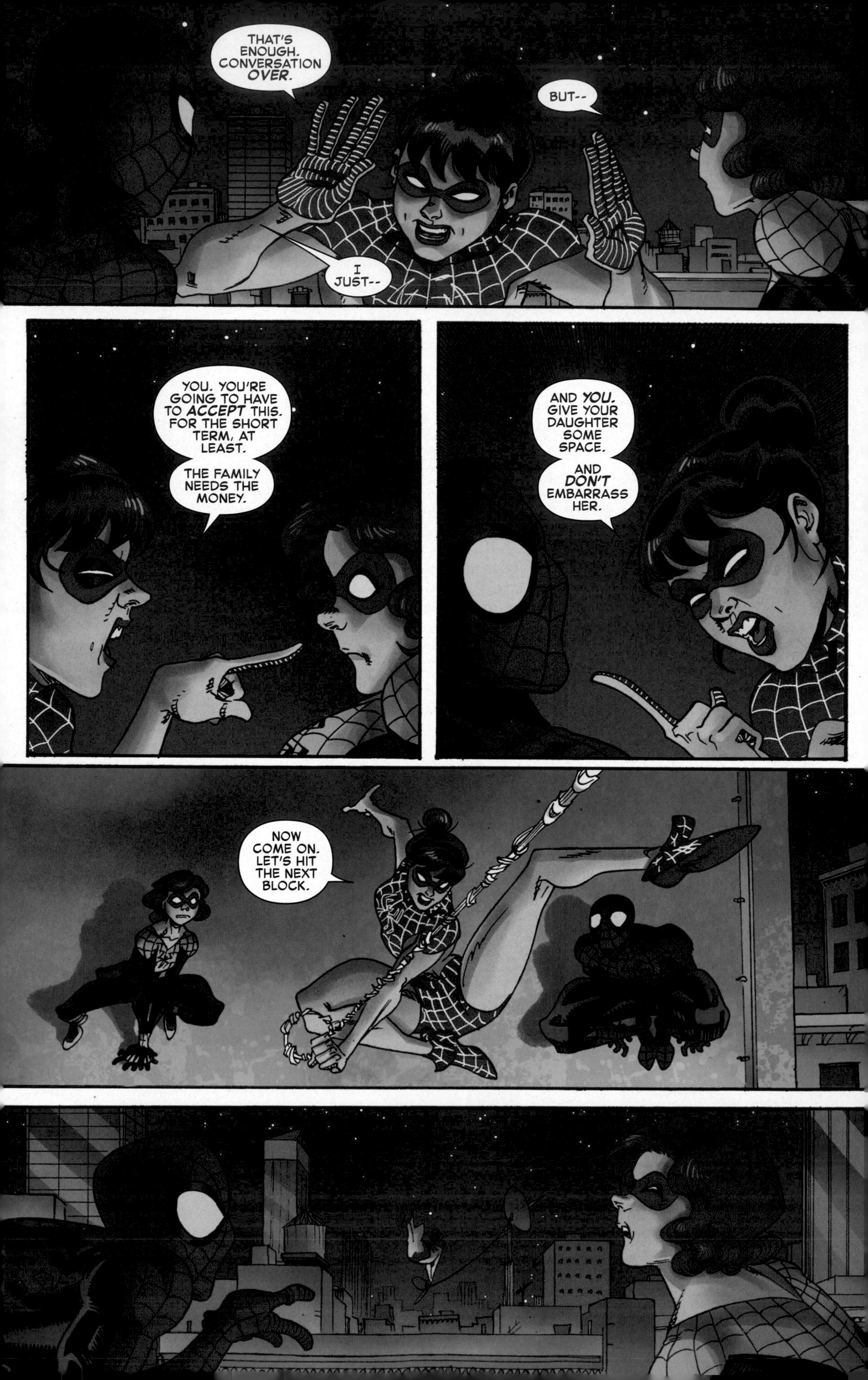
THAT'S ENOUGH. CONVERSATION OVER.
BUT--
I JUST--
YOU. YOU'RE GOING TO HAVE TO ACCEPT THIS. FOR THE SHORT TERM, AT LEAST.
THE FAMILY NEEDS THE MONEY.
AND YOU. GIVE YOUR DAUGHTER SOME SPACE.
AND DON'T EMBARRASS HER.
NOW COME ON. LET'S HIT THE NEXT BLOCK.

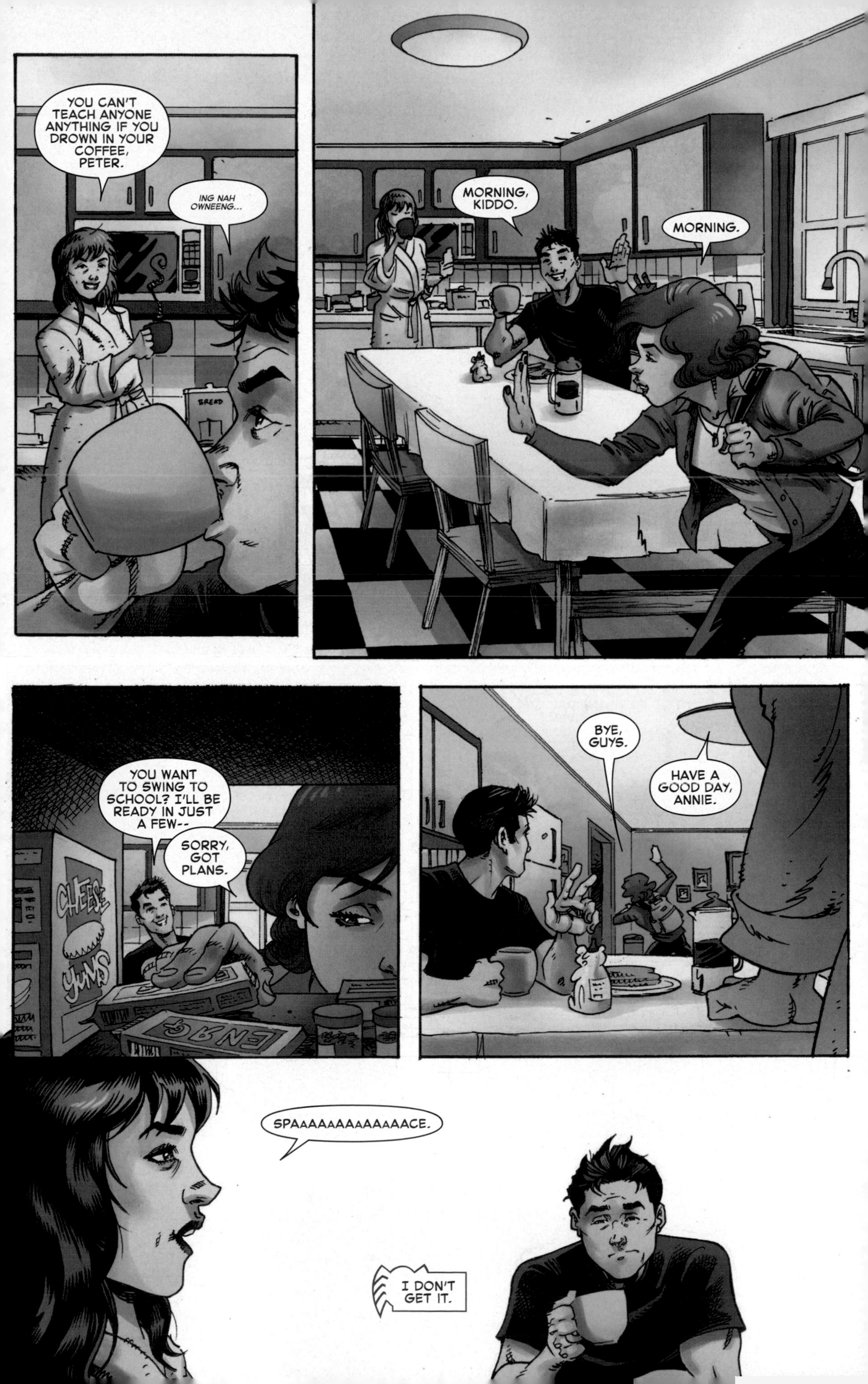
YOU CAN'T TEACH ANYONE ANYTHING IF YOU DROWN IN YOUR COFFEE, PETER.
ING NAH OWNEENG...
MORNING, KIDDO.
MORNING.
YOU WANT TO SWING TO SCHOOL? I'LL BE READY IN JUST A FEW--
SORRY, GOT PLANS.
BYE, GUYS.
HAVE A GOOD DAY, ANNIE.
SPAAAAAAAAAAAAACE.
I DON'T GET IT.

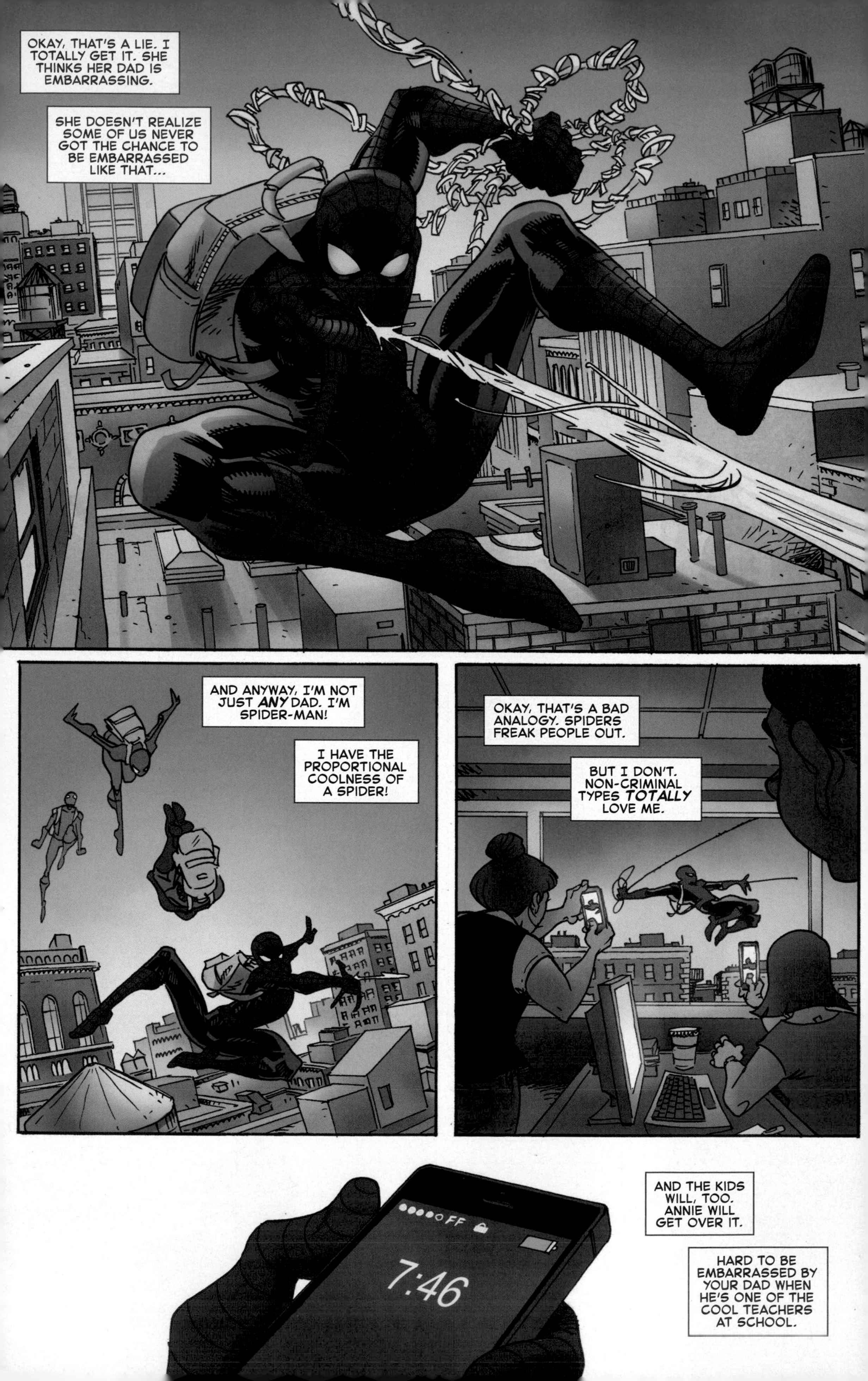
OKAY, THAT'S A LIE. I TOTALLY GET IT. SHE THINKS HER DAD IS EMBARRASSING.
SHE DOESN'T REALIZE SOME OF US NEVER GOT THE CHANCE TO BE EMBARRASSED LIKE THAT...
AND ANYWAY, I'M NOT JUST *ANY* DAD. I'M SPIDER-MAN!
I HAVE THE PROPORTIONAL COOLNESS OF A SPIDER!
OKAY, THAT'S A BAD ANALOGY. SPIDERS FREAK PEOPLE OUT.
BUT I DON'T. NON-CRIMINAL TYPES *TOTALLY* LOVE ME.
7:46
AND THE KIDS WILL, TOO. ANNIE WILL GET OVER IT.
HARD TO BE EMBARRASSED BY YOUR DAD WHEN HE'S ONE OF THE COOL TEACHERS AT SCHOOL.

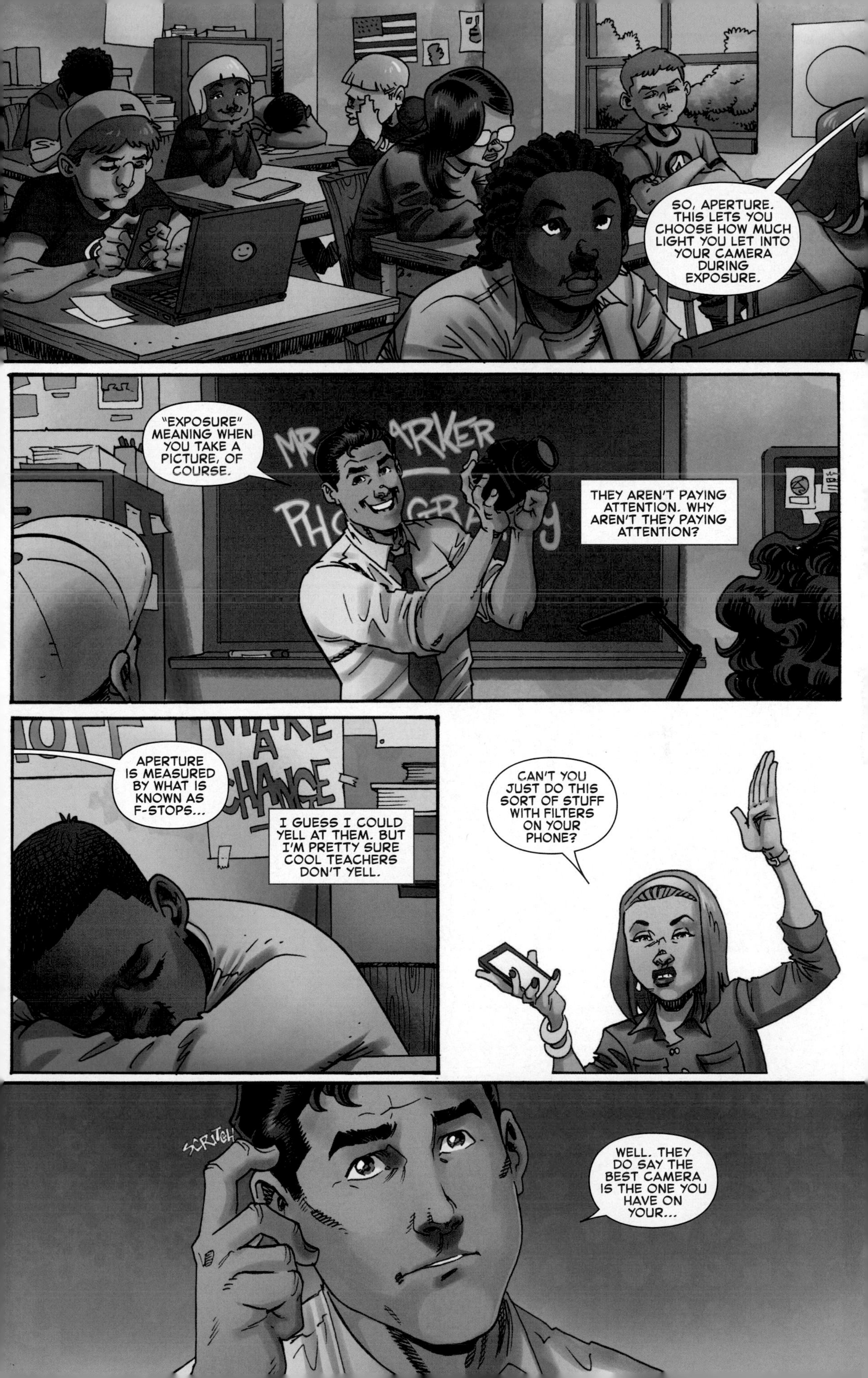
SO, APERTURE. THIS LETS YOU CHOOSE HOW MUCH LIGHT YOU LET INTO YOUR CAMERA DURING EXPOSURE.
MR. PARKER PHOTOGRAPHY
"EXPOSURE" MEANING WHEN YOU TAKE A PICTURE, OF COURSE.
THEY AREN'T PAYING ATTENTION. WHY AREN'T THEY PAYING ATTENTION?
MAKE A CHANGE
APERTURE IS MEASURED BY WHAT IS KNOWN AS F-STOPS...
I GUESS I COULD YELL AT THEM. BUT I'M PRETTY SURE COOL TEACHERS DON'T YELL.
CAN'T YOU JUST DO THIS SORT OF STUFF WITH FILTERS ON YOUR PHONE?
SCRITCH
WELL. THEY DO SAY THE BEST CAMERA IS THE ONE YOU HAVE ON YOUR...

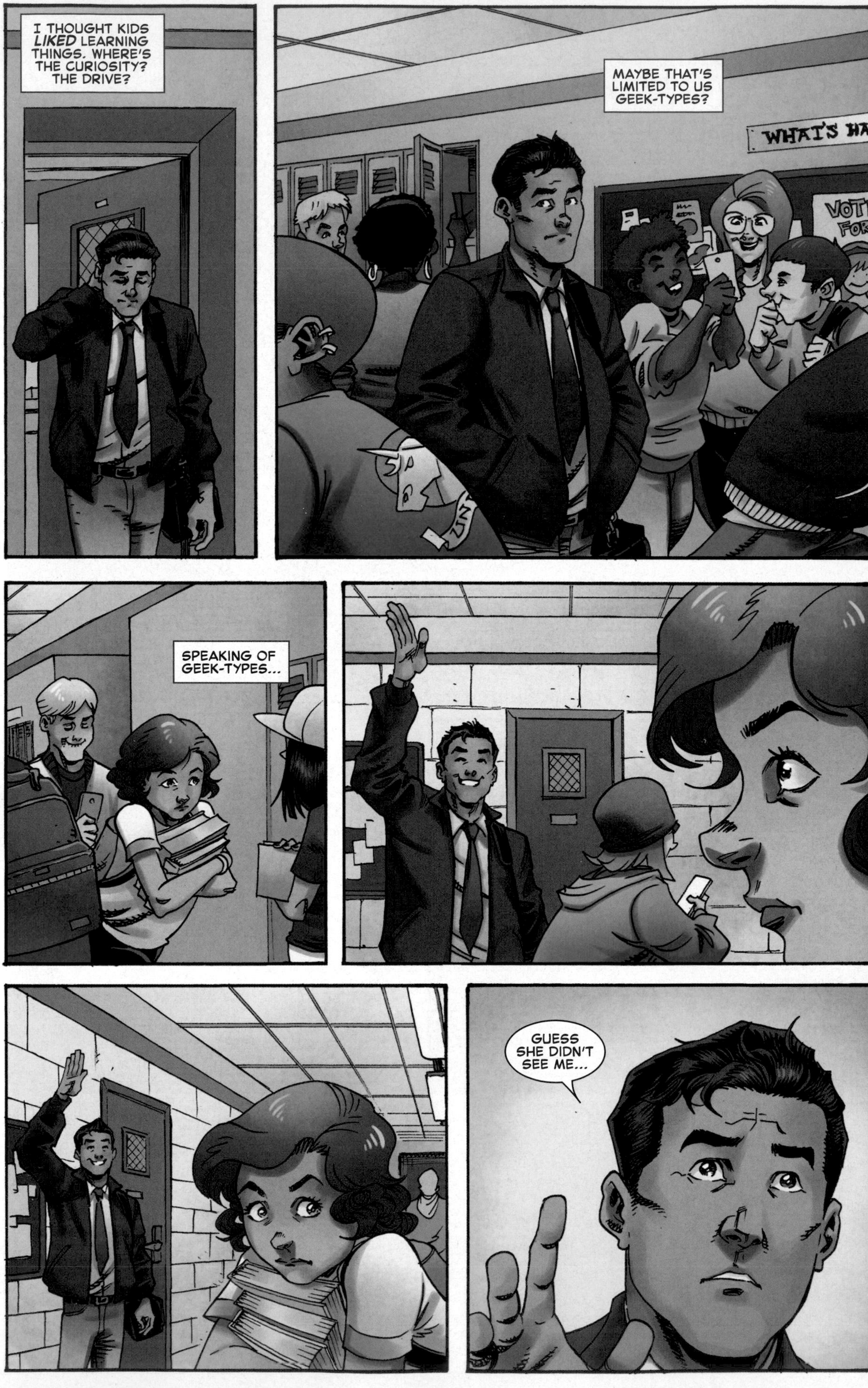
I THOUGHT KIDS *LIKED* LEARNING THINGS. WHERE'S THE CURIOSITY? THE DRIVE?
MAYBE THAT'S LIMITED TO US GEEK-TYPES?
WHAT'S HA
VOTE FOR
SPEAKING OF GEEK-TYPES...
GUESS SHE DIDN'T SEE ME...

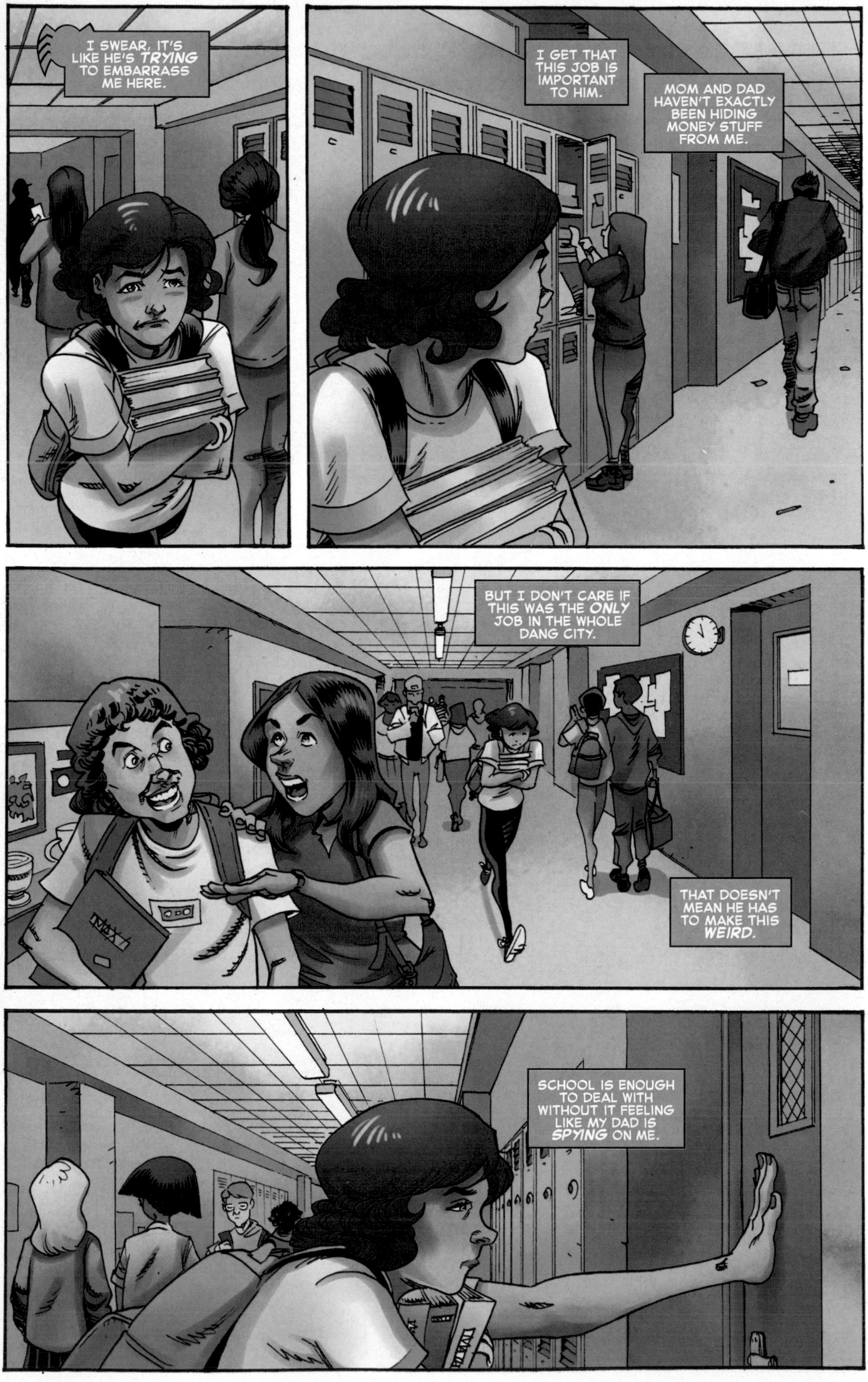
I SWEAR, IT'S LIKE HE'S TRYING TO EMBARRASS ME HERE.
I GET THAT THIS JOB IS IMPORTANT TO HIM.
MOM AND DAD HAVEN'T EXACTLY BEEN HIDING MONEY STUFF FROM ME.
BUT I DON'T CARE IF THIS WAS THE ONLY JOB IN THE WHOLE DANG CITY.
THAT DOESN'T MEAN HE HAS TO MAKE THIS WEIRD.
SCHOOL IS ENOUGH TO DEAL WITH WITHOUT IT FEELING LIKE MY DAD IS SPYING ON ME.

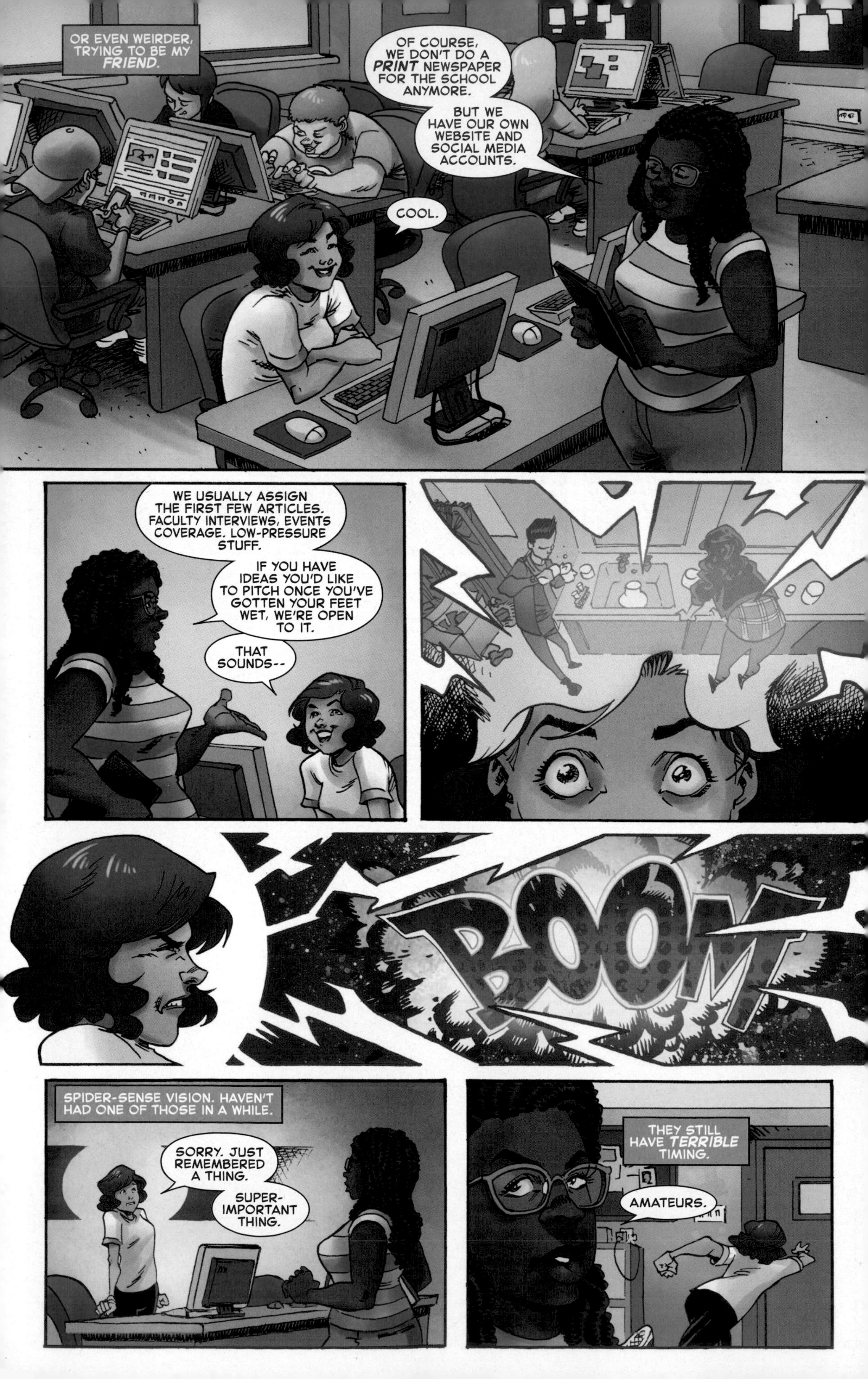
OR EVEN WEIRDER, TRYING TO BE MY FRIEND.
OF COURSE, WE DON'T DO A PRINT NEWSPAPER FOR THE SCHOOL ANYMORE.
BUT WE HAVE OUR OWN WEBSITE AND SOCIAL MEDIA ACCOUNTS.
COOL.
WE USUALLY ASSIGN THE FIRST FEW ARTICLES. FACULTY INTERVIEWS, EVENTS COVERAGE. LOW-PRESSURE STUFF.
IF YOU HAVE IDEAS YOU'D LIKE TO PITCH ONCE YOU'VE GOTTEN YOUR FEET WET, WE'RE OPEN TO IT.
THAT SOUNDS--
BOOM
SPIDER-SENSE VISION. HAVEN'T HAD ONE OF THOSE IN A WHILE.
SORRY. JUST REMEMBERED A THING.
SUPER-IMPORTANT THING.
THEY STILL HAVE TERRIBLE TIMING.
AMATEURS.

WELL, I GUESS SCHOOL NEWSPAPER IS OUT FOR NOW.

CAN THERE BE A "KEEP THE SCHOOL FROM BLOWING UP" CLUB?

I'D BE A SHOO-IN FOR PRESIDENT.

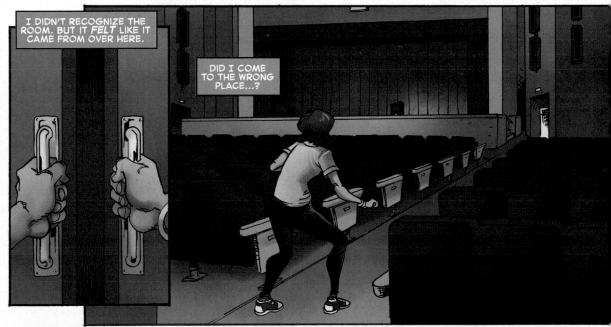

I DIDN'T RECOGNIZE THE ROOM. BUT IT *FELT* LIKE IT CAME FROM OVER HERE.

DID I COME TO THE WRONG PLACE...?

...CHEM LAB...

...TOO MANY PEOPLE...

THERE.

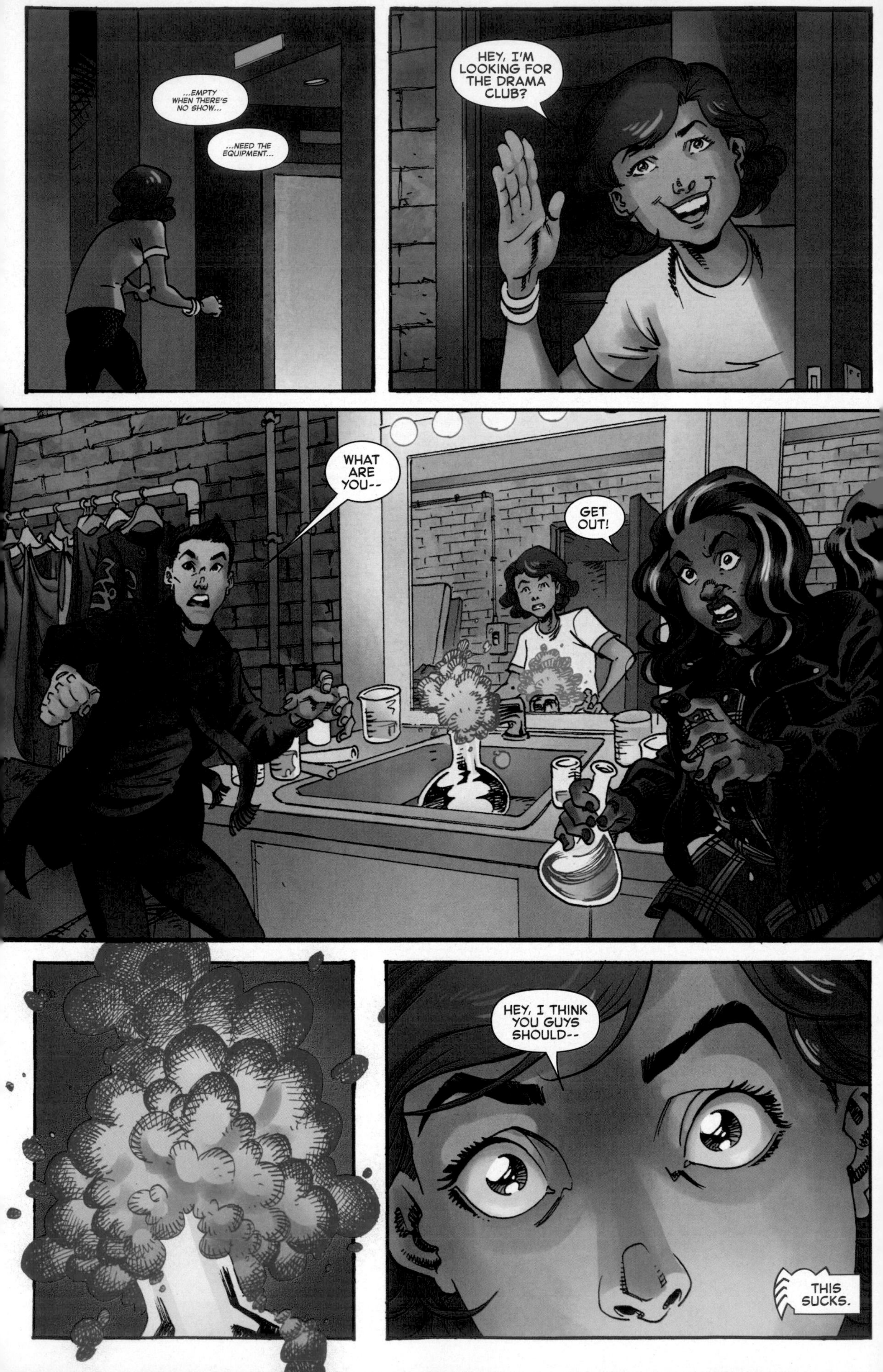
...EMPTY WHEN THERE'S NO SHOW...
...NEED THE EQUIPMENT...
HEY, I'M LOOKING FOR THE DRAMA CLUB?
WHAT ARE YOU--
GET OUT!
HEY, I THINK YOU GUYS SHOULD--
THIS SUCKS.

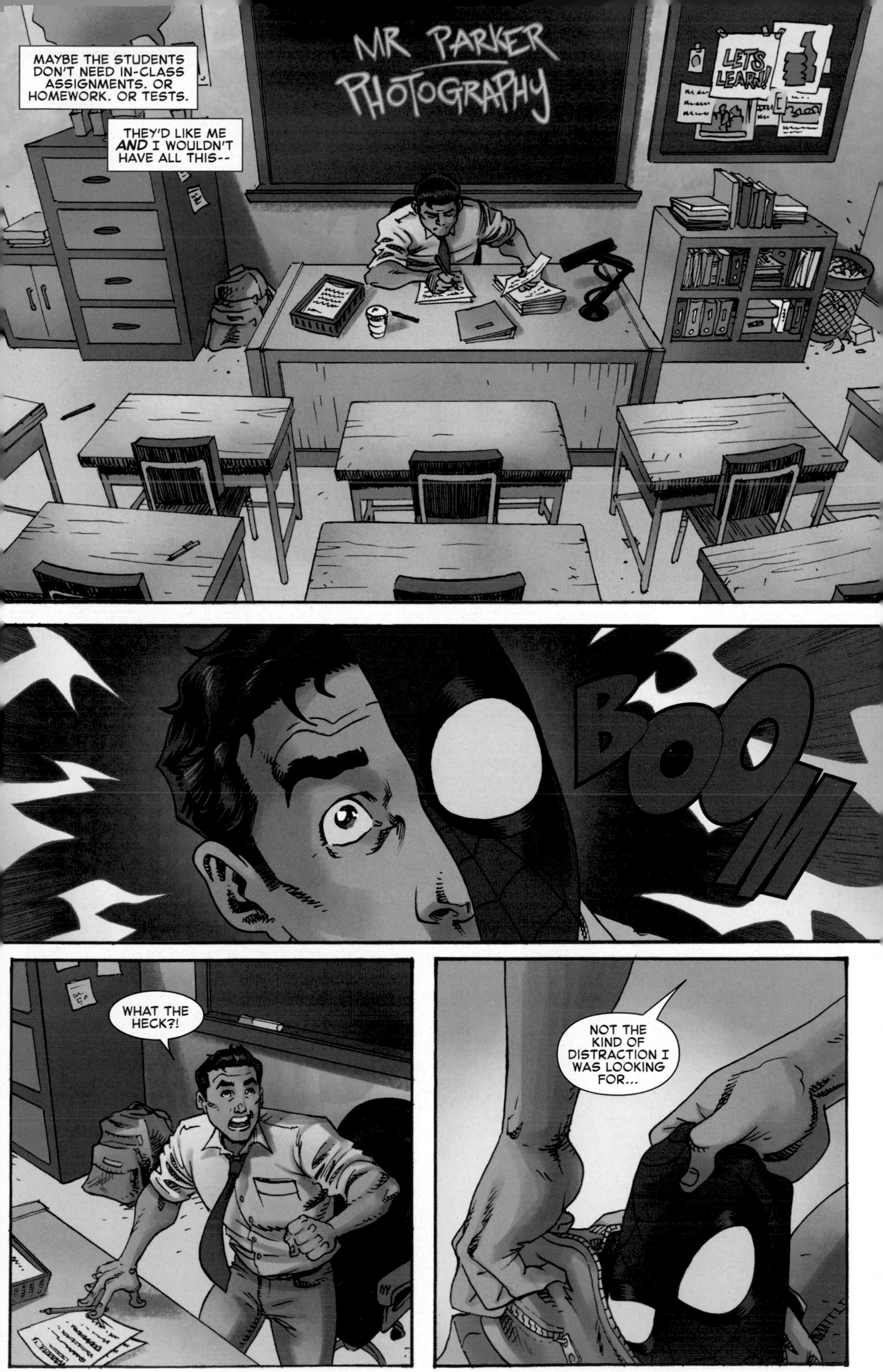
MR PARKER
PHOTOGRAPHY
LETS LEARN!
MAYBE THE STUDENTS DON'T NEED IN-CLASS ASSIGNMENTS. OR HOMEWORK. OR TESTS.
THEY'D LIKE ME AND I WOULDN'T HAVE ALL THIS--
BOOM
WHAT THE HECK?!
NOT THE KIND OF DISTRACTION I WAS LOOKING FOR...

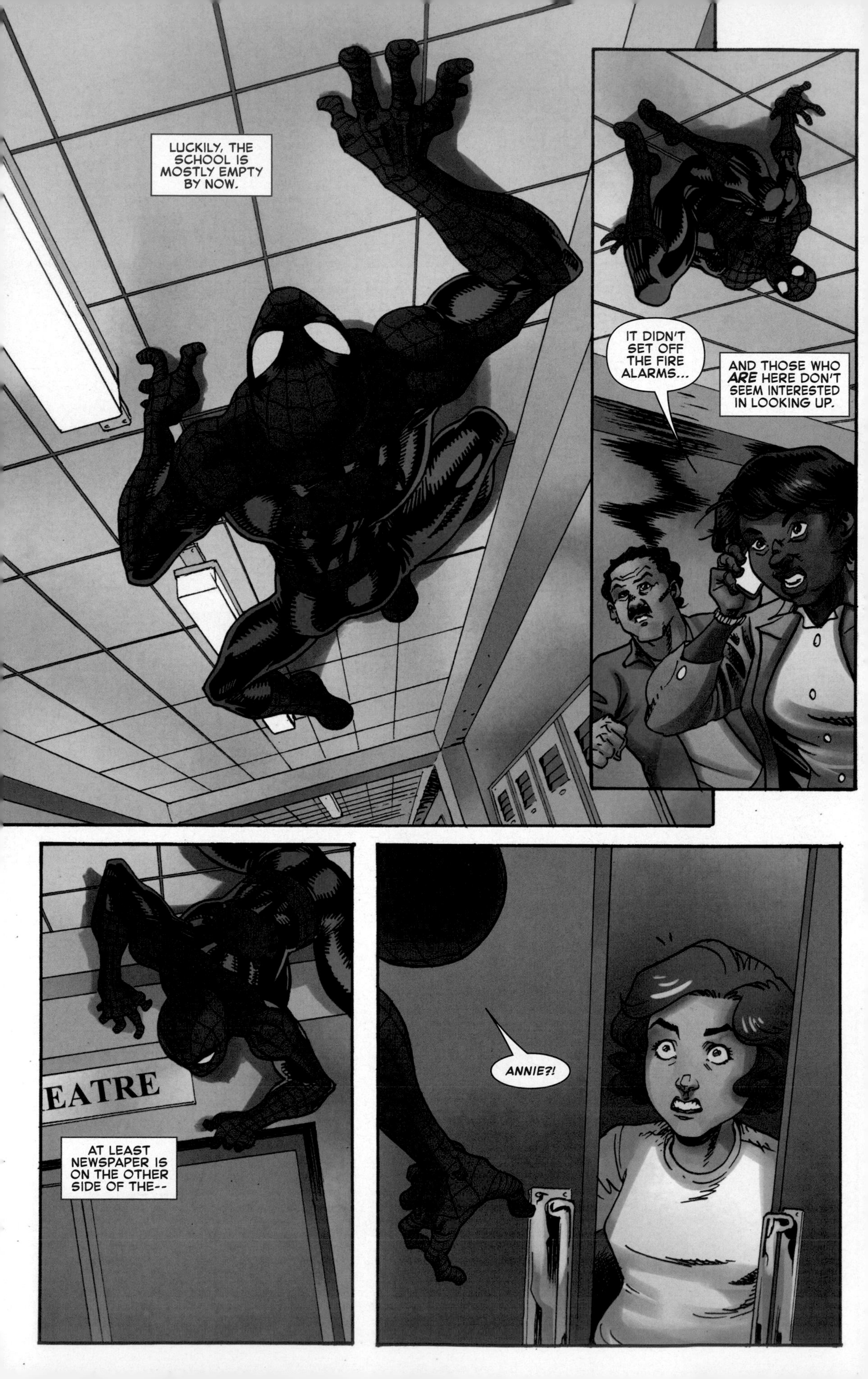
LUCKILY, THE SCHOOL IS MOSTLY EMPTY BY NOW.
IT DIDN'T SET OFF THE FIRE ALARMS...
AND THOSE WHO ARE HERE DON'T SEEM INTERESTED IN LOOKING UP.
EATRE
AT LEAST NEWSPAPER IS ON THE OTHER SIDE OF THE--
ANNIE?!

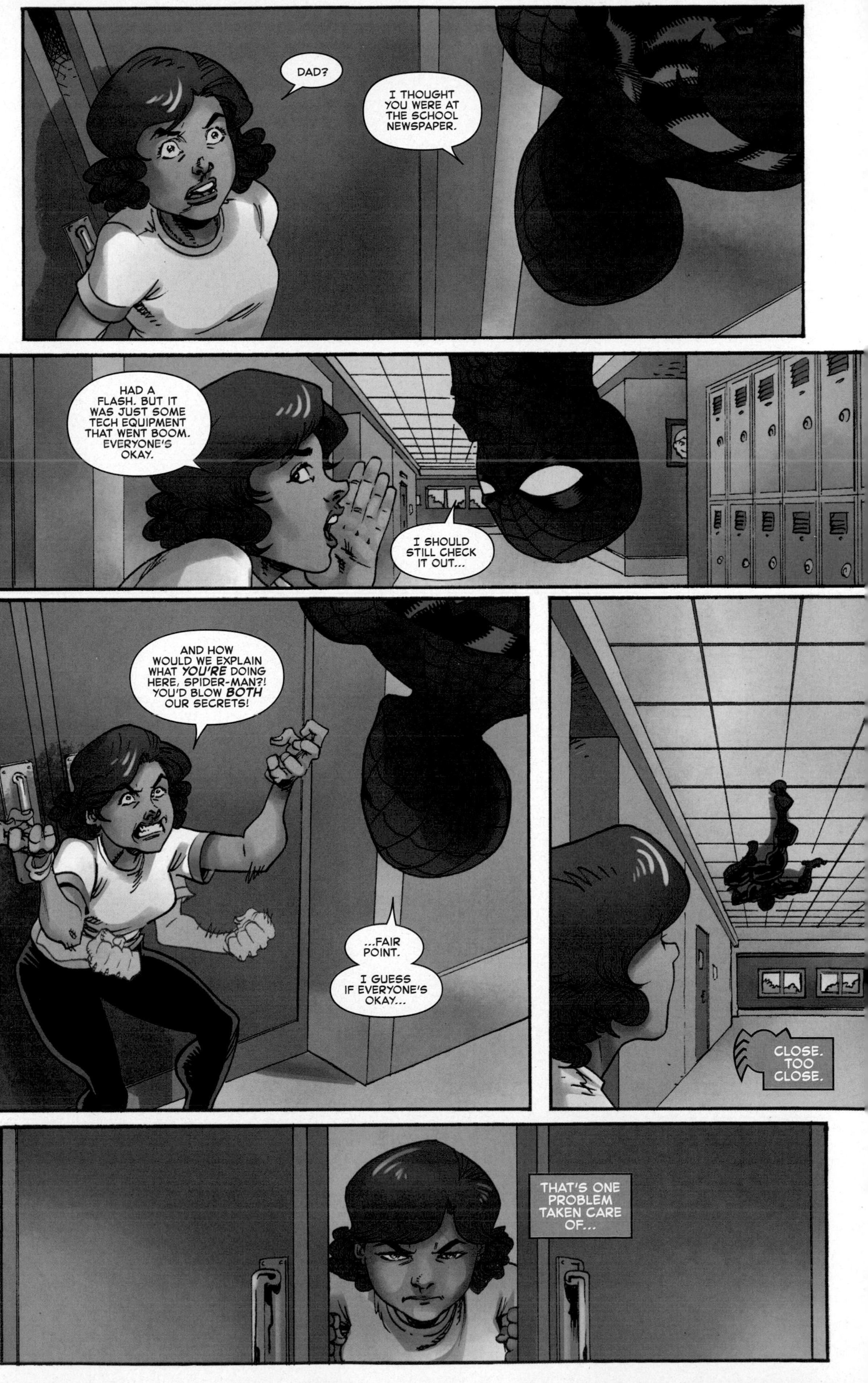
DAD?
I THOUGHT YOU WERE AT THE SCHOOL NEWSPAPER.
HAD A FLASH. BUT IT WAS JUST SOME TECH EQUIPMENT THAT WENT BOOM. EVERYONE'S OKAY.
I SHOULD STILL CHECK IT OUT...
AND HOW WOULD WE EXPLAIN WHAT *YOU'RE* DOING HERE, SPIDER-MAN?! YOU'D BLOW *BOTH* OUR SECRETS!
...FAIR POINT.
I GUESS IF EVERYONE'S OKAY...
CLOSE. TOO CLOSE.
THAT'S ONE PROBLEM TAKEN CARE OF...

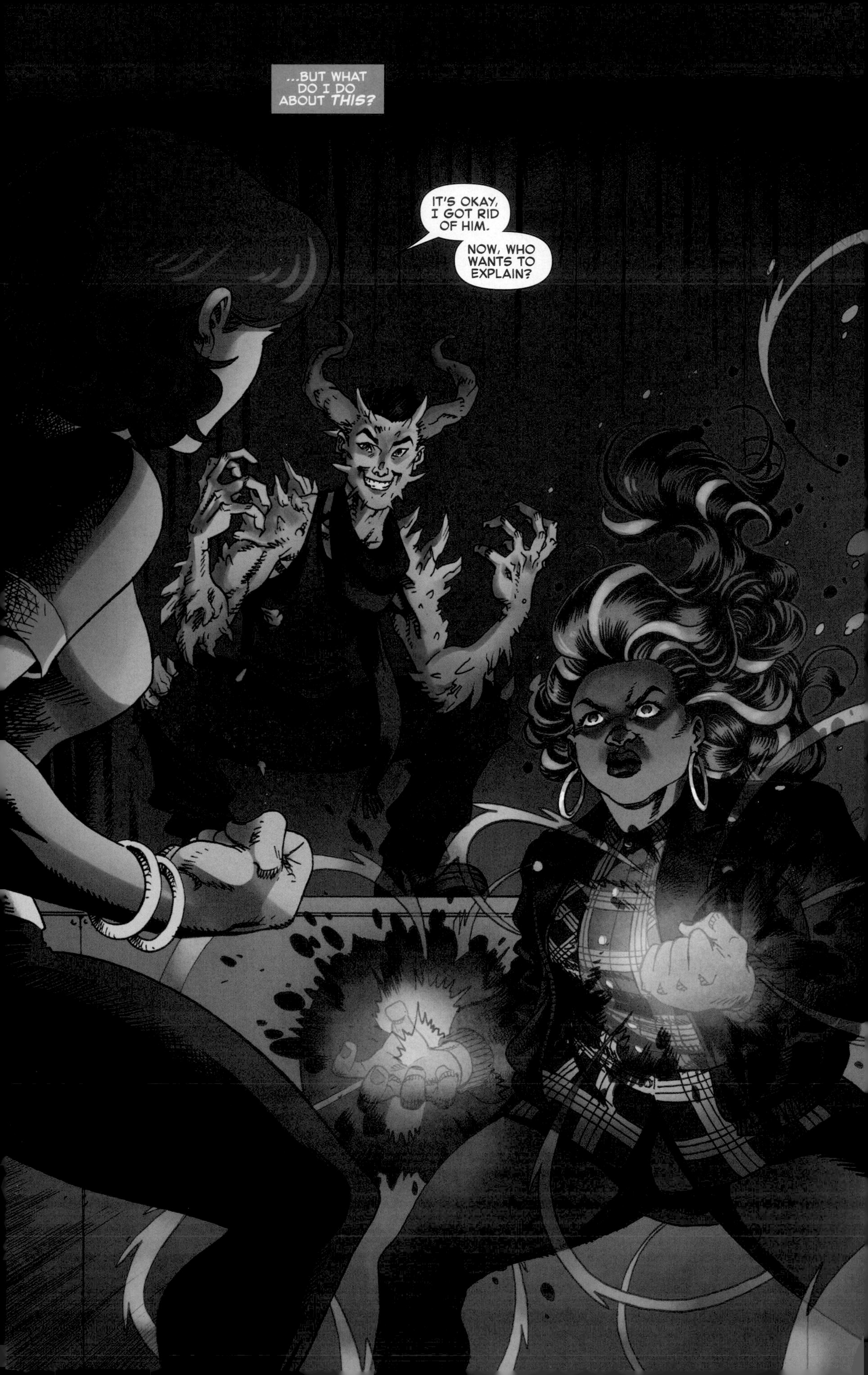
...BUT WHAT DO I DO ABOUT *THIS?*
IT'S OKAY, I GOT RID OF HIM.
NOW, WHO WANTS TO EXPLAIN?

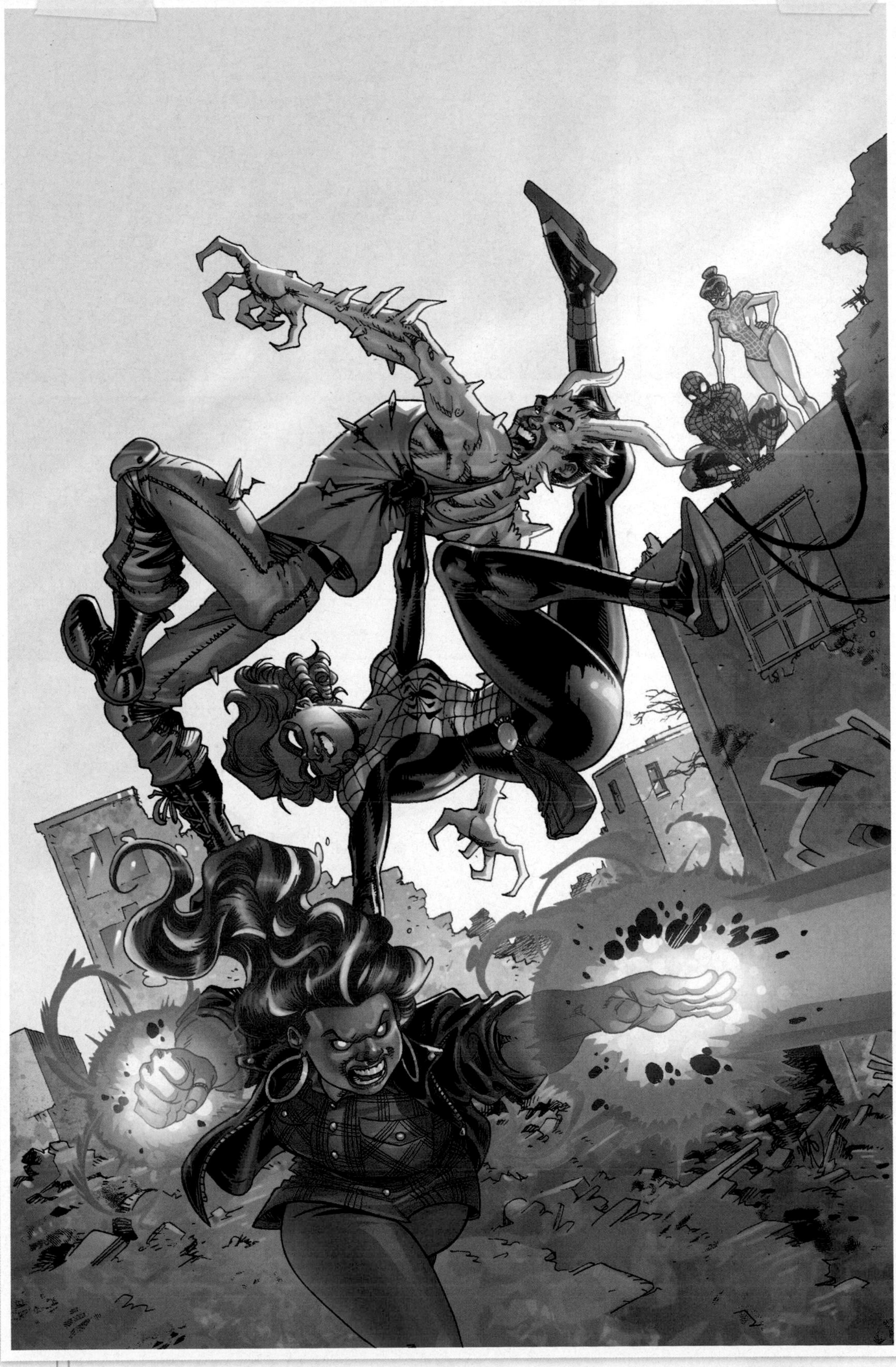

17: FAST TIMES AT MIDTOWN HIGH — PART 2

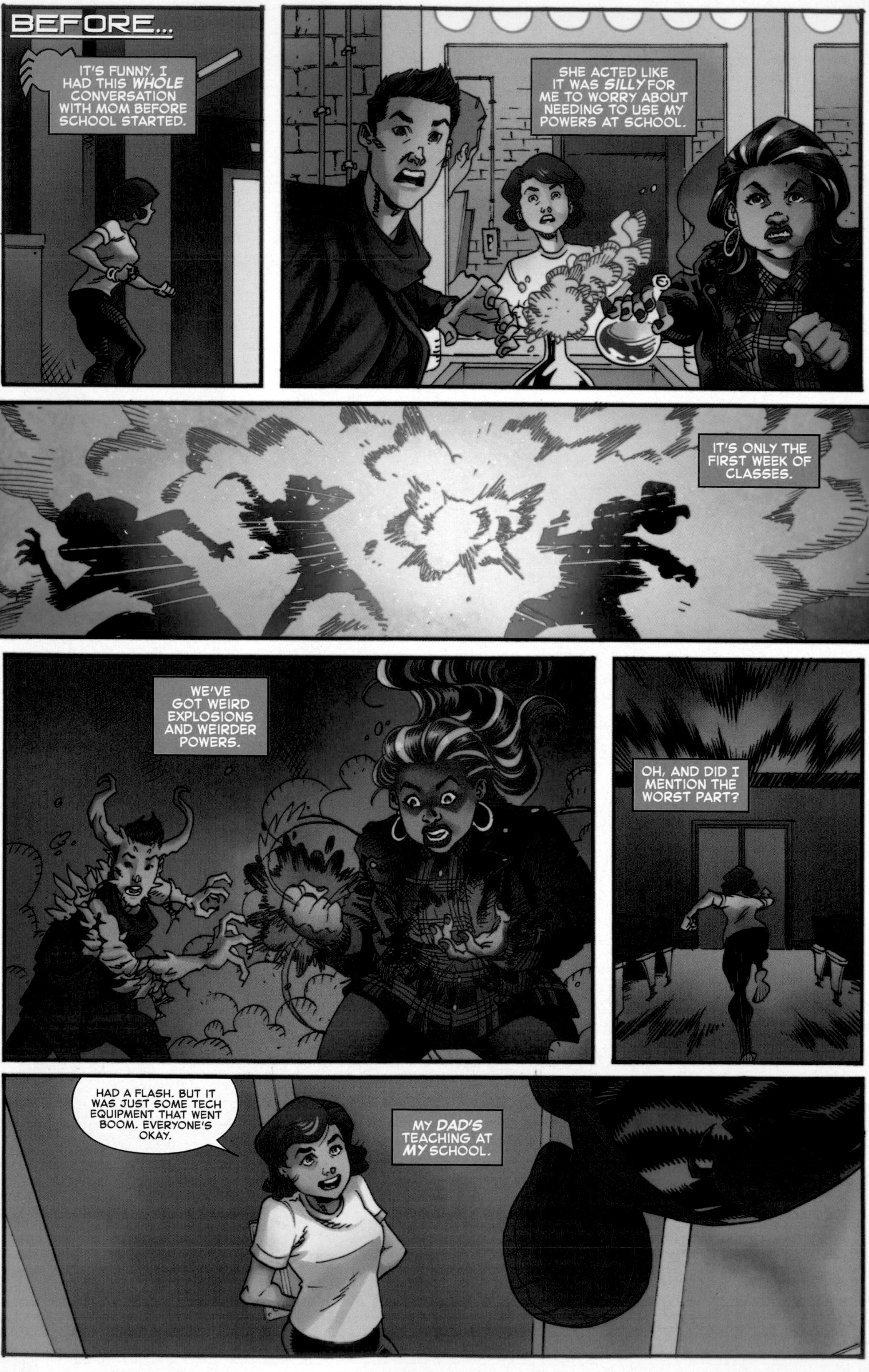

BEFORE...
IT'S FUNNY. I HAD THIS WHOLE CONVERSATION WITH MOM BEFORE SCHOOL STARTED.
SHE ACTED LIKE IT WAS SILLY FOR ME TO WORRY ABOUT NEEDING TO USE MY POWERS AT SCHOOL.
IT'S ONLY THE FIRST WEEK OF CLASSES.
WE'VE GOT WEIRD EXPLOSIONS AND WEIRDER POWERS.
OH, AND DID I MENTION THE WORST PART?
HAD A FLASH. BUT IT WAS JUST SOME TECH EQUIPMENT THAT WENT BOOM. EVERYONE'S OKAY.
MY DAD'S TEACHING AT MY SCHOOL.

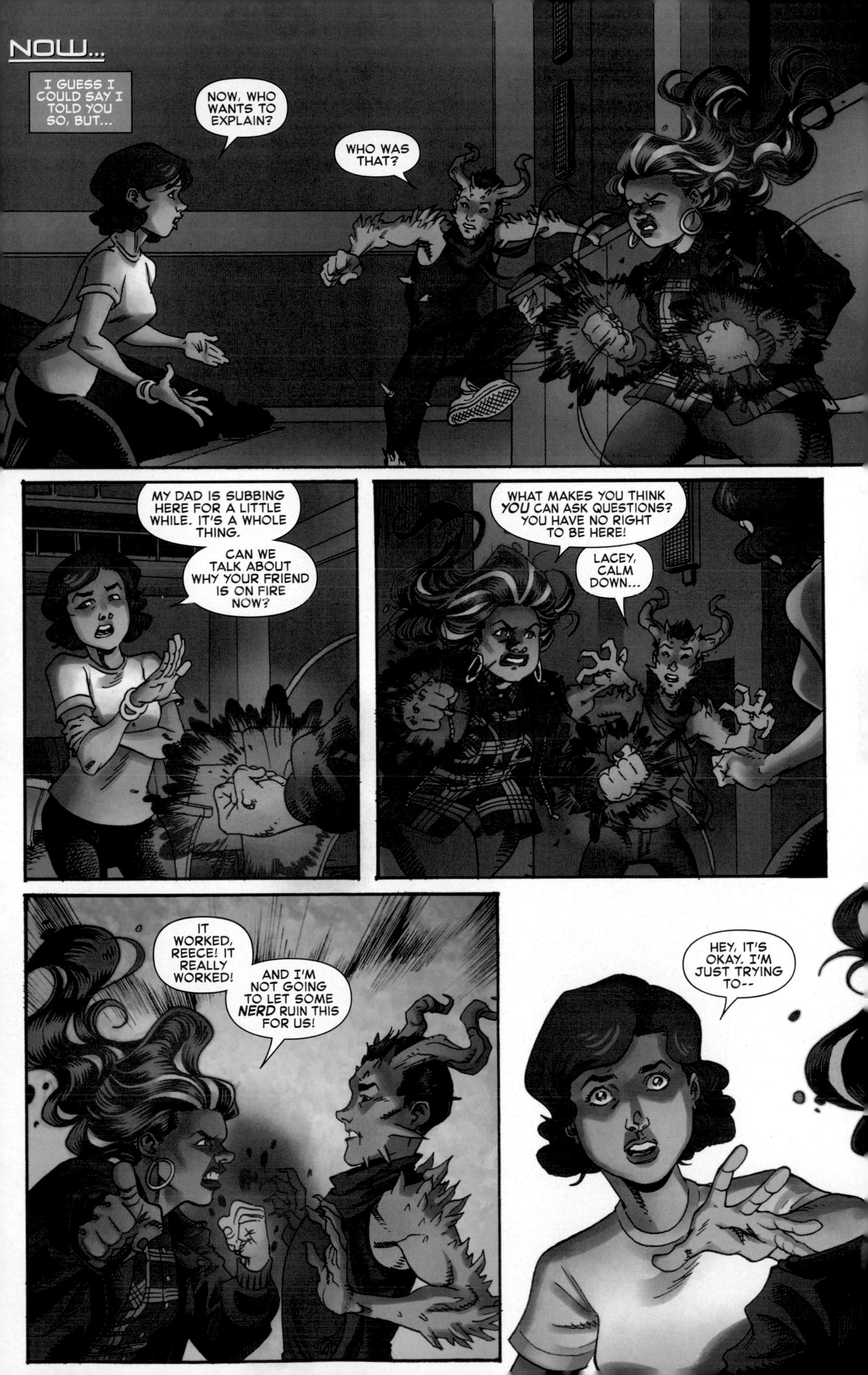
NOW...
I GUESS I COULD SAY I TOLD YOU SO, BUT...
NOW, WHO WANTS TO EXPLAIN?
WHO WAS THAT?
MY DAD IS SUBBING HERE FOR A LITTLE WHILE. IT'S A WHOLE THING.
CAN WE TALK ABOUT WHY YOUR FRIEND IS ON FIRE NOW?
WHAT MAKES YOU THINK YOU CAN ASK QUESTIONS? YOU HAVE NO RIGHT TO BE HERE!
LACEY, CALM DOWN...
IT WORKED, REECE! IT REALLY WORKED!
AND I'M NOT GOING TO LET SOME NERD RUIN THIS FOR US!
HEY, IT'S OKAY. I'M JUST TRYING TO--

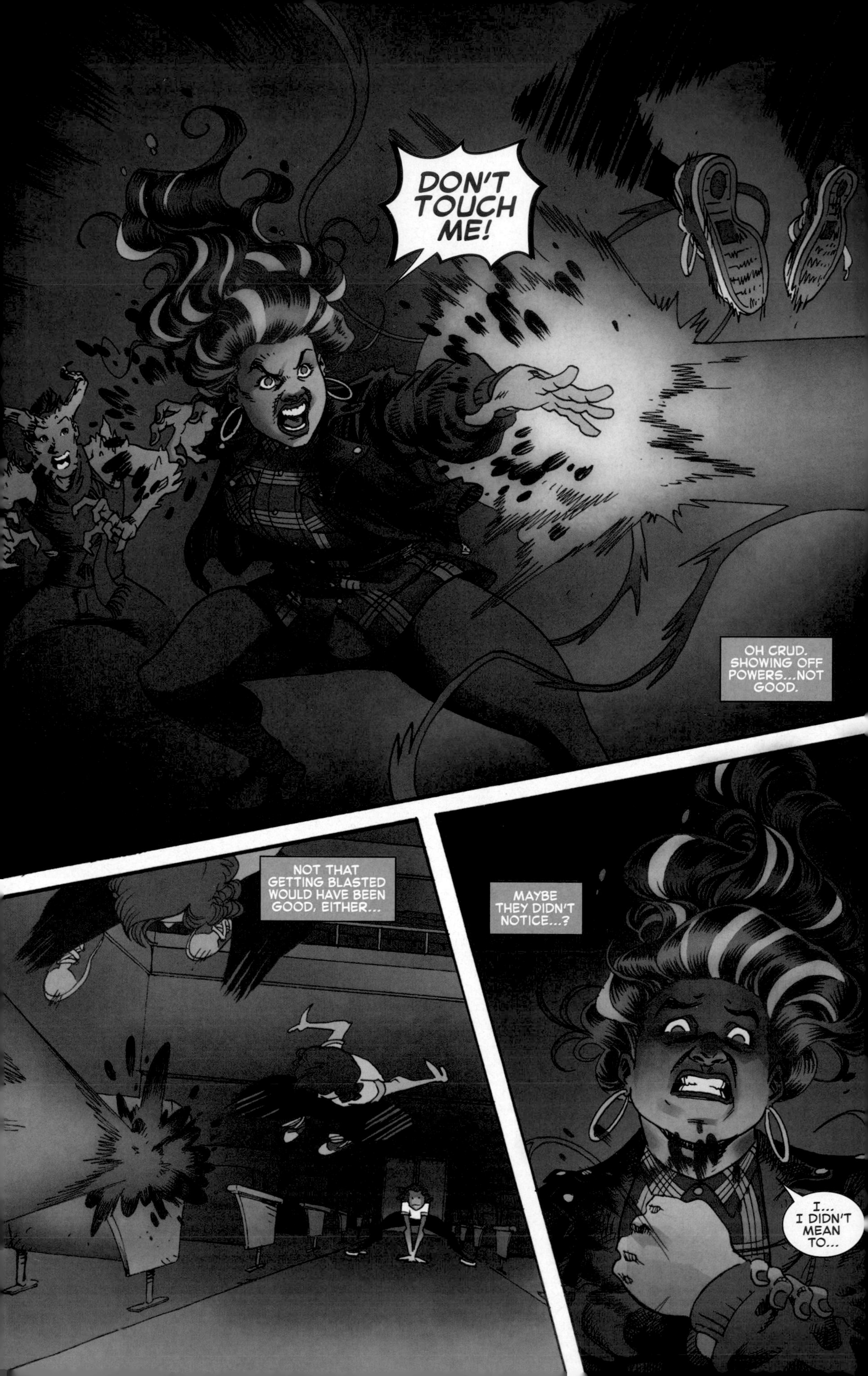
DON'T TOUCH ME!
OH CRUD. SHOWING OFF POWERS...NOT GOOD.
NOT THAT GETTING BLASTED WOULD HAVE BEEN GOOD, EITHER...
MAYBE THEY DIDN'T NOTICE...?
I... I DIDN'T MEAN TO...

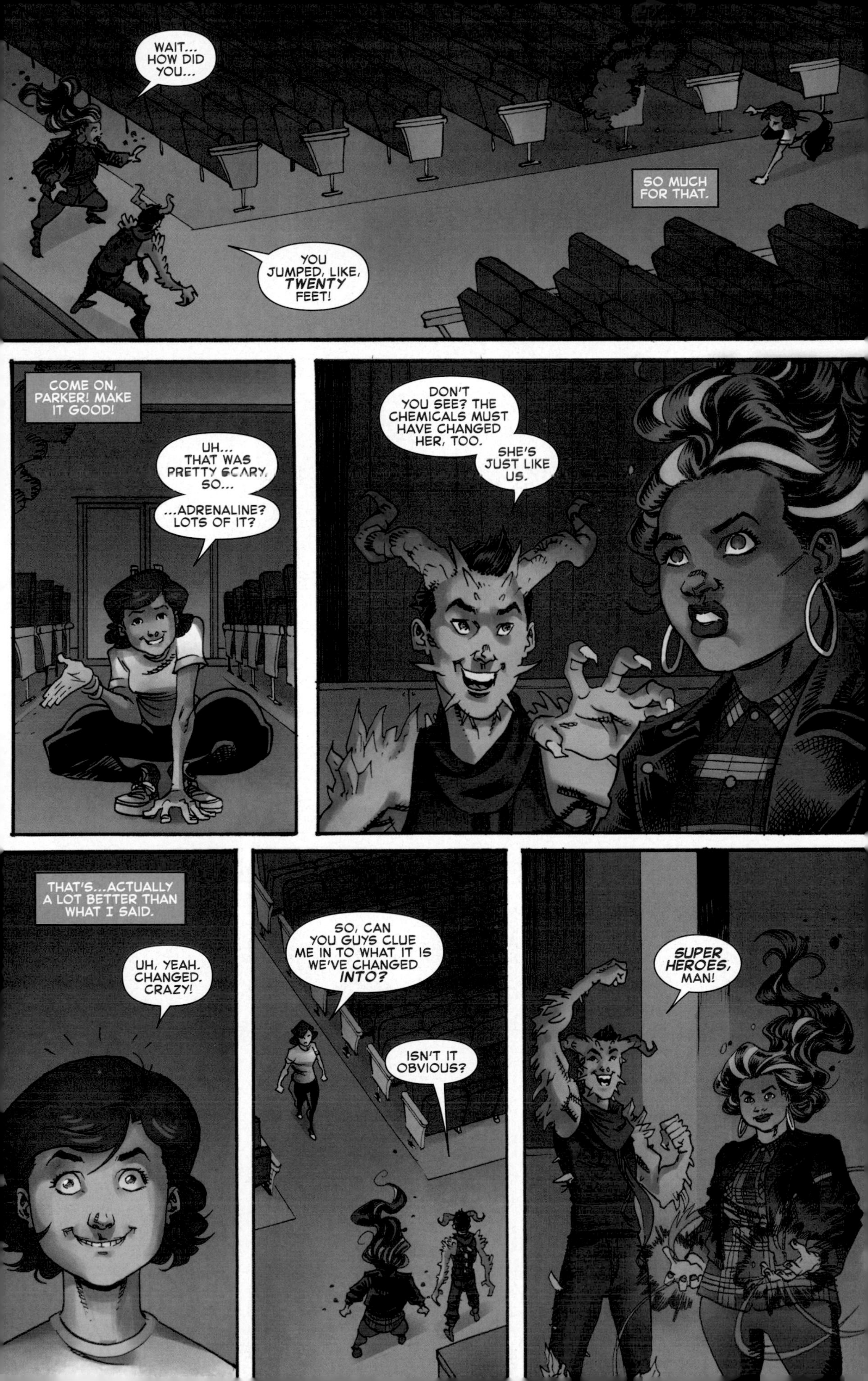

WAIT... HOW DID YOU...
YOU JUMPED, LIKE, TWENTY FEET!
SO MUCH FOR THAT.
COME ON, PARKER! MAKE IT GOOD!
UH... THAT WAS PRETTY SCARY, SO...
...ADRENALINE? LOTS OF IT?
DON'T YOU SEE? THE CHEMICALS MUST HAVE CHANGED HER, TOO.
SHE'S JUST LIKE US.
THAT'S...ACTUALLY A LOT BETTER THAN WHAT I SAID.
UH, YEAH. CHANGED. CRAZY!
SO, CAN YOU GUYS CLUE ME IN TO WHAT IT IS WE'VE CHANGED INTO?
ISN'T IT OBVIOUS?
SUPER HEROES, MAN!

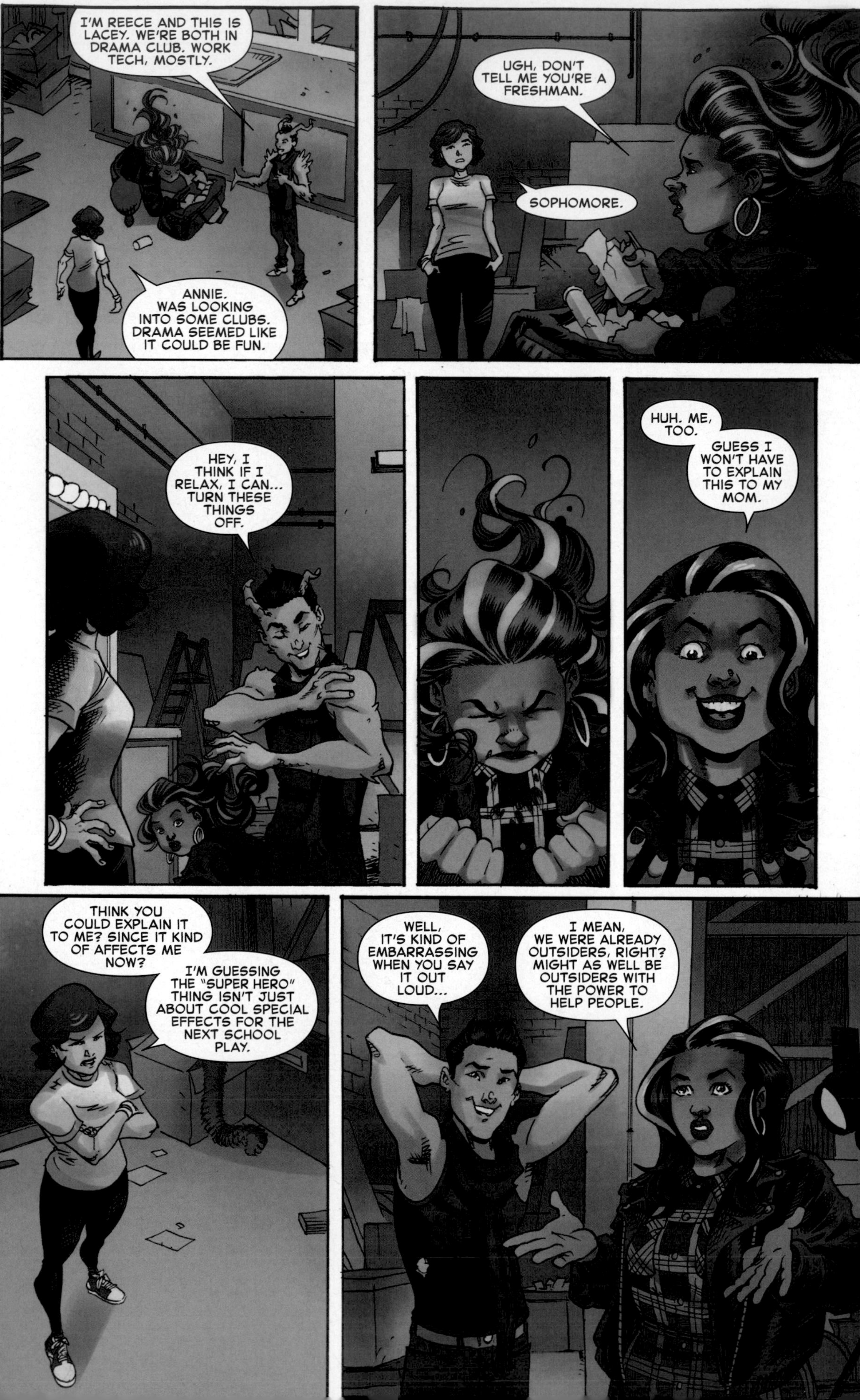
I'M REECE AND THIS IS LACEY. WE'RE BOTH IN DRAMA CLUB. WORK TECH, MOSTLY.
ANNIE. WAS LOOKING INTO SOME CLUBS. DRAMA SEEMED LIKE IT COULD BE FUN.
UGH, DON'T TELL ME YOU'RE A FRESHMAN.
SOPHOMORE.
HEY, I THINK IF I RELAX, I CAN... TURN THESE THINGS OFF.
HUH. ME, TOO.
GUESS I WON'T HAVE TO EXPLAIN THIS TO MY MOM.
THINK YOU COULD EXPLAIN IT TO ME? SINCE IT KIND OF AFFECTS ME NOW?
I'M GUESSING THE "SUPER HERO" THING ISN'T JUST ABOUT COOL SPECIAL EFFECTS FOR THE NEXT SCHOOL PLAY.
WELL, IT'S KIND OF EMBARRASSING WHEN YOU SAY IT OUT LOUD...
I MEAN, WE WERE ALREADY OUTSIDERS, RIGHT? MIGHT AS WELL BE OUTSIDERS WITH THE POWER TO HELP PEOPLE.

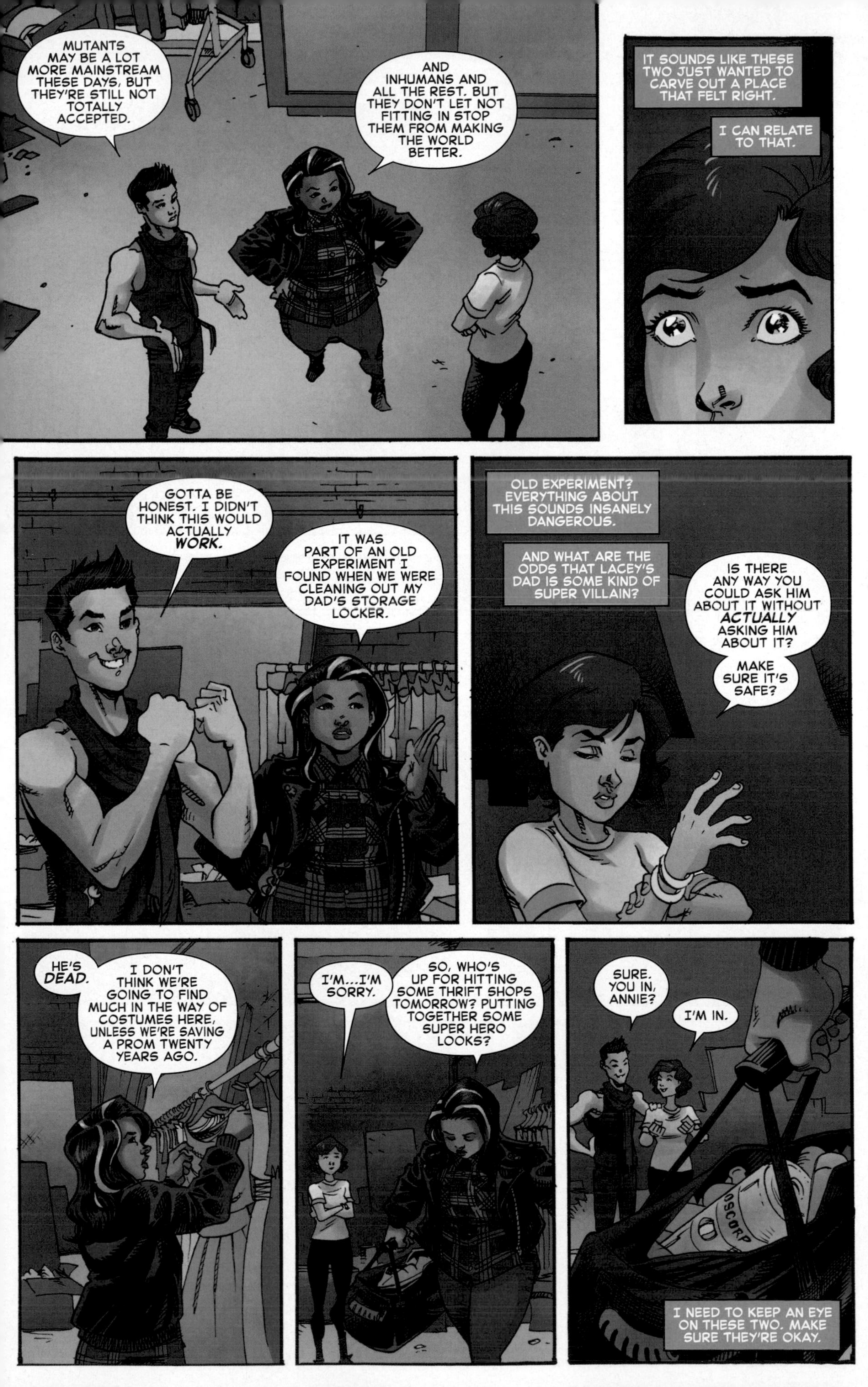
MUTANTS MAY BE A LOT MORE MAINSTREAM THESE DAYS, BUT THEY'RE STILL NOT TOTALLY ACCEPTED.
AND INHUMANS AND ALL THE REST. BUT THEY DON'T LET NOT FITTING IN STOP THEM FROM MAKING THE WORLD BETTER.
IT SOUNDS LIKE THESE TWO JUST WANTED TO CARVE OUT A PLACE THAT FELT RIGHT.
I CAN RELATE TO THAT.
GOTTA BE HONEST. I DIDN'T THINK THIS WOULD ACTUALLY WORK.
IT WAS PART OF AN OLD EXPERIMENT I FOUND WHEN WE WERE CLEANING OUT MY DAD'S STORAGE LOCKER.
OLD EXPERIMENT? EVERYTHING ABOUT THIS SOUNDS INSANELY DANGEROUS.
AND WHAT ARE THE ODDS THAT LACEY'S DAD IS SOME KIND OF SUPER VILLAIN?
IS THERE ANY WAY YOU COULD ASK HIM ABOUT IT WITHOUT ACTUALLY ASKING HIM ABOUT IT?
MAKE SURE IT'S SAFE?
HE'S DEAD.
I DON'T THINK WE'RE GOING TO FIND MUCH IN THE WAY OF COSTUMES HERE, UNLESS WE'RE SAVING A PROM TWENTY YEARS AGO.
I'M...I'M SORRY.
SO, WHO'S UP FOR HITTING SOME THRIFT SHOPS TOMORROW? PUTTING TOGETHER SOME SUPER HERO LOOKS?
SURE. YOU IN, ANNIE?
I'M IN.
OSCORP
I NEED TO KEEP AN EYE ON THESE TWO. MAKE SURE THEY'RE OKAY.

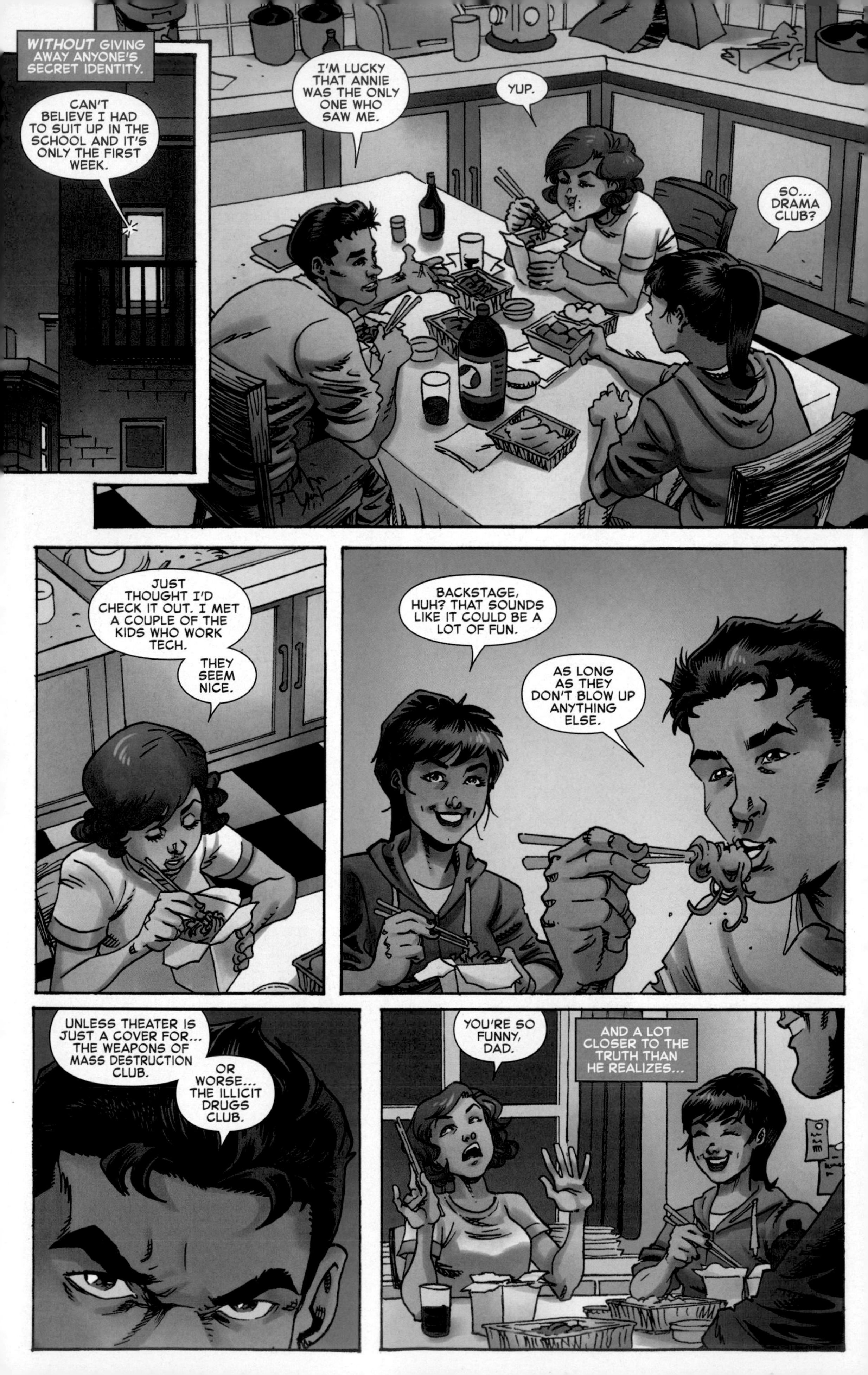
WITHOUT GIVING AWAY ANYONE'S SECRET IDENTITY.
CAN'T BELIEVE I HAD TO SUIT UP IN THE SCHOOL AND IT'S ONLY THE FIRST WEEK.
I'M LUCKY THAT ANNIE WAS THE ONLY ONE WHO SAW ME.
YUP.
SO... DRAMA CLUB?
JUST THOUGHT I'D CHECK IT OUT. I MET A COUPLE OF THE KIDS WHO WORK TECH.
THEY SEEM NICE.
BACKSTAGE, HUH? THAT SOUNDS LIKE IT COULD BE A LOT OF FUN.
AS LONG AS THEY DON'T BLOW UP ANYTHING ELSE.
UNLESS THEATER IS JUST A COVER FOR... THE WEAPONS OF MASS DESTRUCTION CLUB.
OR WORSE... THE ILLICIT DRUGS CLUB.
YOU'RE SO FUNNY, DAD.
AND A LOT CLOSER TO THE TRUTH THAN HE REALIZES...

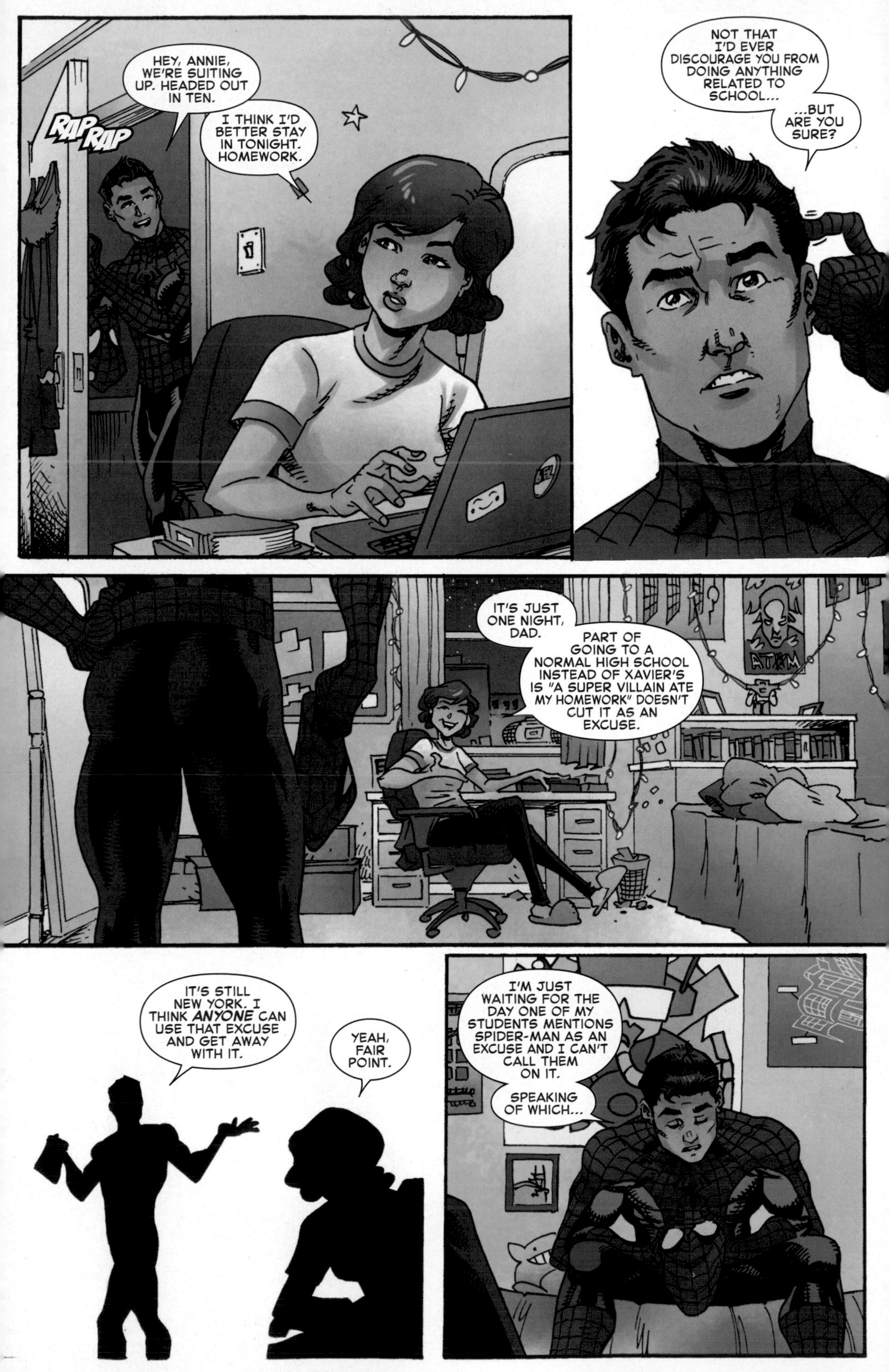
HEY, ANNIE, WE'RE SUITING UP. HEADED OUT IN TEN.
RAP RAP
I THINK I'D BETTER STAY IN TONIGHT. HOMEWORK.
NOT THAT I'D EVER DISCOURAGE YOU FROM DOING ANYTHING RELATED TO SCHOOL...
...BUT ARE YOU SURE?
IT'S JUST ONE NIGHT, DAD.
PART OF GOING TO A NORMAL HIGH SCHOOL INSTEAD OF XAVIER'S IS "A SUPER VILLAIN ATE MY HOMEWORK" DOESN'T CUT IT AS AN EXCUSE.
IT'S STILL NEW YORK. I THINK ANYONE CAN USE THAT EXCUSE AND GET AWAY WITH IT.
YEAH, FAIR POINT.
I'M JUST WAITING FOR THE DAY ONE OF MY STUDENTS MENTIONS SPIDER-MAN AS AN EXCUSE AND I CAN'T CALL THEM ON IT.
SPEAKING OF WHICH...

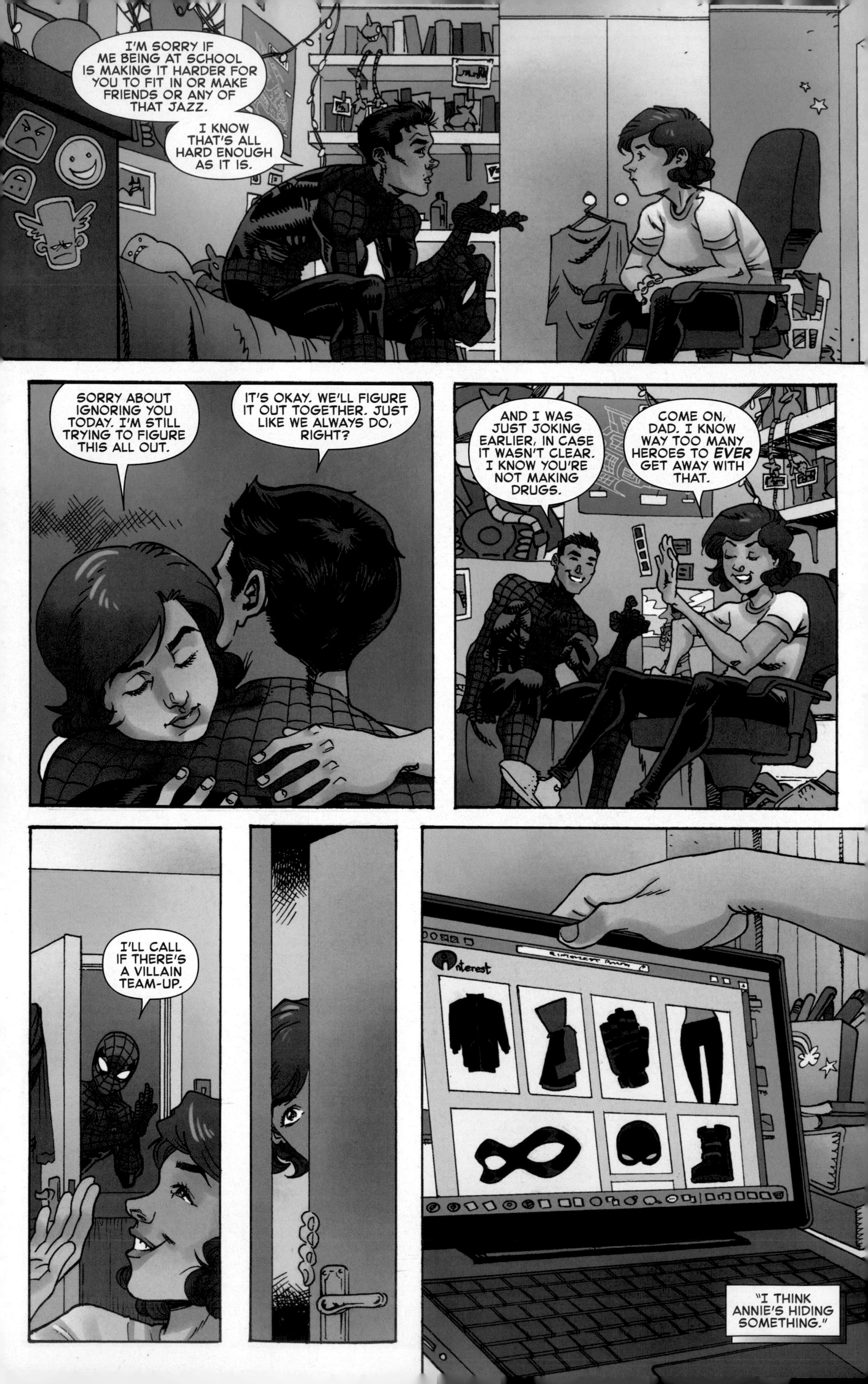

I'M SORRY IF ME BEING AT SCHOOL IS MAKING IT HARDER FOR YOU TO FIT IN OR MAKE FRIENDS OR ANY OF THAT JAZZ.
I KNOW THAT'S ALL HARD ENOUGH AS IT IS.
SORRY ABOUT IGNORING YOU TODAY. I'M STILL TRYING TO FIGURE THIS ALL OUT.
IT'S OKAY. WE'LL FIGURE IT OUT TOGETHER. JUST LIKE WE ALWAYS DO, RIGHT?
AND I WAS JUST JOKING EARLIER, IN CASE IT WASN'T CLEAR. I KNOW YOU'RE NOT MAKING DRUGS.
COME ON, DAD. I KNOW WAY TOO MANY HEROES TO *EVER* GET AWAY WITH THAT.
I'LL CALL IF THERE'S A VILLAIN TEAM-UP.
Interest
"I THINK ANNIE'S HIDING SOMETHING."

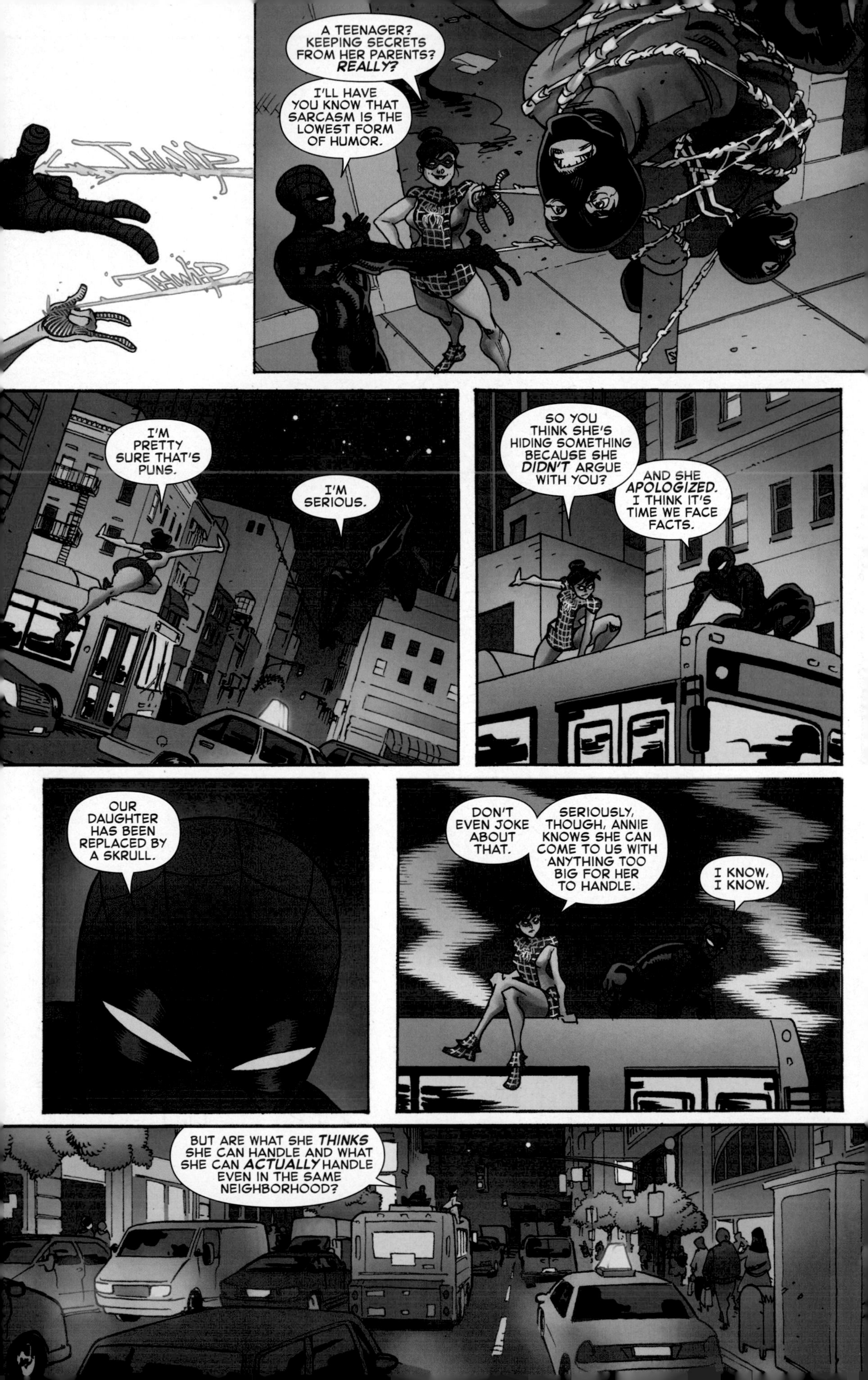
A TEENAGER? KEEPING SECRETS FROM HER PARENTS? REALLY?
I'LL HAVE YOU KNOW THAT SARCASM IS THE LOWEST FORM OF HUMOR.
I'M PRETTY SURE THAT'S PUNS.
I'M SERIOUS.
SO YOU THINK SHE'S HIDING SOMETHING BECAUSE SHE DIDN'T ARGUE WITH YOU?
AND SHE APOLOGIZED. I THINK IT'S TIME WE FACE FACTS.
OUR DAUGHTER HAS BEEN REPLACED BY A SKRULL.
DON'T EVEN JOKE ABOUT THAT.
SERIOUSLY, THOUGH, ANNIE KNOWS SHE CAN COME TO US WITH ANYTHING TOO BIG FOR HER TO HANDLE.
I KNOW, I KNOW.
BUT ARE WHAT SHE THINKS SHE CAN HANDLE AND WHAT SHE CAN ACTUALLY HANDLE EVEN IN THE SAME NEIGHBORHOOD?

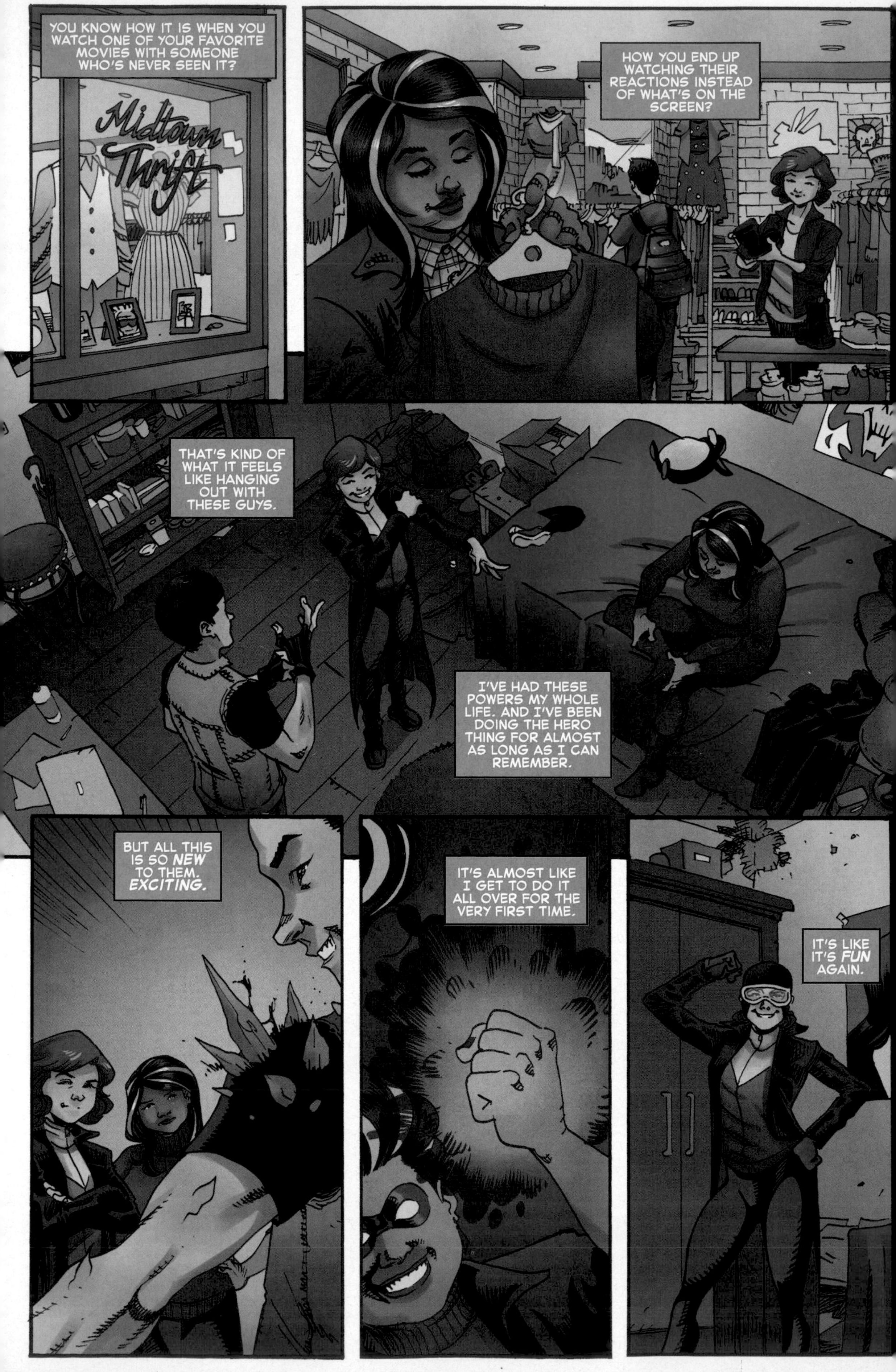
YOU KNOW HOW IT IS WHEN YOU WATCH ONE OF YOUR FAVORITE MOVIES WITH SOMEONE WHO'S NEVER SEEN IT?
Midtown Thrift
HOW YOU END UP WATCHING THEIR REACTIONS INSTEAD OF WHAT'S ON THE SCREEN?
THAT'S KIND OF WHAT IT FEELS LIKE HANGING OUT WITH THESE GUYS.
I'VE HAD THESE POWERS MY WHOLE LIFE. AND I'VE BEEN DOING THE HERO THING FOR ALMOST AS LONG AS I CAN REMEMBER.
BUT ALL THIS IS SO *NEW* TO THEM. *EXCITING.*
IT'S ALMOST LIKE I GET TO DO IT ALL OVER FOR THE VERY FIRST TIME.
IT'S LIKE IT'S *FUN* AGAIN.

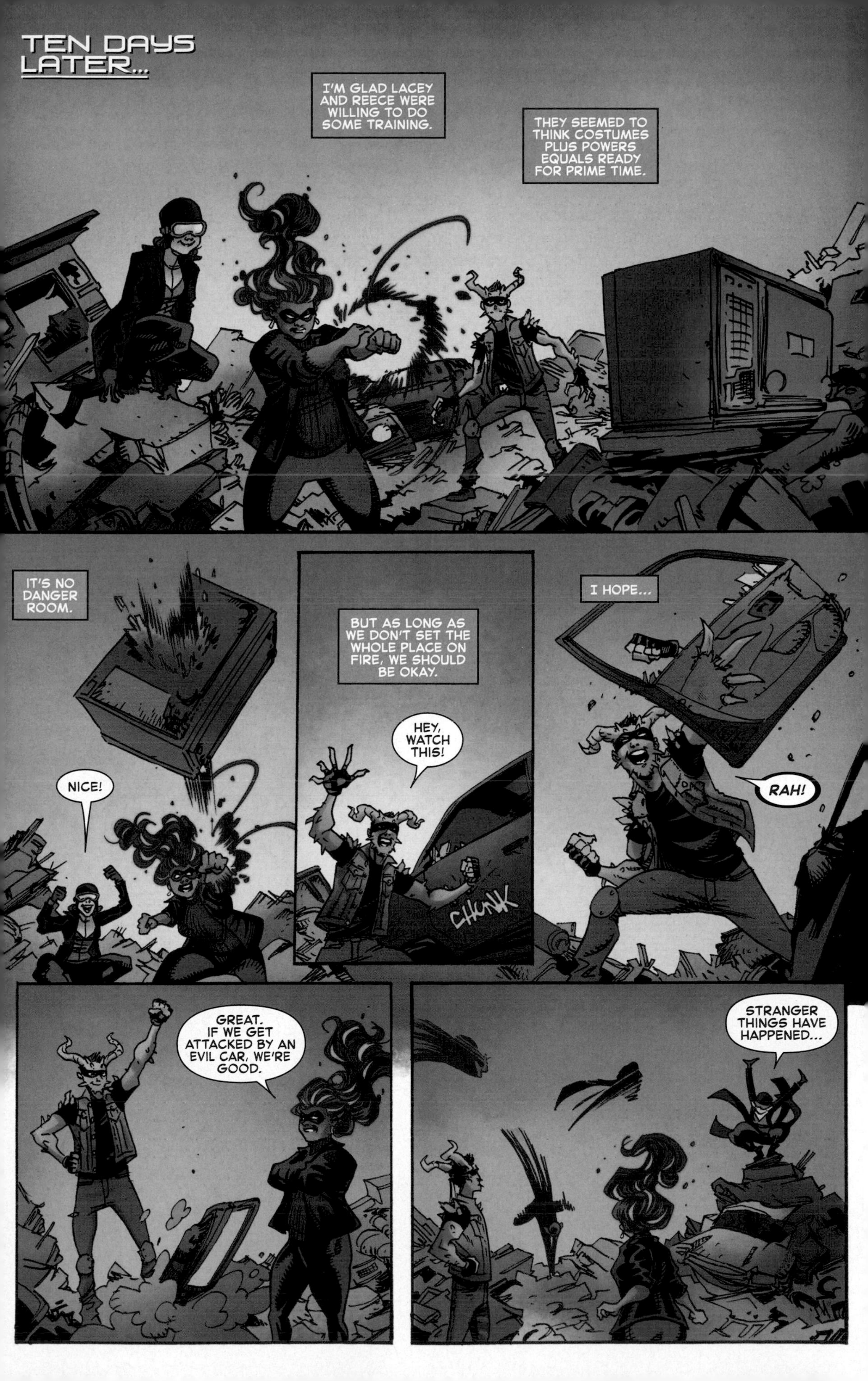
TEN DAYS LATER...
I'M GLAD LACEY AND REECE WERE WILLING TO DO SOME TRAINING.
THEY SEEMED TO THINK COSTUMES PLUS POWERS EQUALS READY FOR PRIME TIME.
IT'S NO DANGER ROOM.
NICE!
BUT AS LONG AS WE DON'T SET THE WHOLE PLACE ON FIRE, WE SHOULD BE OKAY.
HEY, WATCH THIS!
CHUNK
I HOPE...
RAH!
GREAT. IF WE GET ATTACKED BY AN EVIL CAR, WE'RE GOOD.
STRANGER THINGS HAVE HAPPENED...

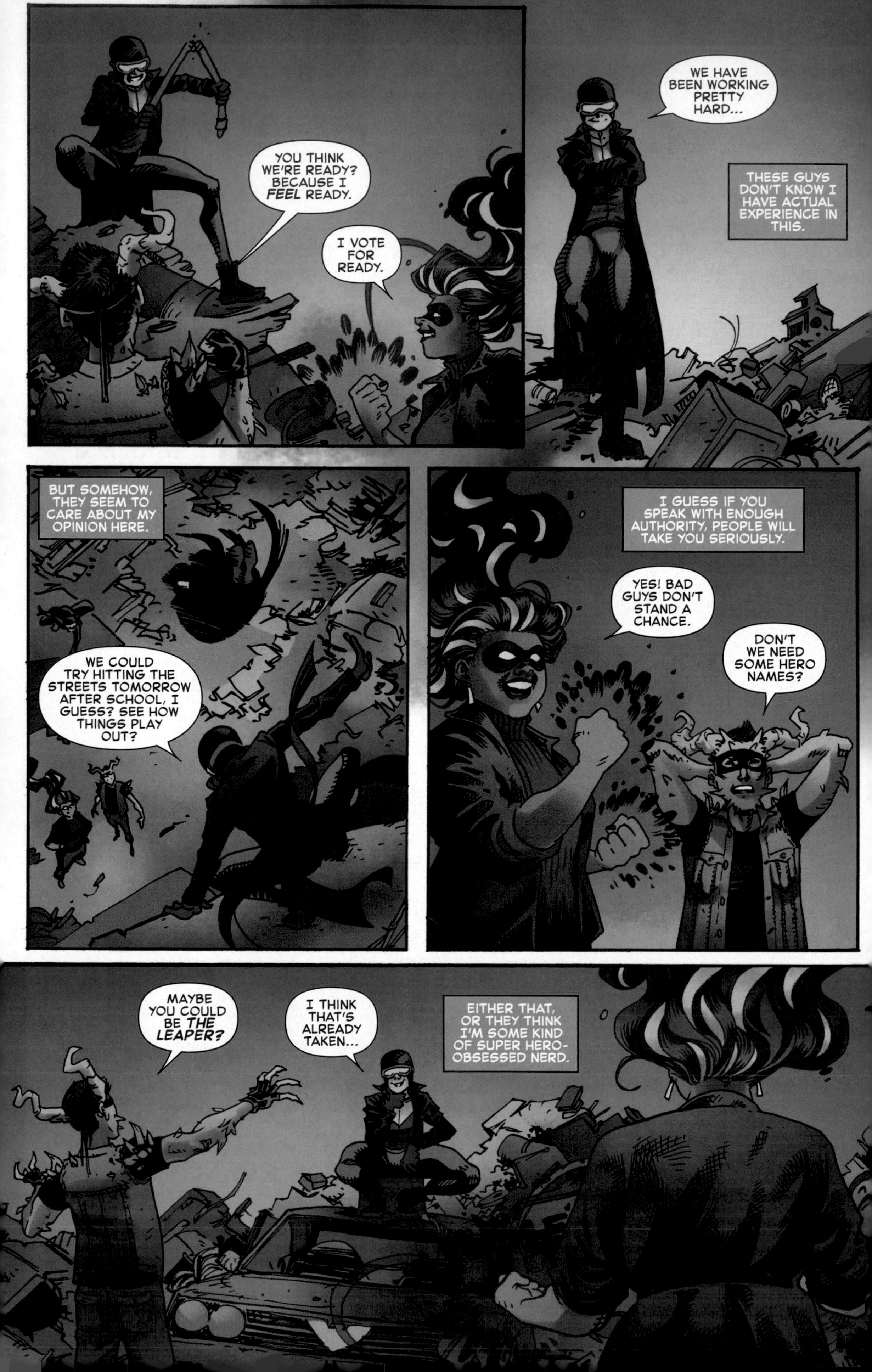
YOU THINK WE'RE READY? BECAUSE I *FEEL* READY.
I VOTE FOR READY.
WE HAVE BEEN WORKING PRETTY HARD...
THESE GUYS DON'T KNOW I HAVE ACTUAL EXPERIENCE IN THIS.
BUT SOMEHOW, THEY SEEM TO CARE ABOUT MY OPINION HERE.
WE COULD TRY HITTING THE STREETS TOMORROW AFTER SCHOOL, I GUESS? SEE HOW THINGS PLAY OUT?
I GUESS IF YOU SPEAK WITH ENOUGH AUTHORITY, PEOPLE WILL TAKE YOU SERIOUSLY.
YES! BAD GUYS DON'T STAND A CHANCE.
DON'T WE NEED SOME HERO NAMES?
MAYBE YOU COULD BE *THE LEAPER?*
I THINK THAT'S ALREADY TAKEN...
EITHER THAT, OR THEY THINK I'M SOME KIND OF SUPER HERO-OBSESSED NERD.

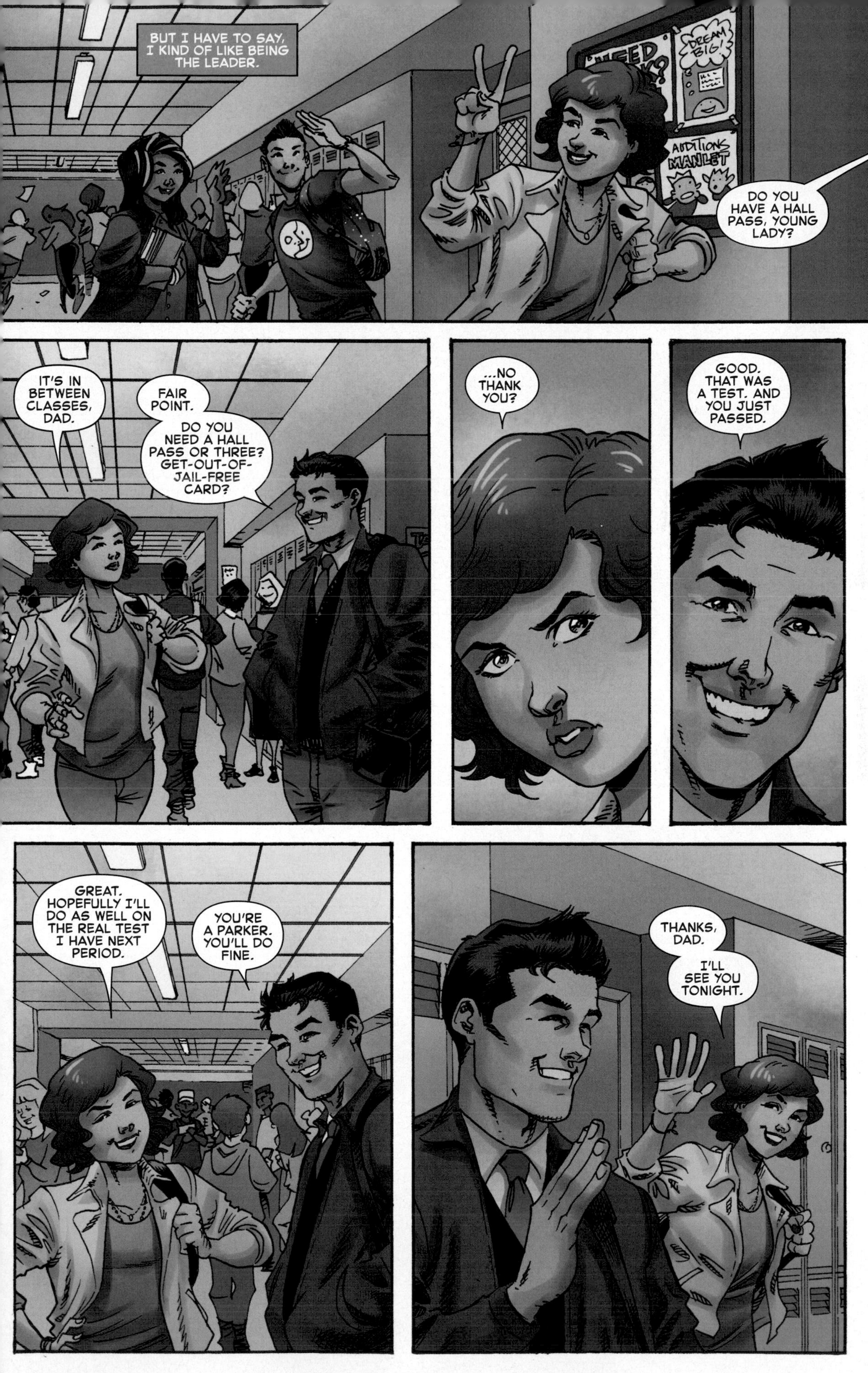
BUT I HAVE TO SAY, I KIND OF LIKE BEING THE LEADER.
NEED
DREAM BIG!
AUDITIONS HAMLET
DO YOU HAVE A HALL PASS, YOUNG LADY?
IT'S IN BETWEEN CLASSES, DAD.
FAIR POINT.
DO YOU NEED A HALL PASS OR THREE? GET-OUT-OF-JAIL-FREE CARD?
...NO THANK YOU?
GOOD. THAT WAS A TEST. AND YOU JUST PASSED.
GREAT. HOPEFULLY I'LL DO AS WELL ON THE REAL TEST I HAVE NEXT PERIOD.
YOU'RE A PARKER. YOU'LL DO FINE.
THANKS, DAD.
I'LL SEE YOU TONIGHT.

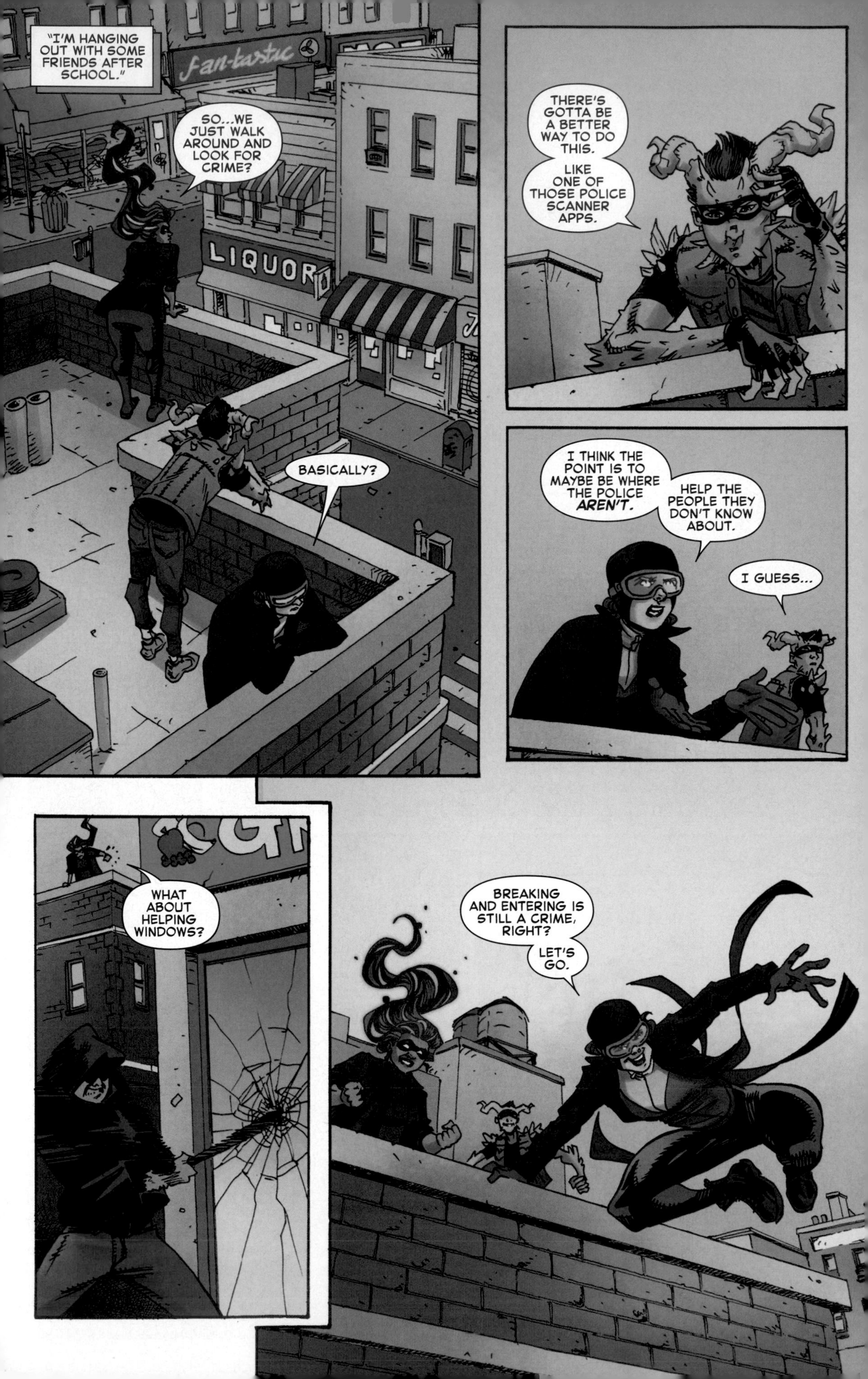
"I'M HANGING OUT WITH SOME FRIENDS AFTER SCHOOL."
Fan-tastic
LIQUOR
SO...WE JUST WALK AROUND AND LOOK FOR CRIME?
BASICALLY?
THERE'S GOTTA BE A BETTER WAY TO DO THIS.
LIKE ONE OF THOSE POLICE SCANNER APPS.
I THINK THE POINT IS TO MAYBE BE WHERE THE POLICE *AREN'T.*
HELP THE PEOPLE THEY DON'T KNOW ABOUT.
I GUESS...
WHAT ABOUT HELPING WINDOWS?
BREAKING AND ENTERING IS STILL A CRIME, RIGHT?
LET'S GO.

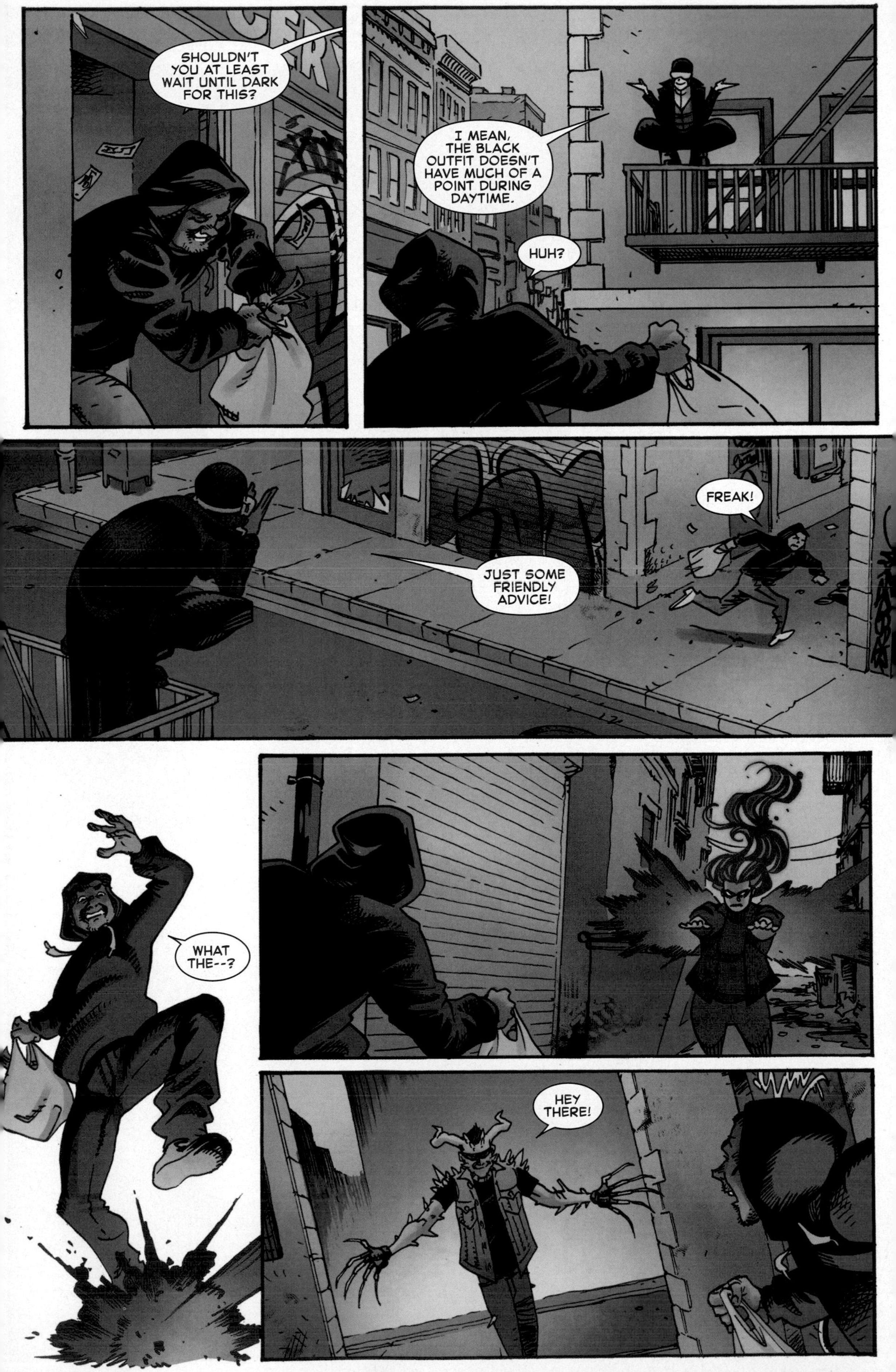
SHOULDN'T YOU AT LEAST WAIT UNTIL DARK FOR THIS?
I MEAN, THE BLACK OUTFIT DOESN'T HAVE MUCH OF A POINT DURING DAYTIME.
HUH?
FREAK!
JUST SOME FRIENDLY ADVICE!
WHAT THE--?
HEY THERE!

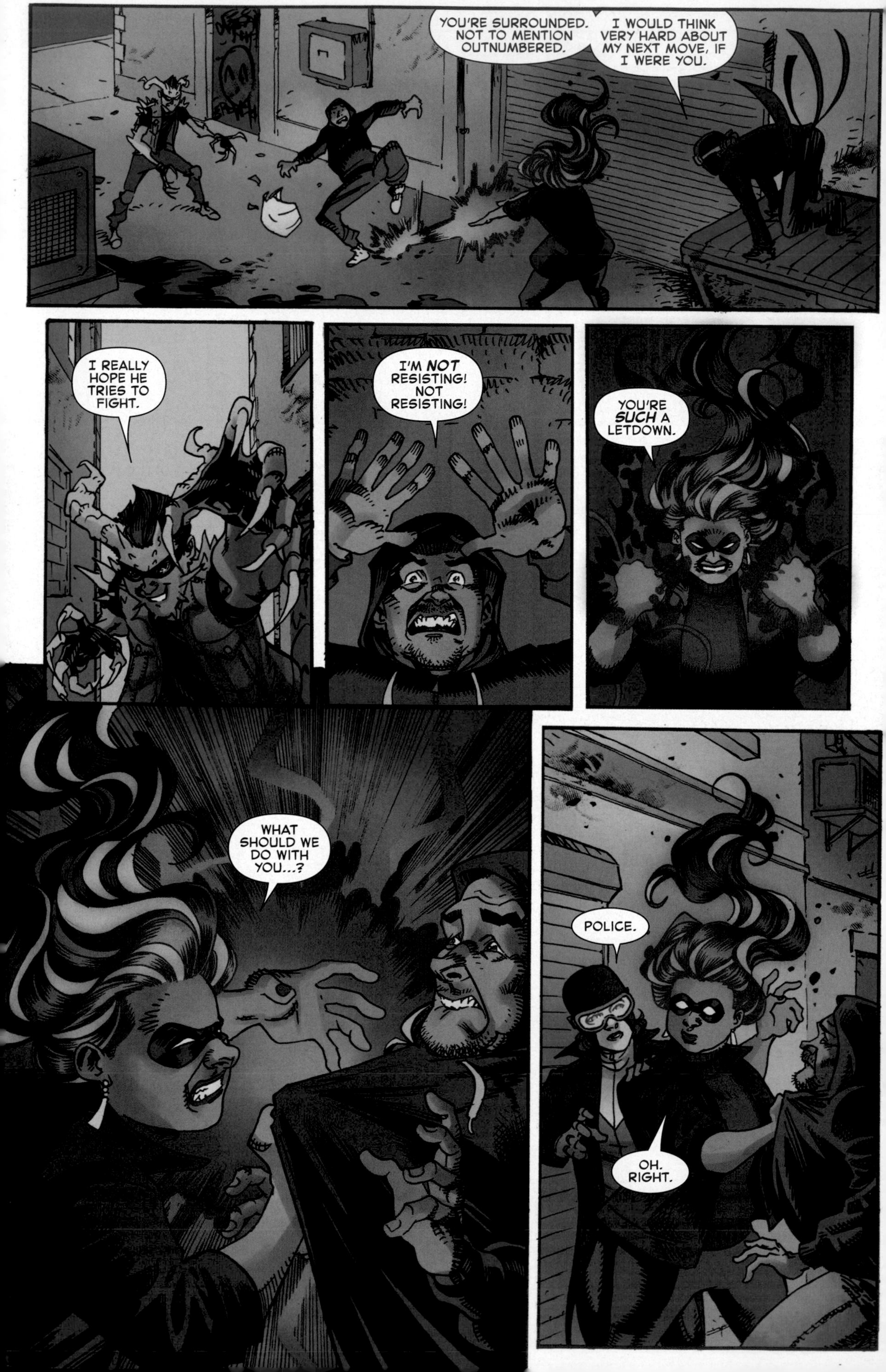
YOU'RE SURROUNDED. NOT TO MENTION OUTNUMBERED.
I WOULD THINK VERY HARD ABOUT MY NEXT MOVE, IF I WERE YOU.
I REALLY HOPE HE TRIES TO FIGHT.
I'M *NOT* RESISTING! NOT RESISTING!
YOU'RE *SUCH* A LETDOWN.
WHAT SHOULD WE DO WITH YOU...?
POLICE.
OH. RIGHT.

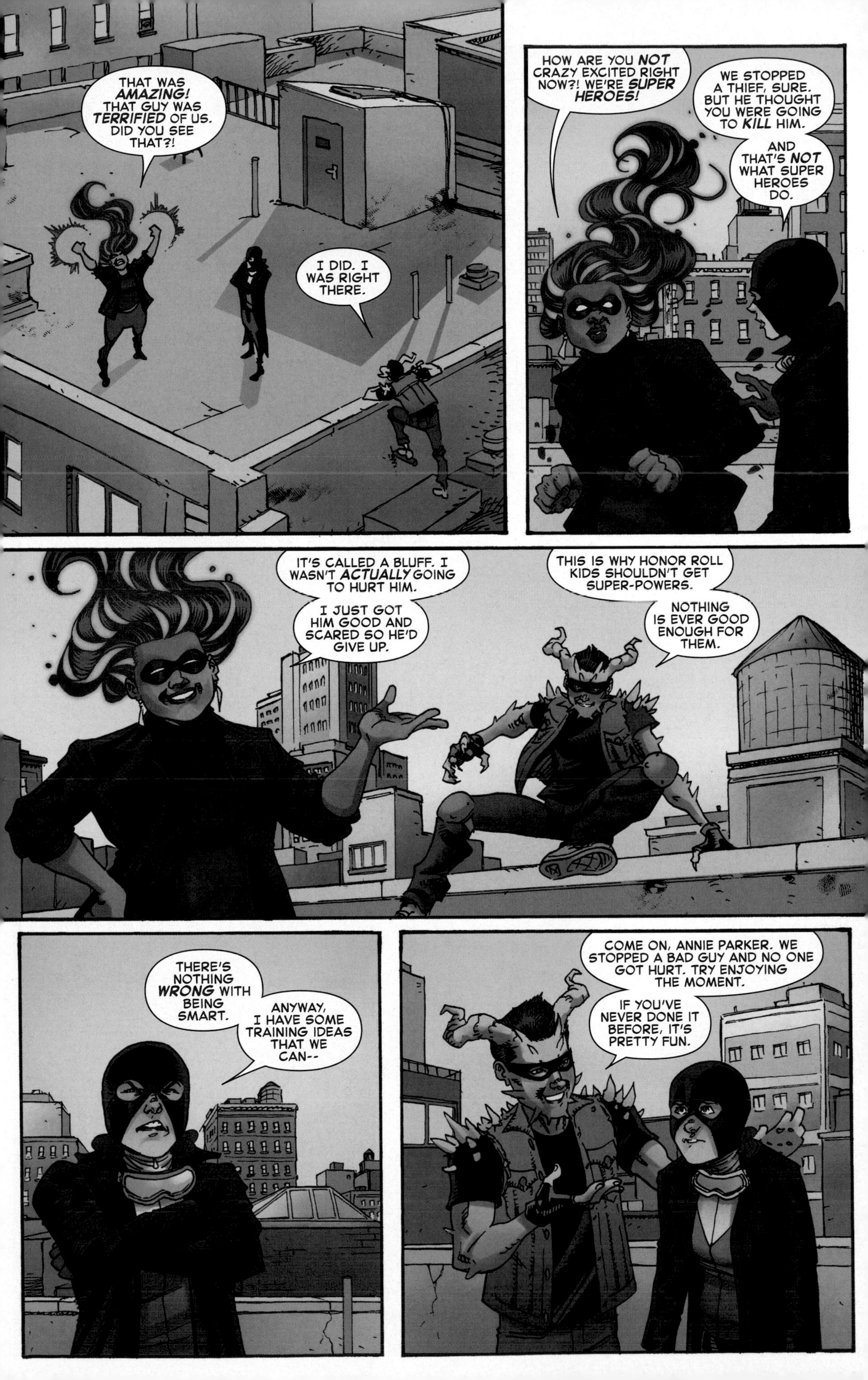

THAT WAS AMAZING! THAT GUY WAS TERRIFIED OF US. DID YOU SEE THAT?!
I DID. I WAS RIGHT THERE.
HOW ARE YOU NOT CRAZY EXCITED RIGHT NOW?! WE'RE SUPER HEROES!
WE STOPPED A THIEF, SURE. BUT HE THOUGHT YOU WERE GOING TO KILL HIM.
AND THAT'S NOT WHAT SUPER HEROES DO.
IT'S CALLED A BLUFF. I WASN'T ACTUALLY GOING TO HURT HIM.
I JUST GOT HIM GOOD AND SCARED SO HE'D GIVE UP.
THIS IS WHY HONOR ROLL KIDS SHOULDN'T GET SUPER-POWERS.
NOTHING IS EVER GOOD ENOUGH FOR THEM.
THERE'S NOTHING WRONG WITH BEING SMART.
ANYWAY, I HAVE SOME TRAINING IDEAS THAT WE CAN--
COME ON, ANNIE PARKER. WE STOPPED A BAD GUY AND NO ONE GOT HURT. TRY ENJOYING THE MOMENT.
IF YOU'VE NEVER DONE IT BEFORE, IT'S PRETTY FUN.

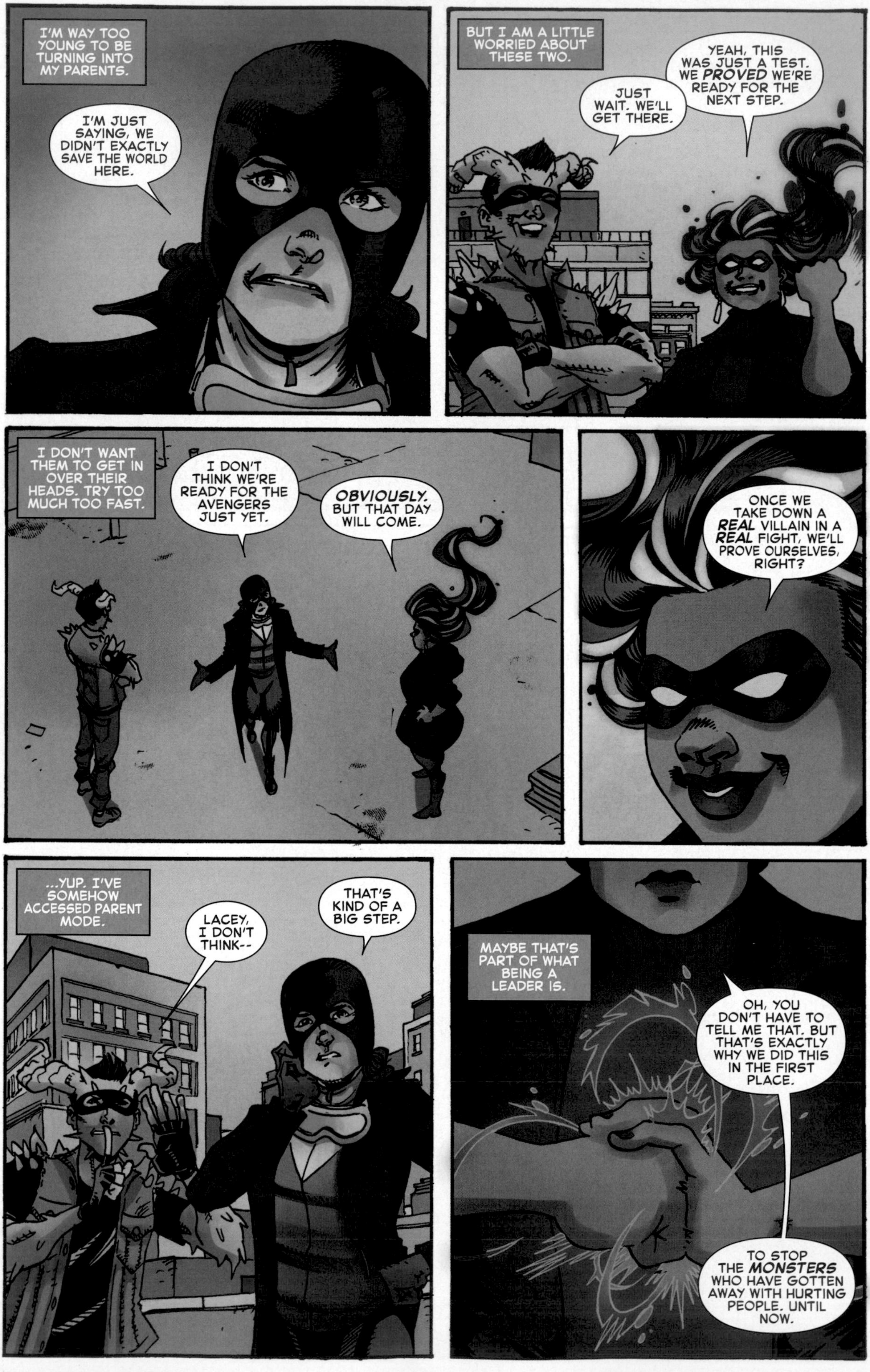
I'M WAY TOO YOUNG TO BE TURNING INTO MY PARENTS.
I'M JUST SAYING, WE DIDN'T EXACTLY SAVE THE WORLD HERE.
BUT I AM A LITTLE WORRIED ABOUT THESE TWO.
JUST WAIT. WE'LL GET THERE.
YEAH, THIS WAS JUST A TEST. WE PROVED WE'RE READY FOR THE NEXT STEP.
I DON'T WANT THEM TO GET IN OVER THEIR HEADS. TRY TOO MUCH TOO FAST.
I DON'T THINK WE'RE READY FOR THE AVENGERS JUST YET.
OBVIOUSLY. BUT THAT DAY WILL COME.
ONCE WE TAKE DOWN A REAL VILLAIN IN A REAL FIGHT, WE'LL PROVE OURSELVES, RIGHT?
...YUP. I'VE SOMEHOW ACCESSED PARENT MODE.
LACEY, I DON'T THINK--
THAT'S KIND OF A BIG STEP.
MAYBE THAT'S PART OF WHAT BEING A LEADER IS.
OH, YOU DON'T HAVE TO TELL ME THAT. BUT THAT'S EXACTLY WHY WE DID THIS IN THE FIRST PLACE.
TO STOP THE MONSTERS WHO HAVE GOTTEN AWAY WITH HURTING PEOPLE. UNTIL NOW.

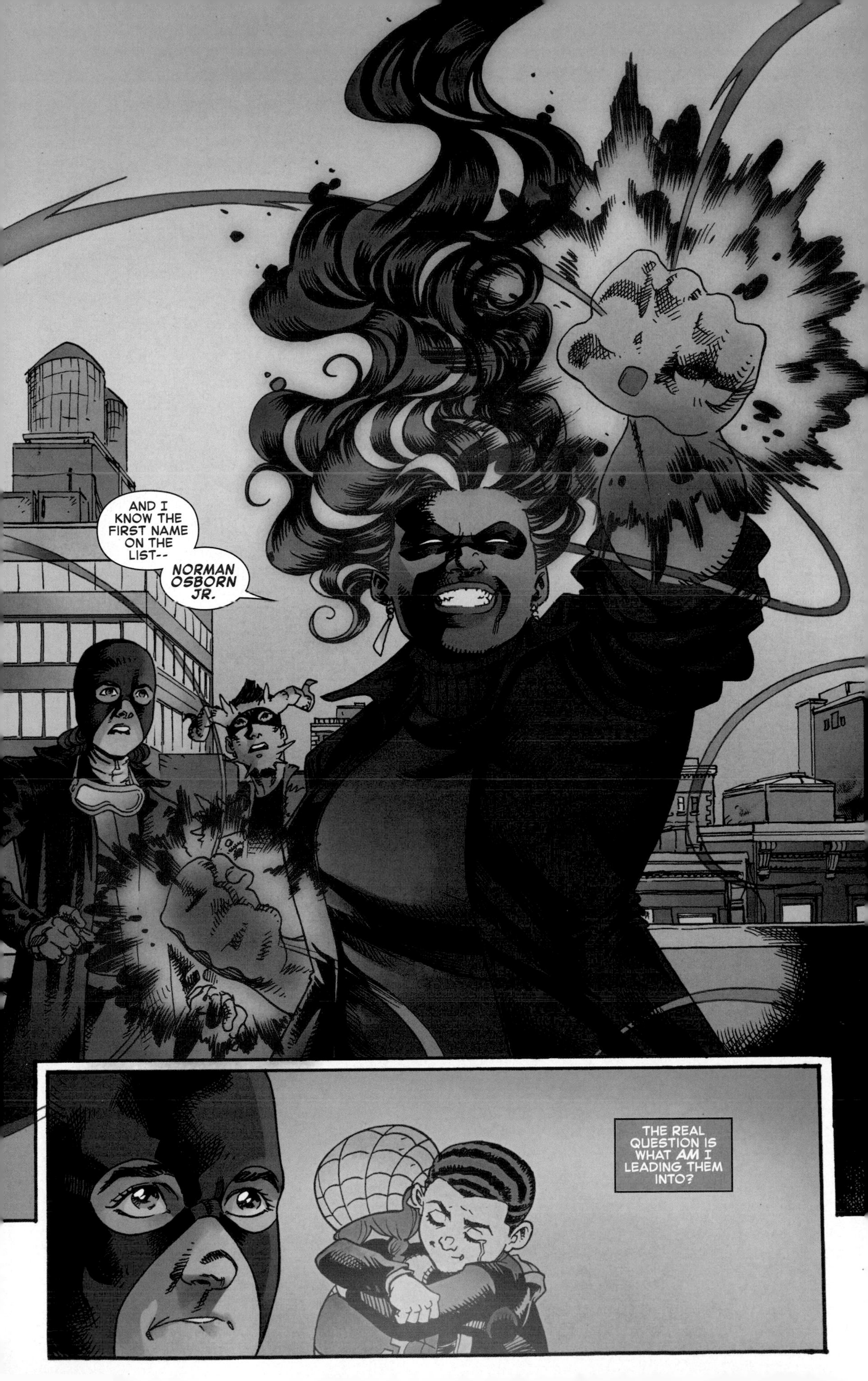

AND I KNOW THE FIRST NAME ON THE LIST--
NORMAN OSBORN JR.
THE REAL QUESTION IS WHAT AM I LEADING THEM INTO?

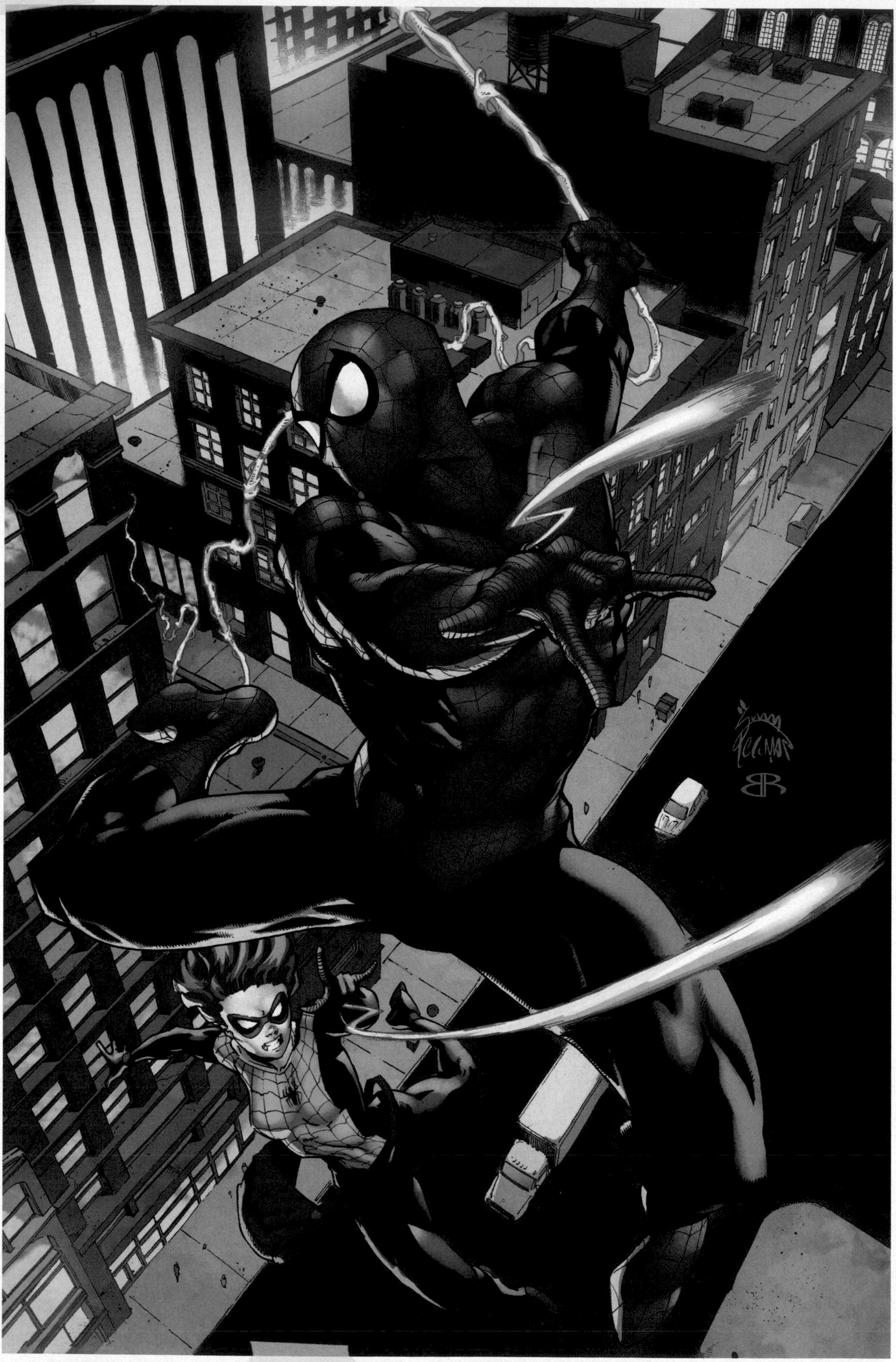

18: FAST TIMES AT MIDTOWN HIGH — PART 3

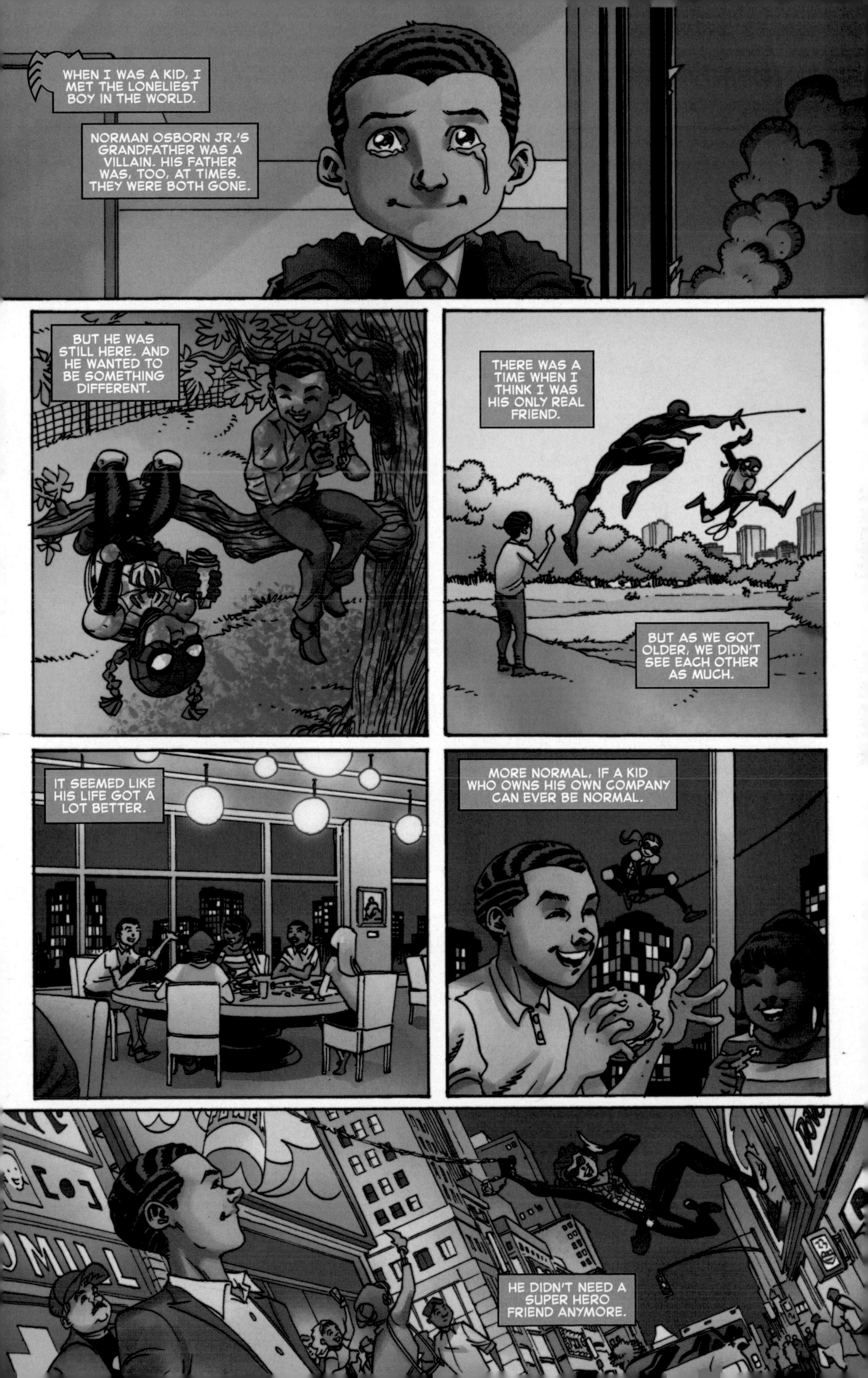

WHEN I WAS A KID, I MET THE LONELIEST BOY IN THE WORLD.
NORMAN OSBORN JR.'S GRANDFATHER WAS A VILLAIN. HIS FATHER WAS, TOO, AT TIMES. THEY WERE BOTH GONE.
BUT HE WAS STILL HERE. AND HE WANTED TO BE SOMETHING DIFFERENT.
THERE WAS A TIME WHEN I THINK I WAS HIS ONLY REAL FRIEND.
BUT AS WE GOT OLDER, WE DIDN'T SEE EACH OTHER AS MUCH.
IT SEEMED LIKE HIS LIFE GOT A LOT BETTER.
MORE NORMAL, IF A KID WHO OWNS HIS OWN COMPANY CAN EVER BE NORMAL.
HE DIDN'T NEED A SUPER HERO FRIEND ANYMORE.

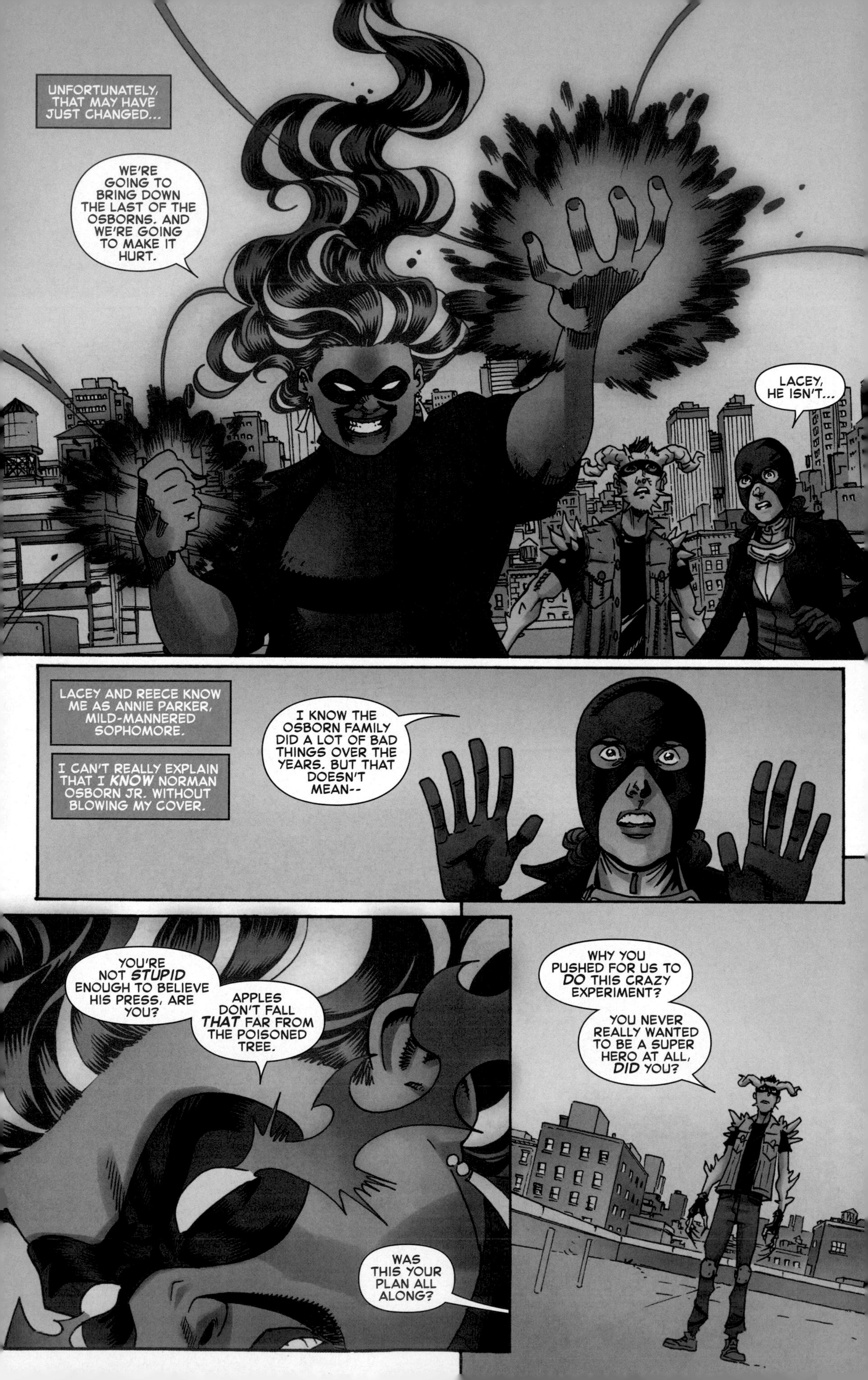
UNFORTUNATELY, THAT MAY HAVE JUST CHANGED...
WE'RE GOING TO BRING DOWN THE LAST OF THE OSBORNS. AND WE'RE GOING TO MAKE IT HURT.
LACEY, HE ISN'T...
LACEY AND REECE KNOW ME AS ANNIE PARKER, MILD-MANNERED SOPHOMORE.
I CAN'T REALLY EXPLAIN THAT I *KNOW* NORMAN OSBORN JR. WITHOUT BLOWING MY COVER.
I KNOW THE OSBORN FAMILY DID A LOT OF BAD THINGS OVER THE YEARS. BUT THAT DOESN'T MEAN--
YOU'RE NOT *STUPID* ENOUGH TO BELIEVE HIS PRESS, ARE YOU?
APPLES DON'T FALL *THAT* FAR FROM THE POISONED TREE.
WAS THIS YOUR PLAN ALL ALONG?
WHY YOU PUSHED FOR US TO *DO* THIS CRAZY EXPERIMENT?
YOU NEVER REALLY WANTED TO BE A SUPER HERO AT ALL, *DID* YOU?

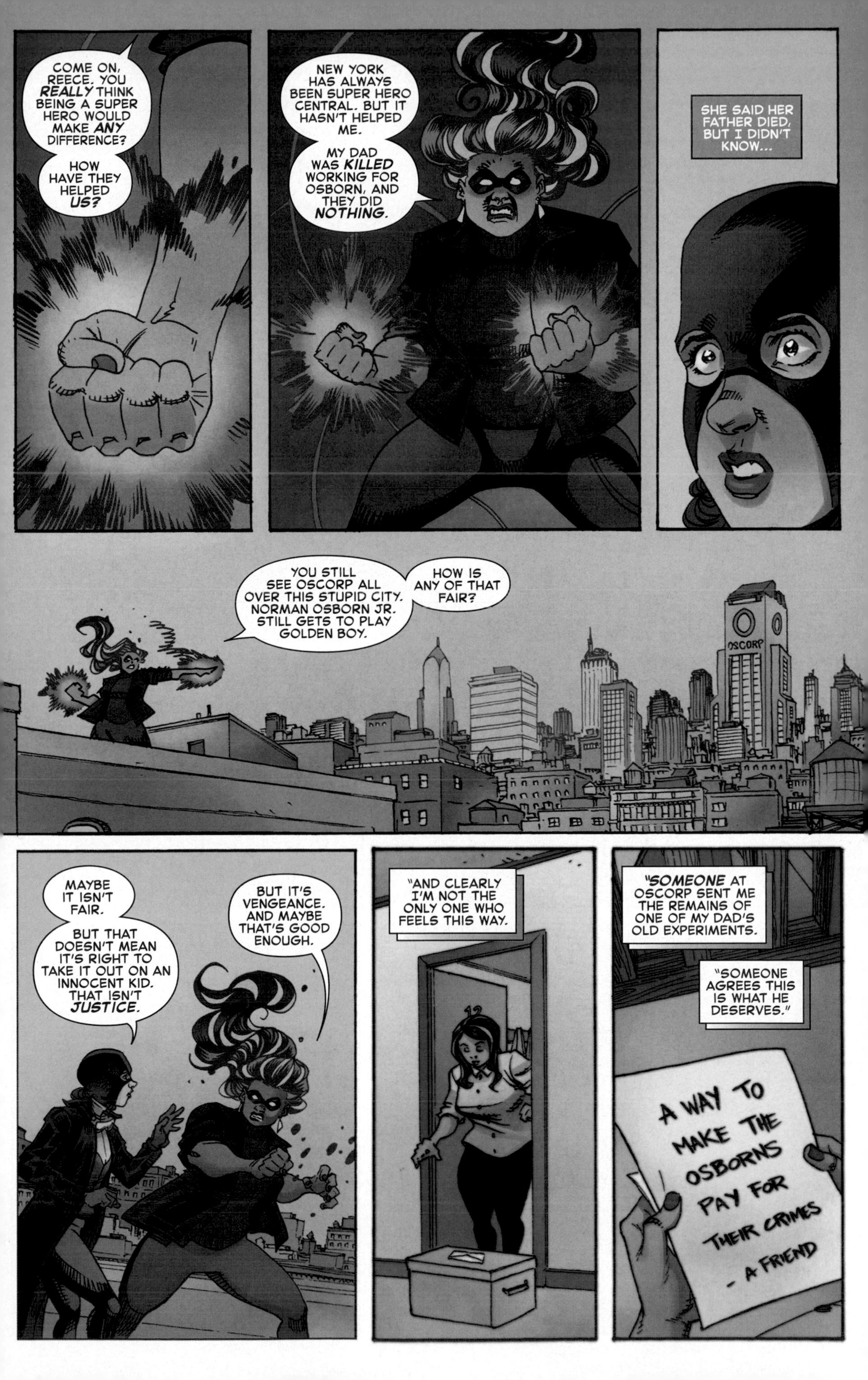
COME ON, REECE. YOU REALLY THINK BEING A SUPER HERO WOULD MAKE ANY DIFFERENCE?
HOW HAVE THEY HELPED US?
NEW YORK HAS ALWAYS BEEN SUPER HERO CENTRAL. BUT IT HASN'T HELPED ME.
MY DAD WAS KILLED WORKING FOR OSBORN, AND THEY DID NOTHING.
SHE SAID HER FATHER DIED, BUT I DIDN'T KNOW...
YOU STILL SEE OSCORP ALL OVER THIS STUPID CITY. NORMAN OSBORN JR. STILL GETS TO PLAY GOLDEN BOY.
HOW IS ANY OF THAT FAIR?
OSCORP
MAYBE IT ISN'T FAIR.
BUT THAT DOESN'T MEAN IT'S RIGHT TO TAKE IT OUT ON AN INNOCENT KID. THAT ISN'T JUSTICE.
BUT IT'S VENGEANCE. AND MAYBE THAT'S GOOD ENOUGH.
"AND CLEARLY I'M NOT THE ONLY ONE WHO FEELS THIS WAY.
"SOMEONE AT OSCORP SENT ME THE REMAINS OF ONE OF MY DAD'S OLD EXPERIMENTS.
"SOMEONE AGREES THIS IS WHAT HE DESERVES."
A WAY TO MAKE THE OSBORNS PAY FOR THEIR CRIMES
- A FRIEND

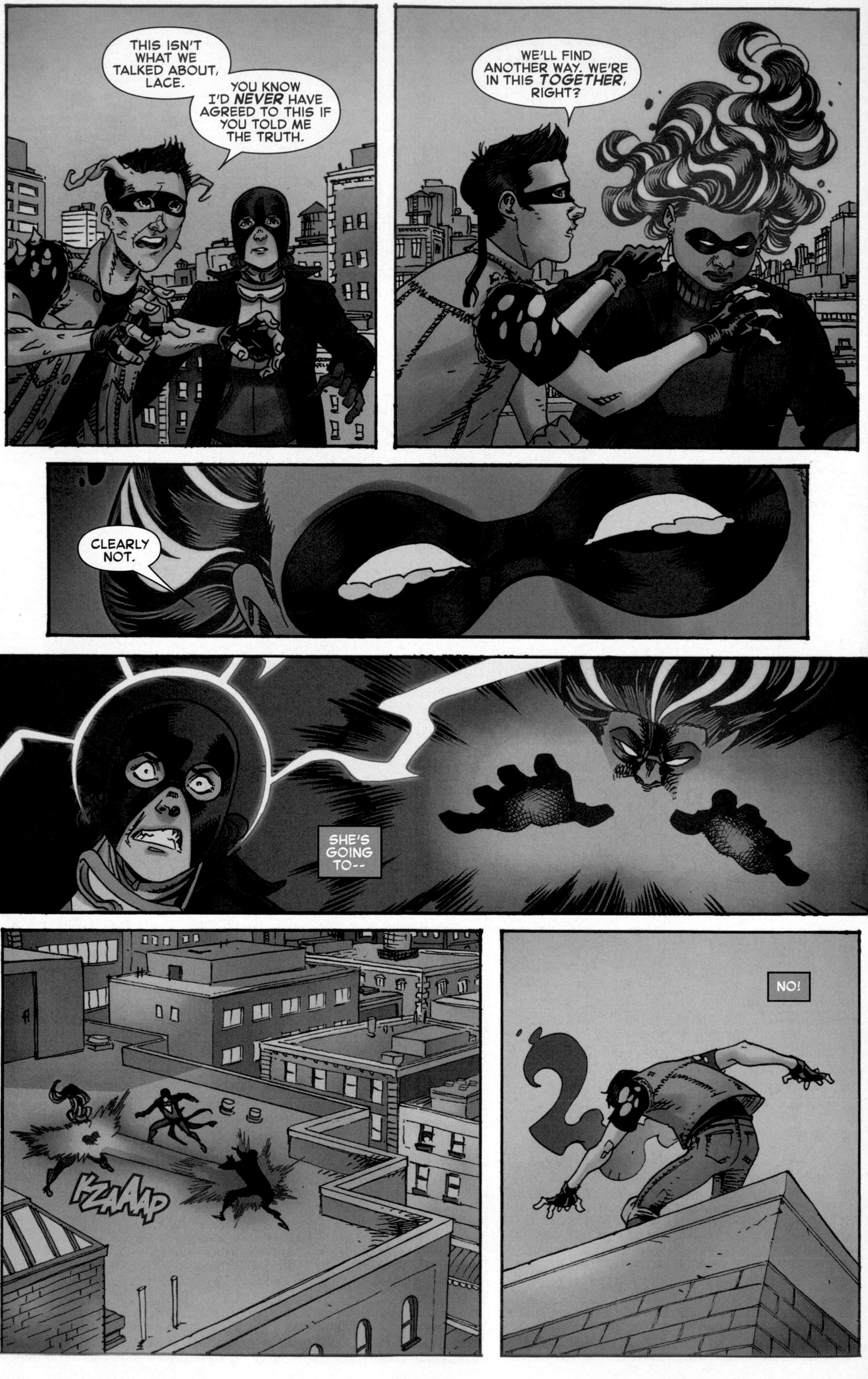
THIS ISN'T WHAT WE TALKED ABOUT, LACE.
YOU KNOW I'D NEVER HAVE AGREED TO THIS IF YOU TOLD ME THE TRUTH.
WE'LL FIND ANOTHER WAY. WE'RE IN THIS TOGETHER, RIGHT?
CLEARLY NOT.
SHE'S GOING TO--
KZAAAP
NO!

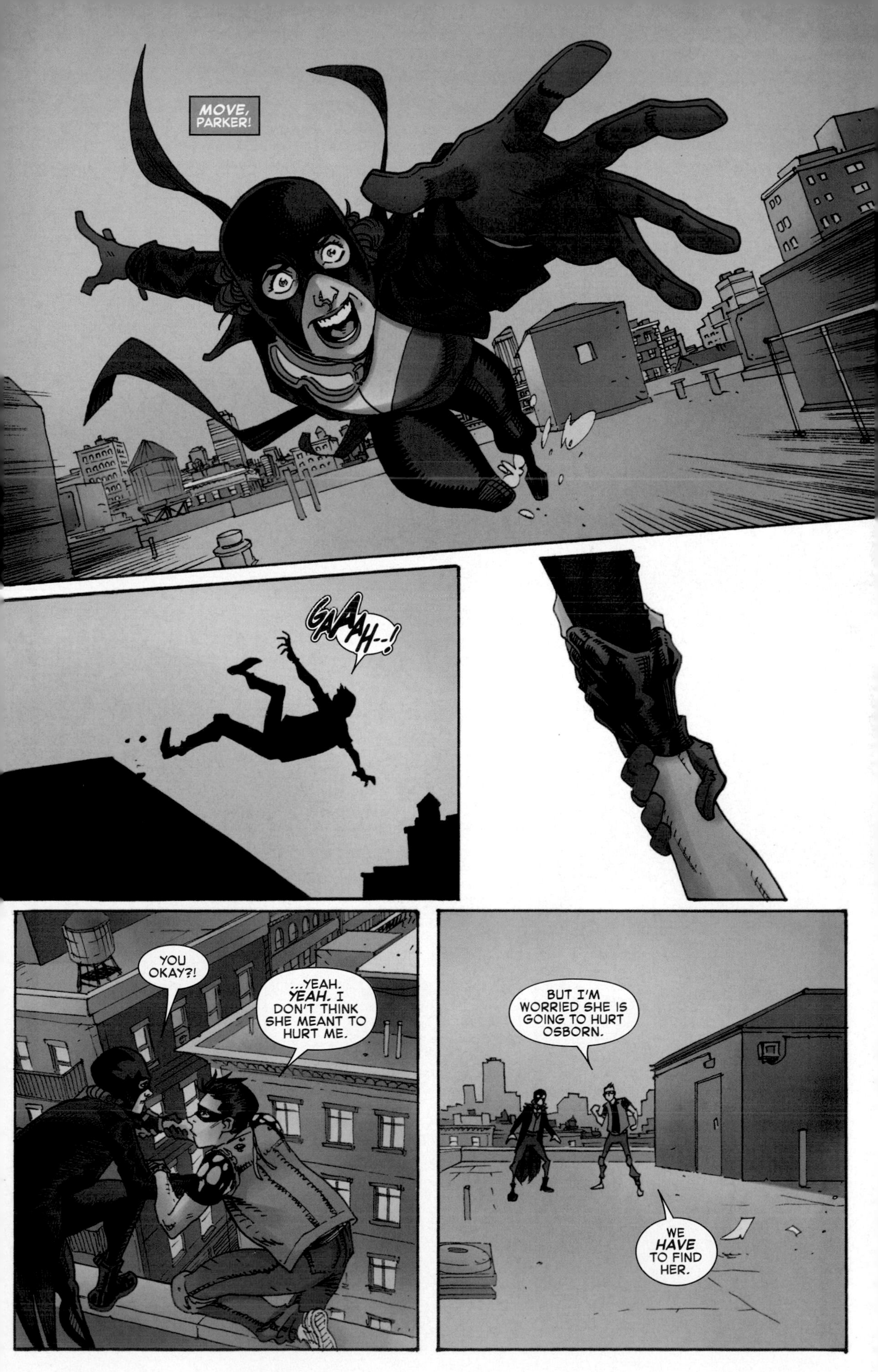
MOVE, PARKER!
GAAAH--!
YOU OKAY?!
...YEAH. YEAH. I DON'T THINK SHE MEANT TO HURT ME.
BUT I'M WORRIED SHE IS GOING TO HURT OSBORN.
WE HAVE TO FIND HER.

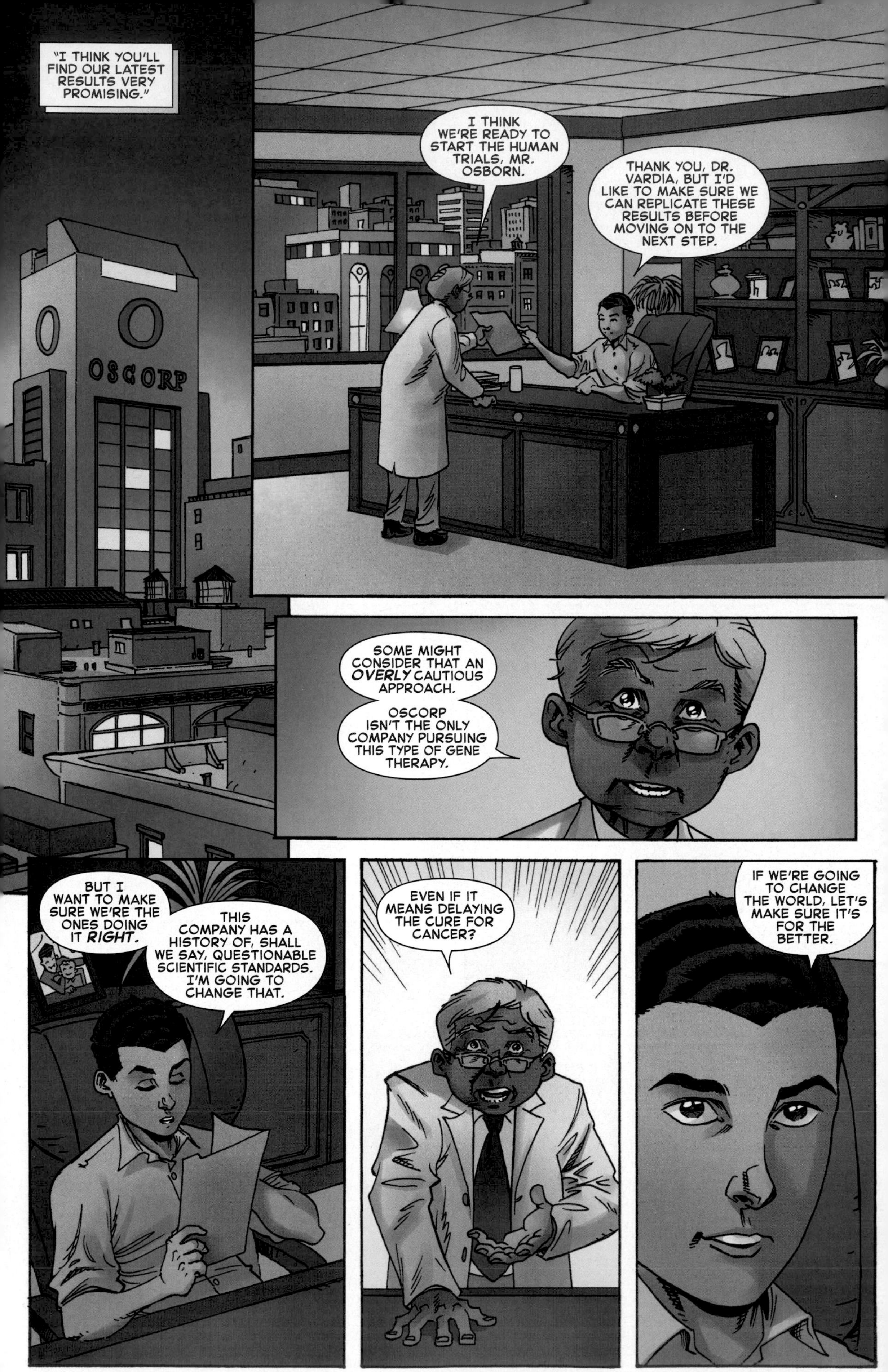
"I THINK YOU'LL FIND OUR LATEST RESULTS VERY PROMISING."
OSCORP
I THINK WE'RE READY TO START THE HUMAN TRIALS, MR. OSBORN.
THANK YOU, DR. VARDIA, BUT I'D LIKE TO MAKE SURE WE CAN REPLICATE THESE RESULTS BEFORE MOVING ON TO THE NEXT STEP.
SOME MIGHT CONSIDER THAT AN *OVERLY* CAUTIOUS APPROACH.
OSCORP ISN'T THE ONLY COMPANY PURSUING THIS TYPE OF GENE THERAPY.
BUT I WANT TO MAKE SURE WE'RE THE ONES DOING IT ***RIGHT.***
THIS COMPANY HAS A HISTORY OF, SHALL WE SAY, QUESTIONABLE SCIENTIFIC STANDARDS. I'M GOING TO CHANGE THAT.
EVEN IF IT MEANS DELAYING THE CURE FOR CANCER?
IF WE'RE GOING TO CHANGE THE WORLD, LET'S MAKE SURE IT'S FOR THE BETTER.

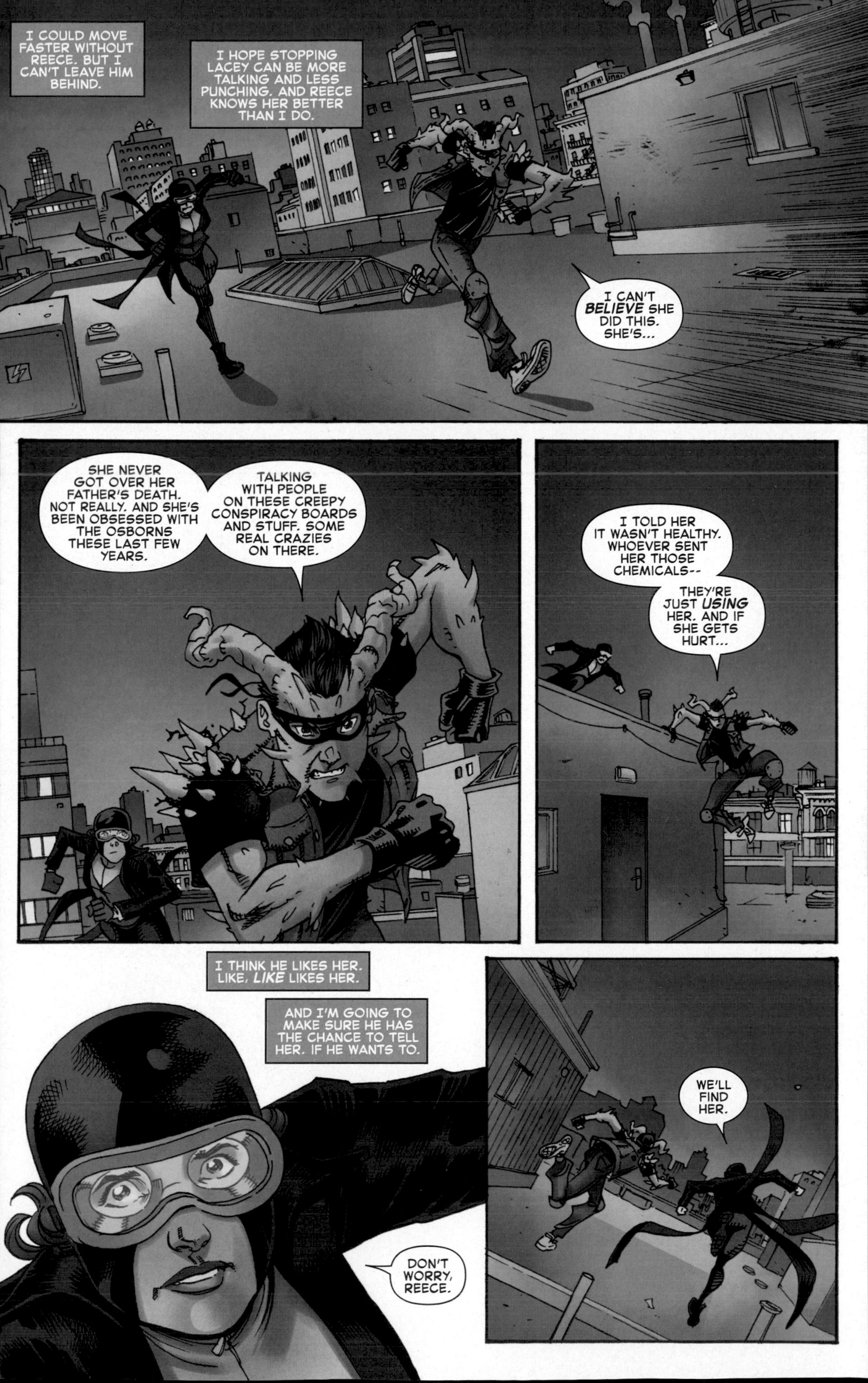
I COULD MOVE FASTER WITHOUT REECE. BUT I CAN'T LEAVE HIM BEHIND.
I HOPE STOPPING LACEY CAN BE MORE TALKING AND LESS PUNCHING. AND REECE KNOWS HER BETTER THAN I DO.
I CAN'T BELIEVE SHE DID THIS. SHE'S...
SHE NEVER GOT OVER HER FATHER'S DEATH. NOT REALLY. AND SHE'S BEEN OBSESSED WITH THE OSBORNS THESE LAST FEW YEARS.
TALKING WITH PEOPLE ON THESE CREEPY CONSPIRACY BOARDS AND STUFF. SOME REAL CRAZIES ON THERE.
I TOLD HER IT WASN'T HEALTHY. WHOEVER SENT HER THOSE CHEMICALS--
THEY'RE JUST USING HER. AND IF SHE GETS HURT...
I THINK HE LIKES HER. LIKE, LIKE LIKES HER.
AND I'M GOING TO MAKE SURE HE HAS THE CHANCE TO TELL HER. IF HE WANTS TO.
DON'T WORRY, REECE.
WE'LL FIND HER.

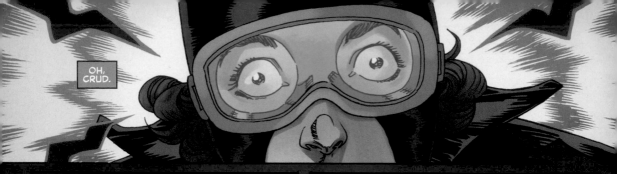

OH, CRUD.

GAH!

YOU OKAY?

TWISTED MY ANKLE... NEED A MINUTE.

KEEP GOING. I'LL CATCH UP.

I'VE GOT THIS. I HOPE...

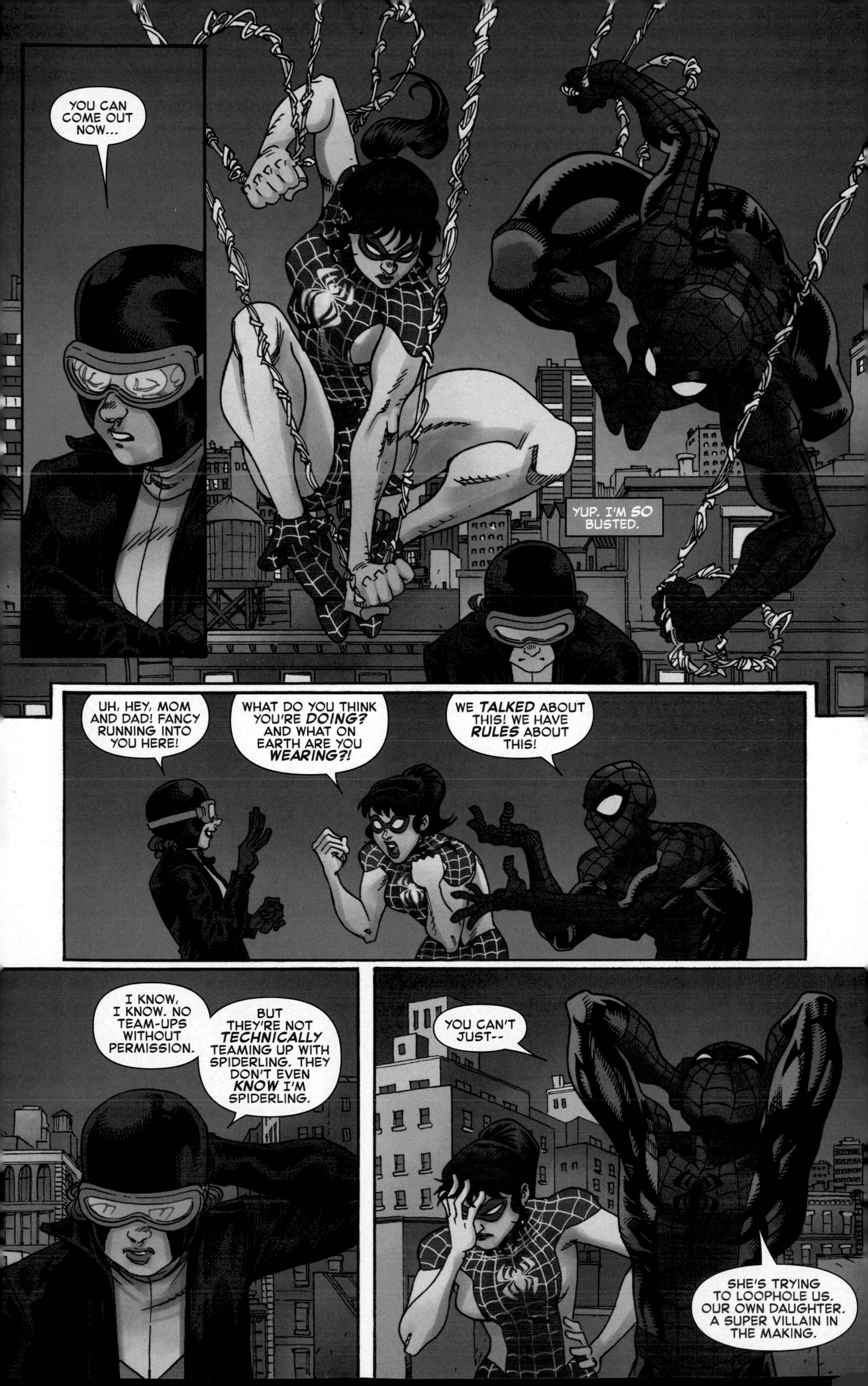
YOU CAN COME OUT NOW...
YUP. I'M SO BUSTED.
UH, HEY, MOM AND DAD! FANCY RUNNING INTO YOU HERE!
WHAT DO YOU THINK YOU'RE DOING? AND WHAT ON EARTH ARE YOU WEARING?!
WE TALKED ABOUT THIS! WE HAVE RULES ABOUT THIS!
I KNOW, I KNOW. NO TEAM-UPS WITHOUT PERMISSION.
BUT THEY'RE NOT TECHNICALLY TEAMING UP WITH SPIDERLING. THEY DON'T EVEN KNOW I'M SPIDERLING.
YOU CAN'T JUST--
SHE'S TRYING TO LOOPHOLE US. OUR OWN DAUGHTER. A SUPER VILLAIN IN THE MAKING.

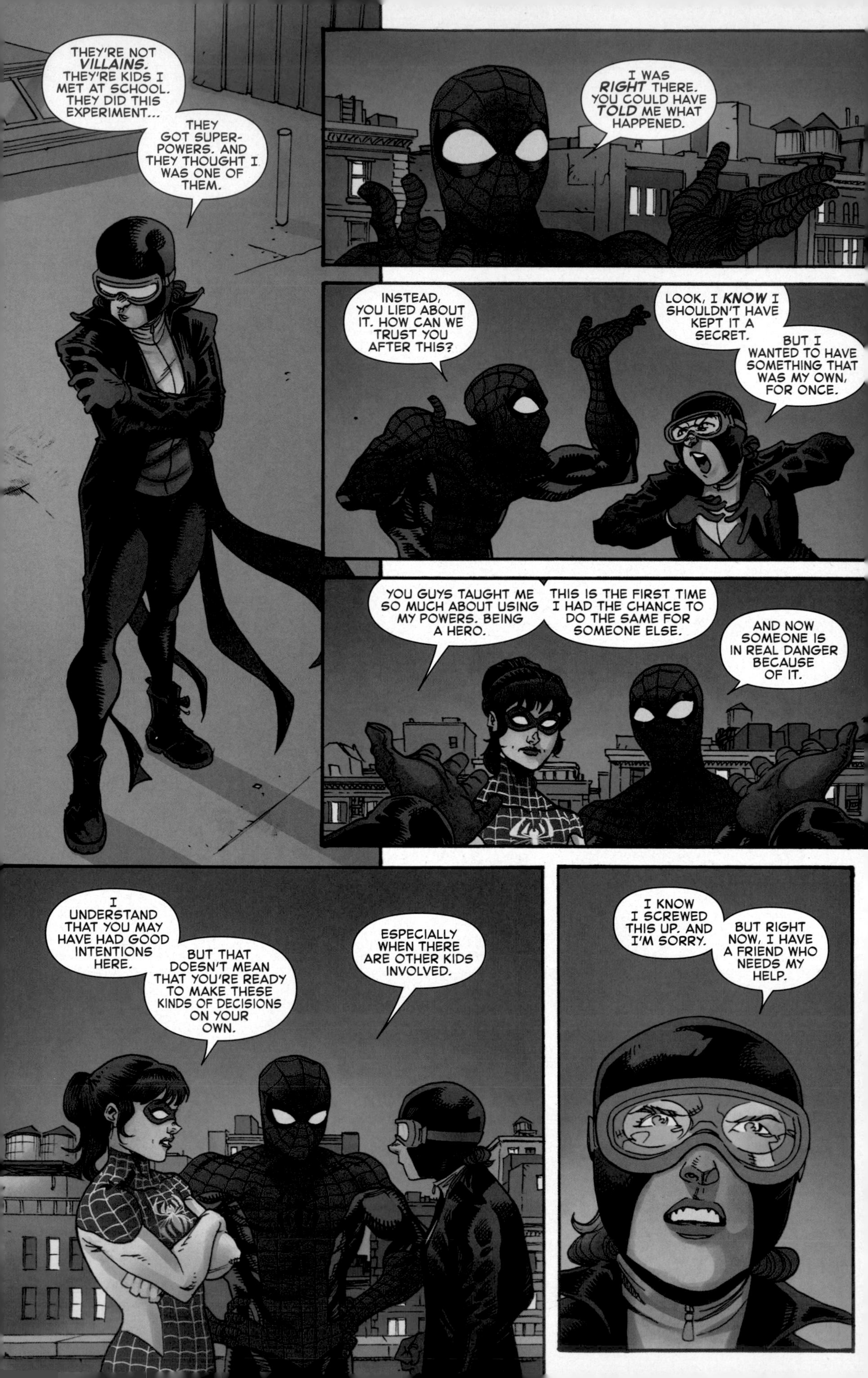
THEY'RE NOT VILLAINS. THEY'RE KIDS I MET AT SCHOOL. THEY DID THIS EXPERIMENT...
THEY GOT SUPER-POWERS. AND THEY THOUGHT I WAS ONE OF THEM.
I WAS RIGHT THERE. YOU COULD HAVE TOLD ME WHAT HAPPENED.
INSTEAD, YOU LIED ABOUT IT. HOW CAN WE TRUST YOU AFTER THIS?
LOOK, I KNOW I SHOULDN'T HAVE KEPT IT A SECRET.
BUT I WANTED TO HAVE SOMETHING THAT WAS MY OWN, FOR ONCE.
YOU GUYS TAUGHT ME SO MUCH ABOUT USING MY POWERS. BEING A HERO.
THIS IS THE FIRST TIME I HAD THE CHANCE TO DO THE SAME FOR SOMEONE ELSE.
AND NOW SOMEONE IS IN REAL DANGER BECAUSE OF IT.
I UNDERSTAND THAT YOU MAY HAVE HAD GOOD INTENTIONS HERE.
BUT THAT DOESN'T MEAN THAT YOU'RE READY TO MAKE THESE KINDS OF DECISIONS ON YOUR OWN.
ESPECIALLY WHEN THERE ARE OTHER KIDS INVOLVED.
I KNOW I SCREWED THIS UP. AND I'M SORRY.
BUT RIGHT NOW, I HAVE A FRIEND WHO NEEDS MY HELP.

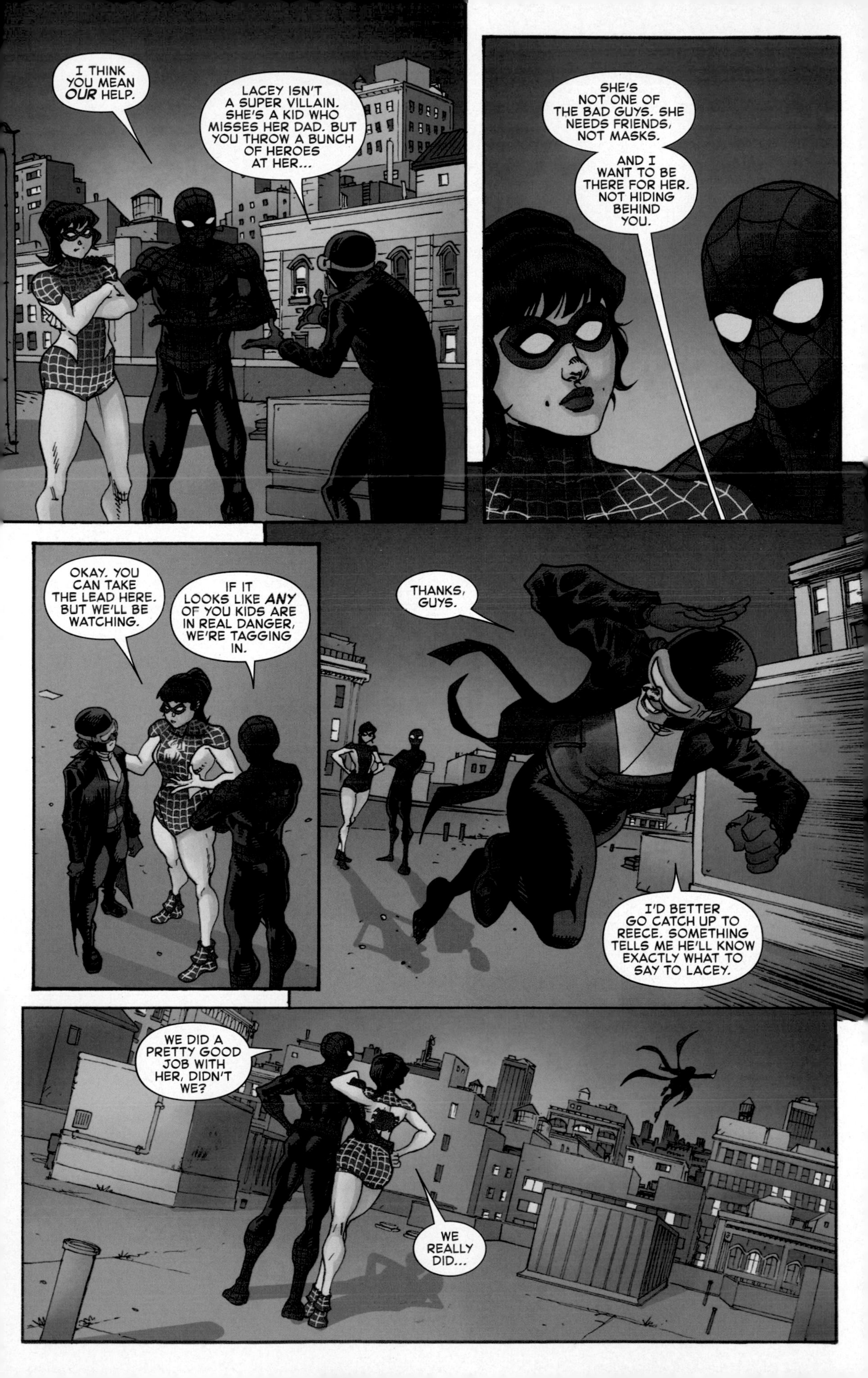

I THINK YOU MEAN OUR HELP.
LACEY ISN'T A SUPER VILLAIN. SHE'S A KID WHO MISSES HER DAD. BUT YOU THROW A BUNCH OF HEROES AT HER...
SHE'S NOT ONE OF THE BAD GUYS. SHE NEEDS FRIENDS, NOT MASKS.
AND I WANT TO BE THERE FOR HER. NOT HIDING BEHIND YOU.
OKAY. YOU CAN TAKE THE LEAD HERE. BUT WE'LL BE WATCHING.
IF IT LOOKS LIKE ANY OF YOU KIDS ARE IN REAL DANGER, WE'RE TAGGING IN.
THANKS, GUYS.
I'D BETTER GO CATCH UP TO REECE. SOMETHING TELLS ME HE'LL KNOW EXACTLY WHAT TO SAY TO LACEY.
WE DID A PRETTY GOOD JOB WITH HER, DIDN'T WE?
WE REALLY DID...

"...I JUST HOPE SHE'S READY FOR THIS."

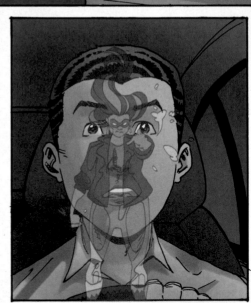

GOING TO TAKE *EVERYTHING* AWAY FROM YOU...

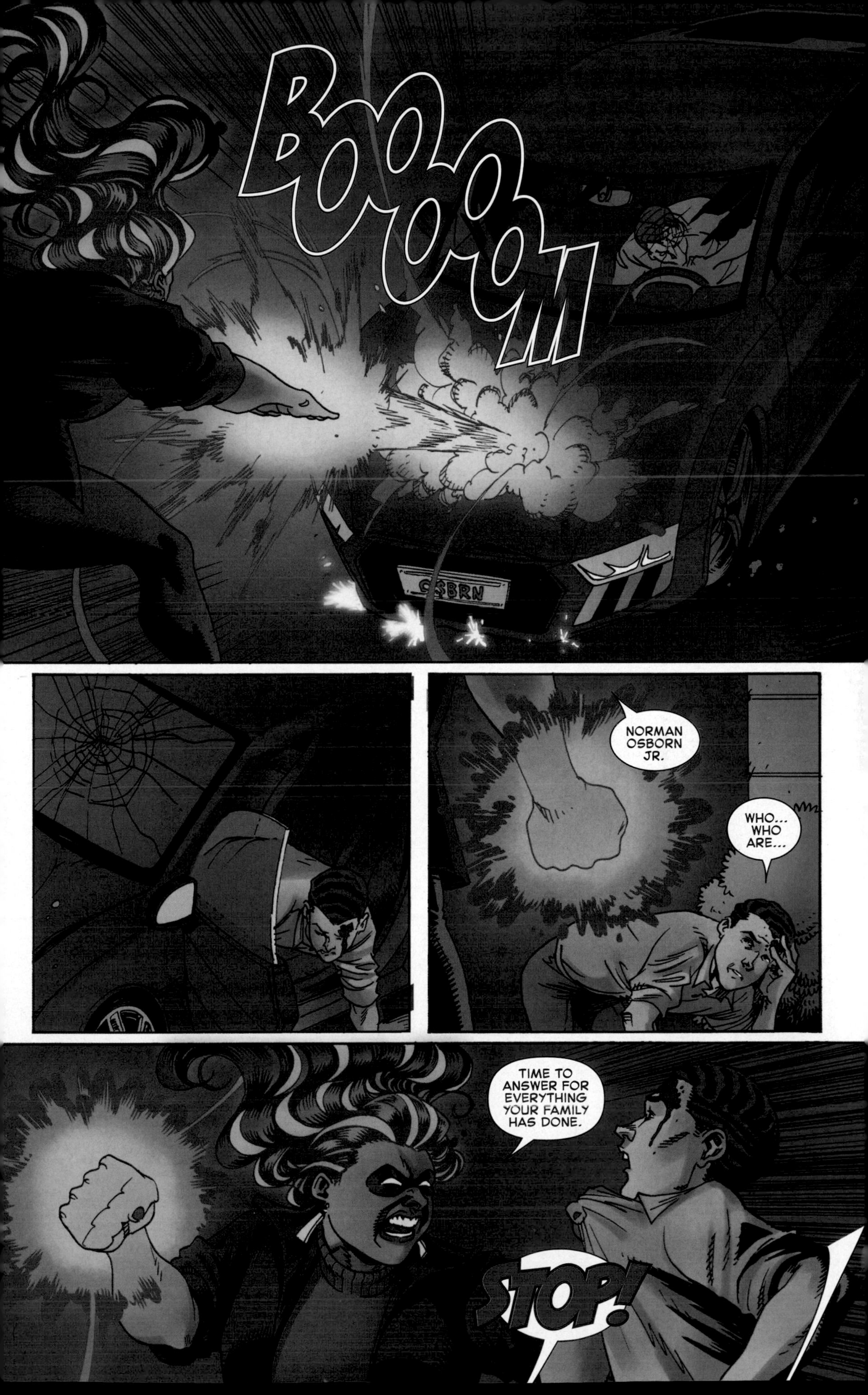
BOOOOOM
OSBRN
NORMAN OSBORN JR.
WHO... WHO ARE...
TIME TO ANSWER FOR EVERYTHING YOUR FAMILY HAS DONE.
STOP!

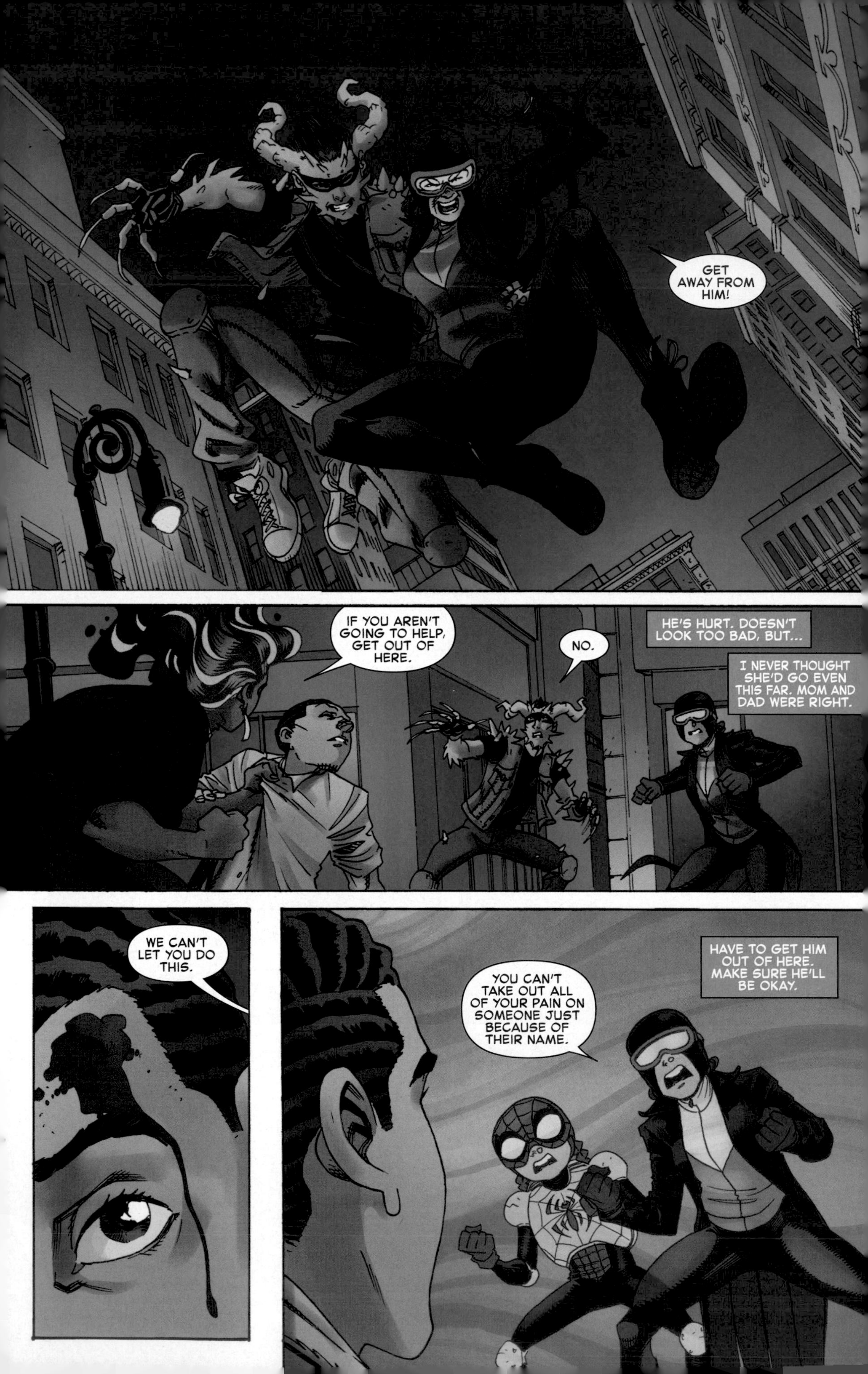
GET AWAY FROM HIM!
IF YOU AREN'T GOING TO HELP, GET OUT OF HERE.
NO.
HE'S HURT. DOESN'T LOOK TOO BAD, BUT...
I NEVER THOUGHT SHE'D GO EVEN THIS FAR. MOM AND DAD WERE RIGHT.
WE CAN'T LET YOU DO THIS.
YOU CAN'T TAKE OUT ALL OF YOUR PAIN ON SOMEONE JUST BECAUSE OF THEIR NAME.
HAVE TO GET HIM OUT OF HERE. MAKE SURE HE'LL BE OKAY.

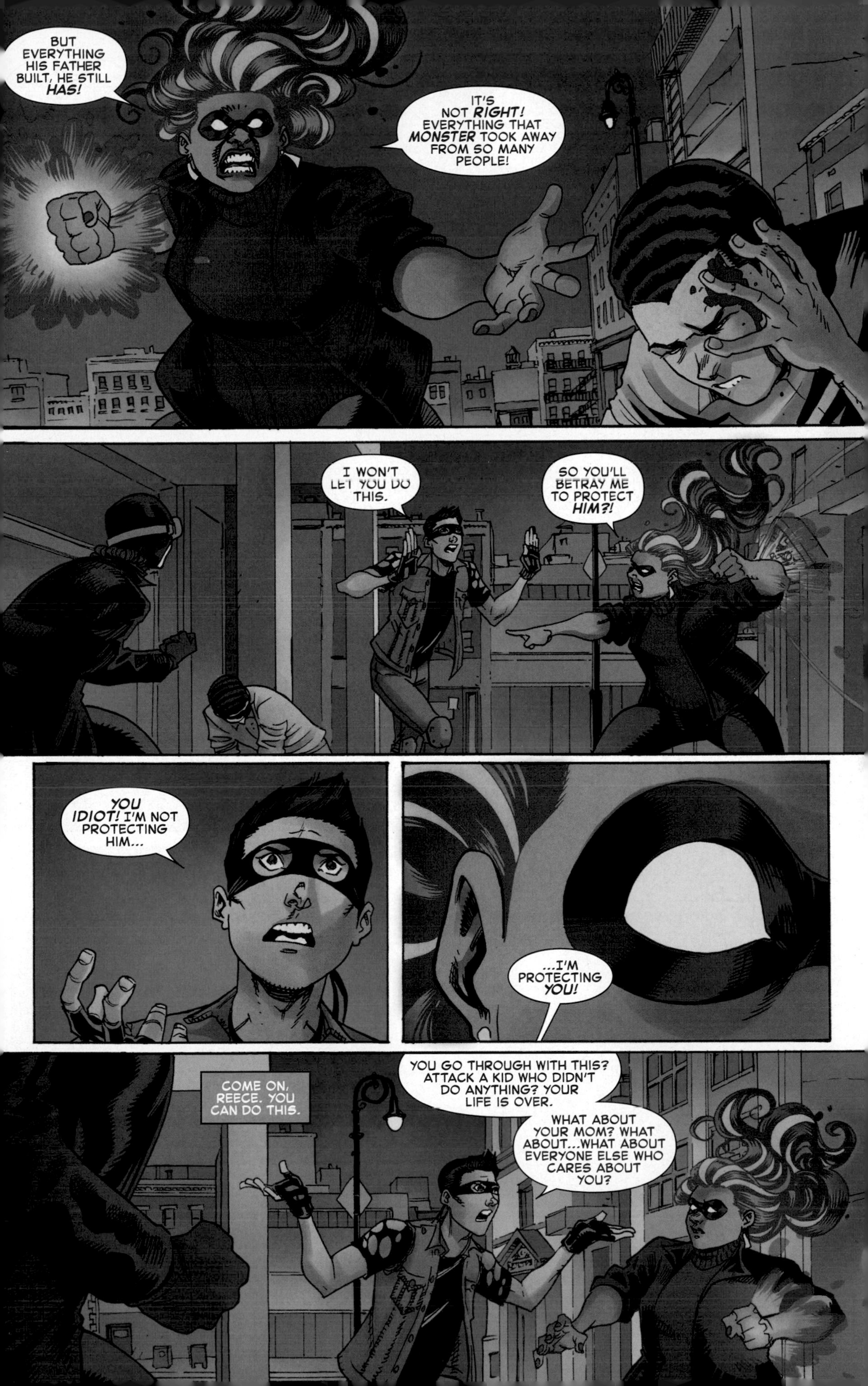
BUT EVERYTHING HIS FATHER BUILT, HE STILL HAS!
IT'S NOT RIGHT! EVERYTHING THAT MONSTER TOOK AWAY FROM SO MANY PEOPLE!
I WON'T LET YOU DO THIS.
SO YOU'LL BETRAY ME TO PROTECT HIM?!
YOU IDIOT! I'M NOT PROTECTING HIM...
...I'M PROTECTING YOU!
COME ON, REECE. YOU CAN DO THIS.
YOU GO THROUGH WITH THIS? ATTACK A KID WHO DIDN'T DO ANYTHING? YOUR LIFE IS OVER.
WHAT ABOUT YOUR MOM? WHAT ABOUT...WHAT ABOUT EVERYONE ELSE WHO CARES ABOUT YOU?

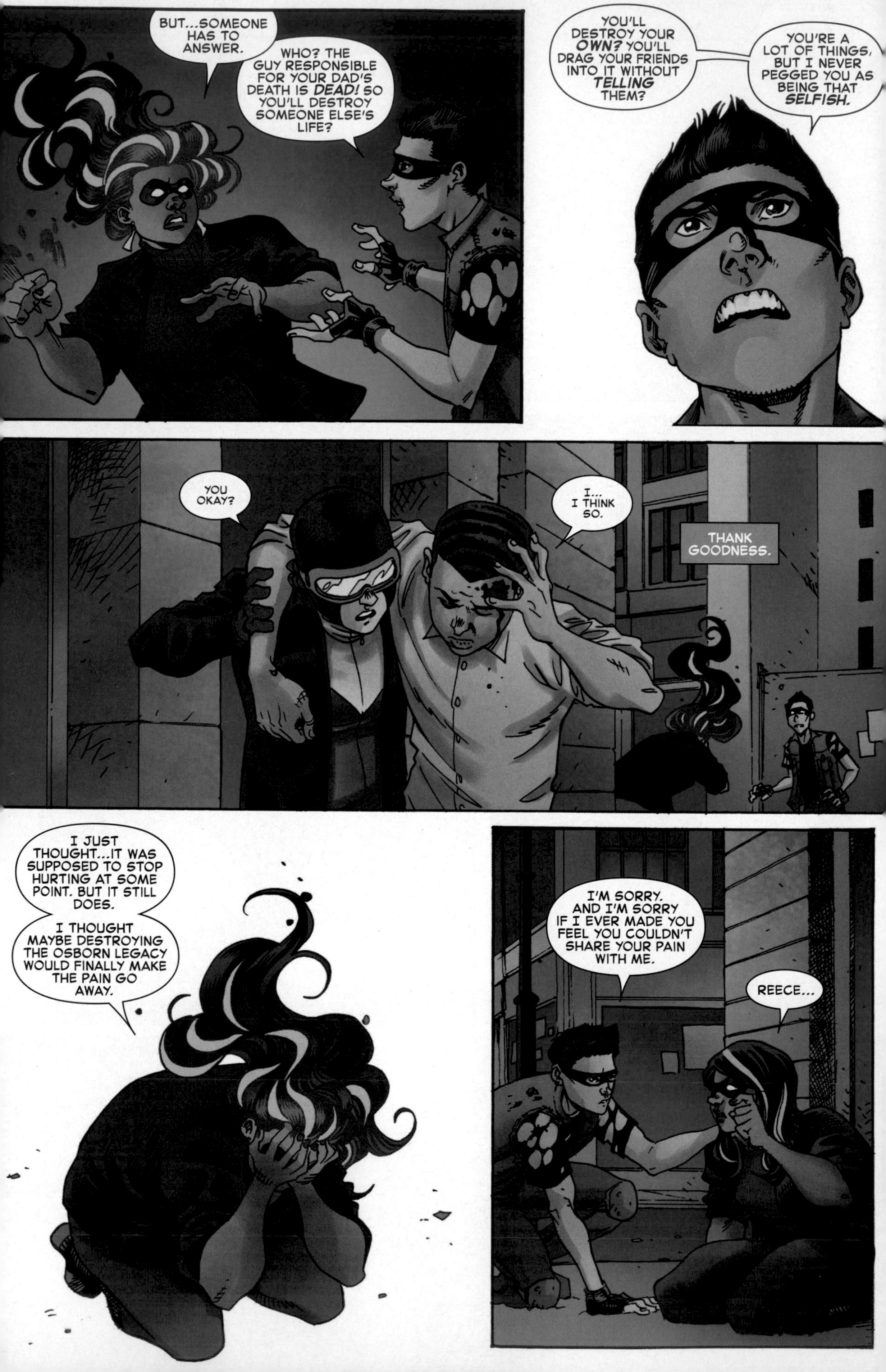
BUT...SOMEONE HAS TO ANSWER.
WHO? THE GUY RESPONSIBLE FOR YOUR DAD'S DEATH IS *DEAD!* SO YOU'LL DESTROY SOMEONE ELSE'S LIFE?
YOU'LL DESTROY YOUR *OWN?* YOU'LL DRAG YOUR FRIENDS INTO IT WITHOUT *TELLING* THEM?
YOU'RE A LOT OF THINGS, BUT I NEVER PEGGED YOU AS BEING THAT *SELFISH.*
YOU OKAY?
I... I THINK SO.
THANK GOODNESS.
I JUST THOUGHT...IT WAS SUPPOSED TO STOP HURTING AT SOME POINT. BUT IT STILL DOES.
I THOUGHT MAYBE DESTROYING THE OSBORN LEGACY WOULD FINALLY MAKE THE PAIN GO AWAY.
I'M SORRY. AND I'M SORRY IF I EVER MADE YOU FEEL YOU COULDN'T SHARE YOUR PAIN WITH ME.
REECE...

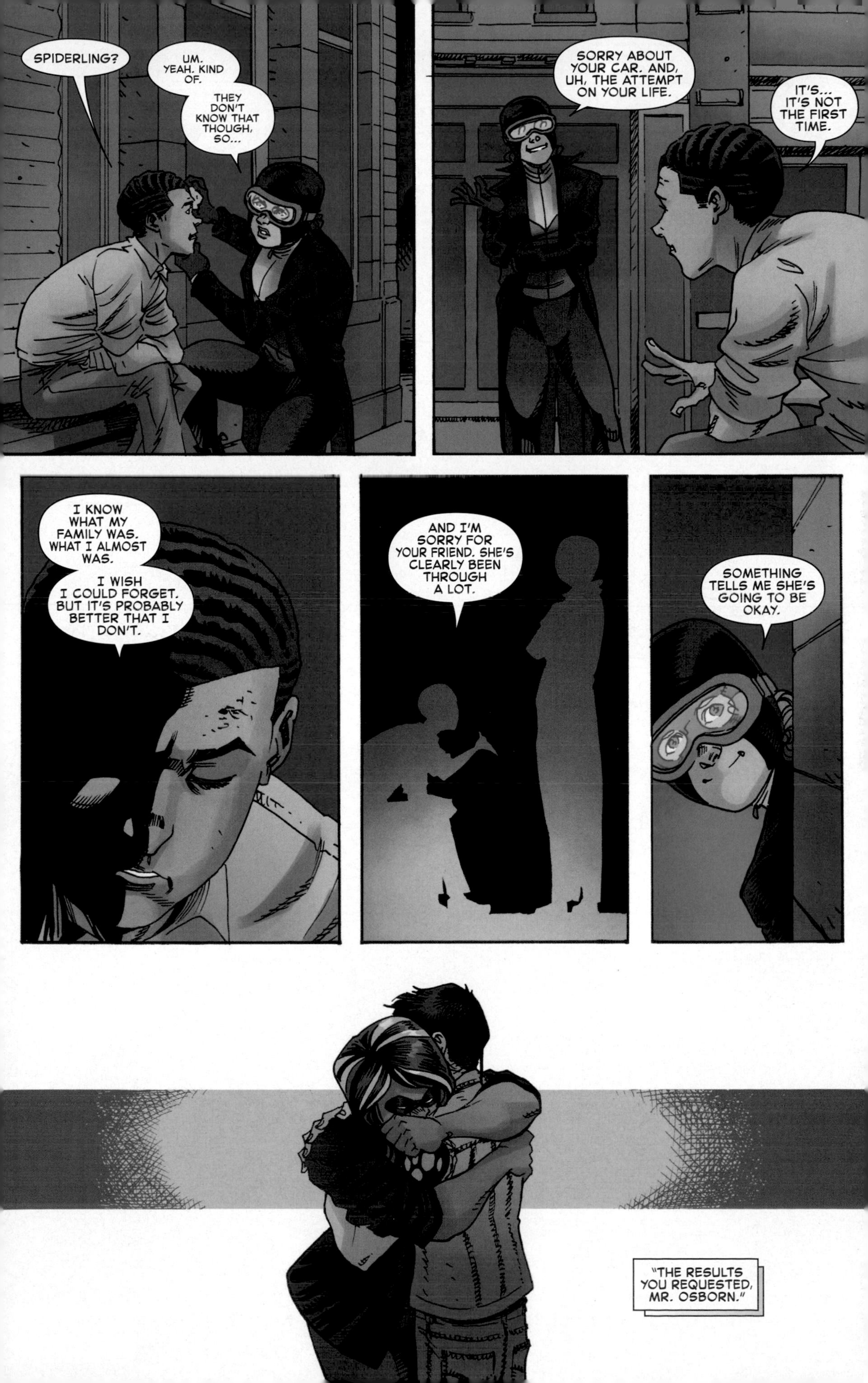
SPIDERLING?
UM. YEAH. KIND OF.
THEY DON'T KNOW THAT THOUGH, SO...
SORRY ABOUT YOUR CAR. AND, UH, THE ATTEMPT ON YOUR LIFE.
IT'S... IT'S NOT THE FIRST TIME.
I KNOW WHAT MY FAMILY WAS. WHAT I ALMOST WAS.
I WISH I COULD FORGET. BUT IT'S PROBABLY BETTER THAT I DON'T.
AND I'M SORRY FOR YOUR FRIEND. SHE'S CLEARLY BEEN THROUGH A LOT.
SOMETHING TELLS ME SHE'S GOING TO BE OKAY.
"THE RESULTS YOU REQUESTED, MR. OSBORN."

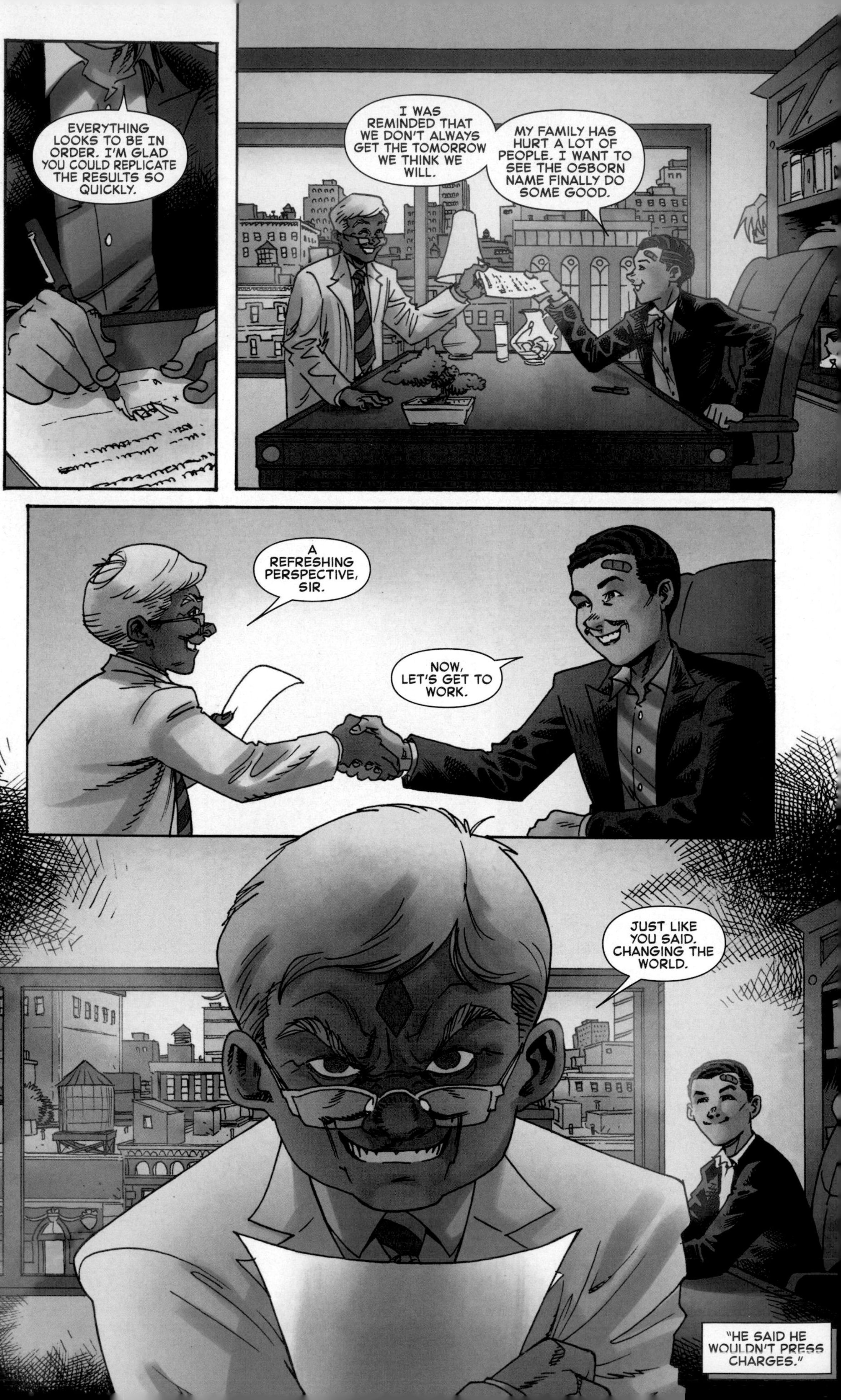
EVERYTHING LOOKS TO BE IN ORDER. I'M GLAD YOU COULD REPLICATE THE RESULTS SO QUICKLY.
I WAS REMINDED THAT WE DON'T ALWAYS GET THE TOMORROW WE THINK WE WILL.
MY FAMILY HAS HURT A LOT OF PEOPLE. I WANT TO SEE THE OSBORN NAME FINALLY DO SOME GOOD.
A REFRESHING PERSPECTIVE, SIR.
NOW, LET'S GET TO WORK.
JUST LIKE YOU SAID. CHANGING THE WORLD.
"HE SAID HE WOULDN'T PRESS CHARGES."

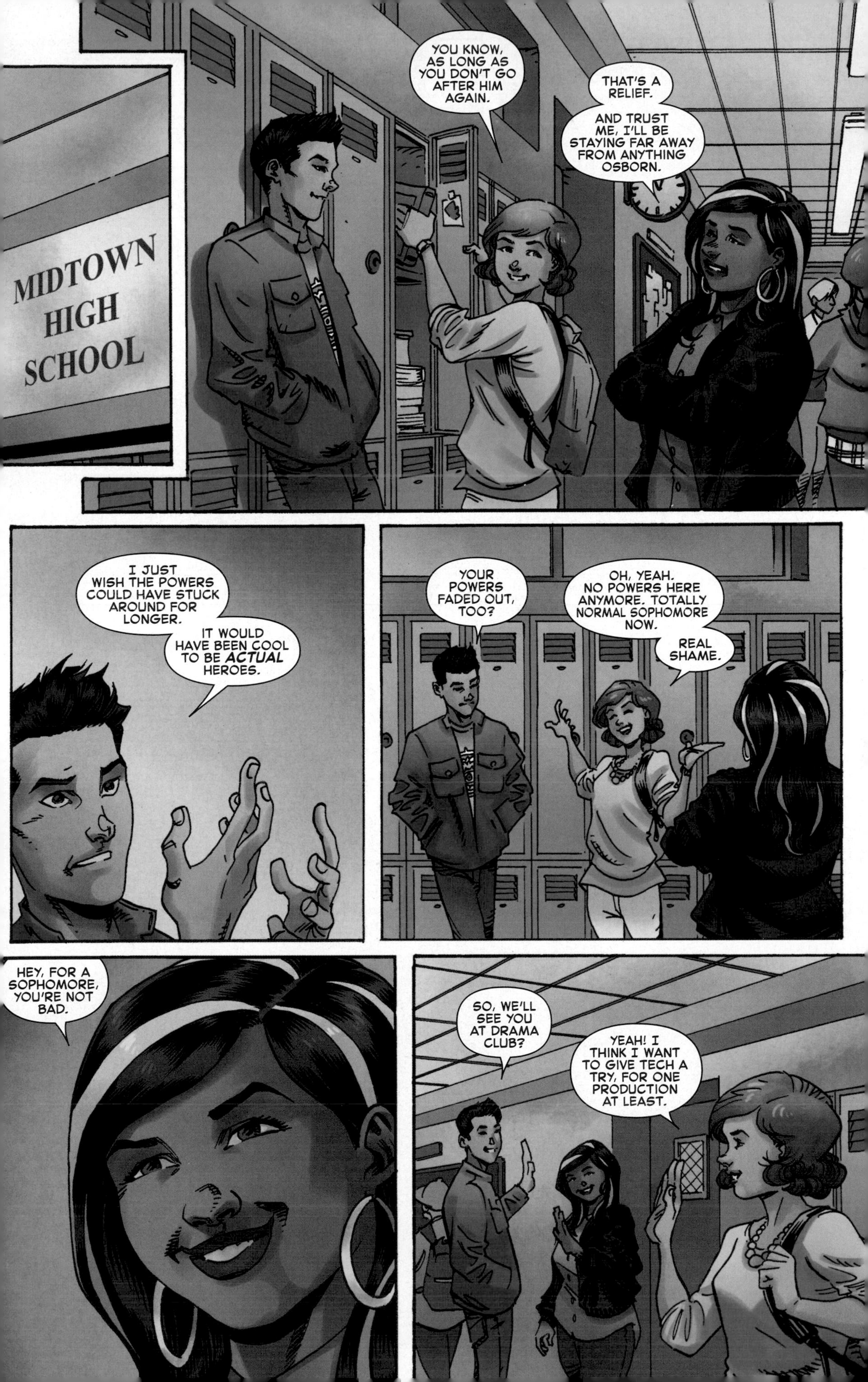
MIDTOWN HIGH SCHOOL
YOU KNOW, AS LONG AS YOU DON'T GO AFTER HIM AGAIN.
THAT'S A RELIEF.
AND TRUST ME, I'LL BE STAYING FAR AWAY FROM ANYTHING OSBORN.
I JUST WISH THE POWERS COULD HAVE STUCK AROUND FOR LONGER.
IT WOULD HAVE BEEN COOL TO BE *ACTUAL* HEROES.
YOUR POWERS FADED OUT, TOO?
OH, YEAH. NO POWERS HERE ANYMORE. TOTALLY NORMAL SOPHOMORE NOW.
REAL SHAME.
HEY, FOR A SOPHOMORE, YOU'RE NOT BAD.
SO, WE'LL SEE YOU AT DRAMA CLUB?
YEAH! I THINK I WANT TO GIVE TECH A TRY, FOR ONE PRODUCTION AT LEAST.

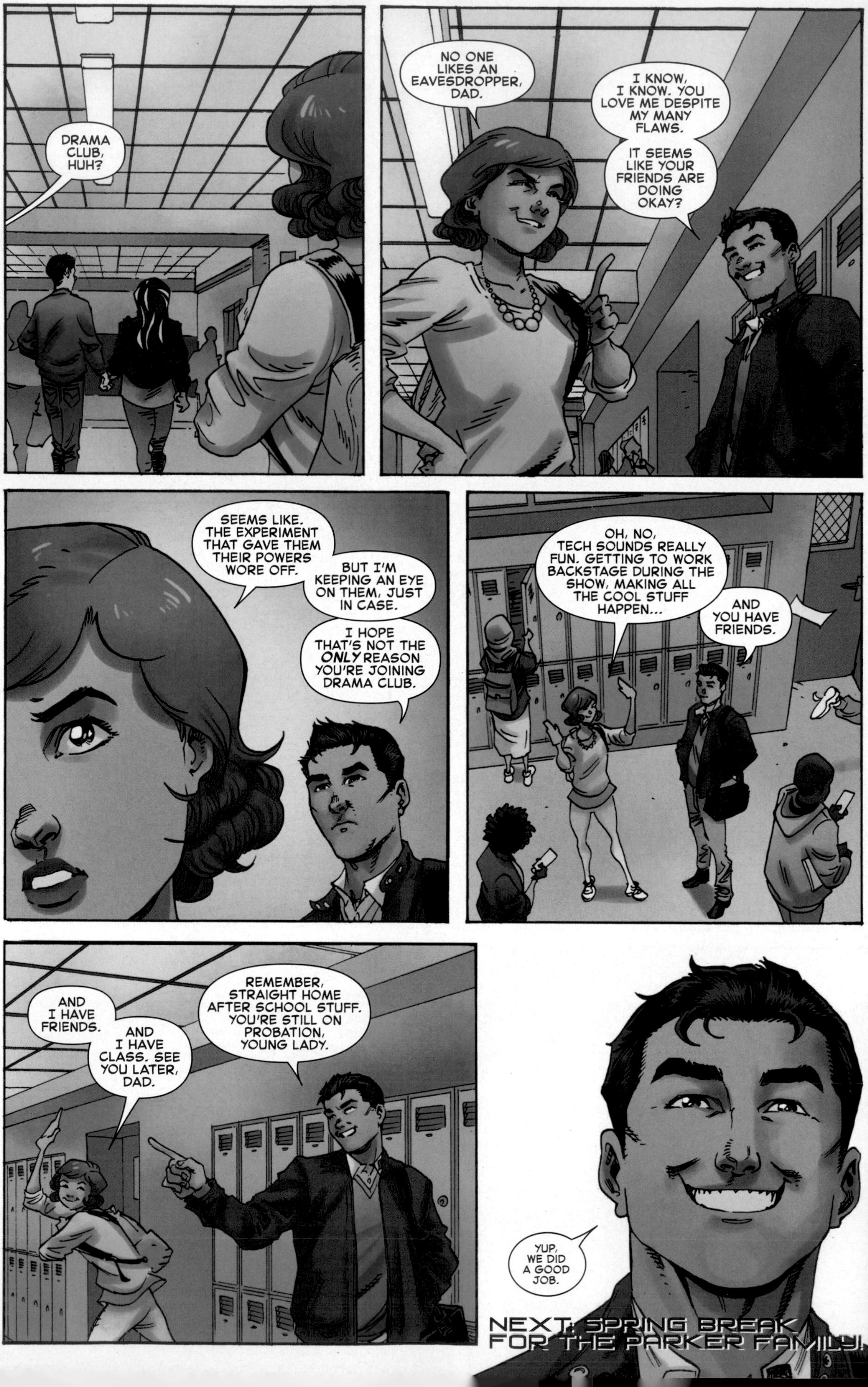
DRAMA CLUB, HUH?
NO ONE LIKES AN EAVESDROPPER, DAD.
I KNOW, I KNOW. YOU LOVE ME DESPITE MY MANY FLAWS.
IT SEEMS LIKE YOUR FRIENDS ARE DOING OKAY?
SEEMS LIKE. THE EXPERIMENT THAT GAVE THEM THEIR POWERS WORE OFF.
BUT I'M KEEPING AN EYE ON THEM, JUST IN CASE.
I HOPE THAT'S NOT THE ONLY REASON YOU'RE JOINING DRAMA CLUB.
OH, NO, TECH SOUNDS REALLY FUN. GETTING TO WORK BACKSTAGE DURING THE SHOW, MAKING ALL THE COOL STUFF HAPPEN...
AND YOU HAVE FRIENDS.
AND I HAVE FRIENDS.
AND I HAVE CLASS. SEE YOU LATER, DAD.
REMEMBER, STRAIGHT HOME AFTER SCHOOL STUFF. YOU'RE STILL ON PROBATION, YOUNG LADY.
YUP, WE DID A GOOD JOB.
NEXT: SPRING BREAK FOR THE PARKER FAMILY!

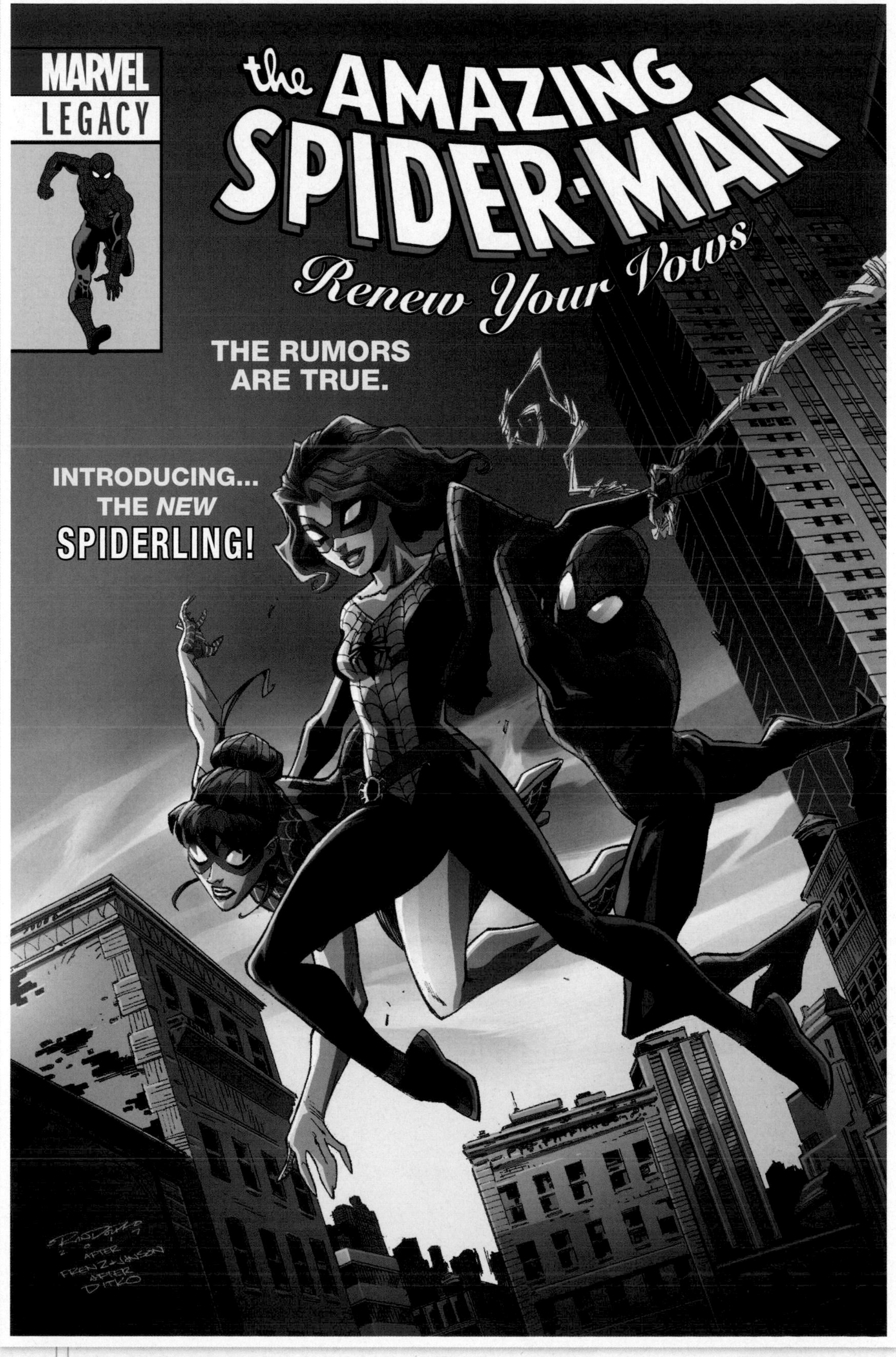
MARVEL
LEGACY
the AMAZING
SPIDER-MAN
Renew Your Vows
THE RUMORS
ARE TRUE.
INTRODUCING...
THE *NEW*
SPIDERLING!

13 HOMAGE VARIANT BY KHARY RANDOLPH & EMILIO LOPEZ

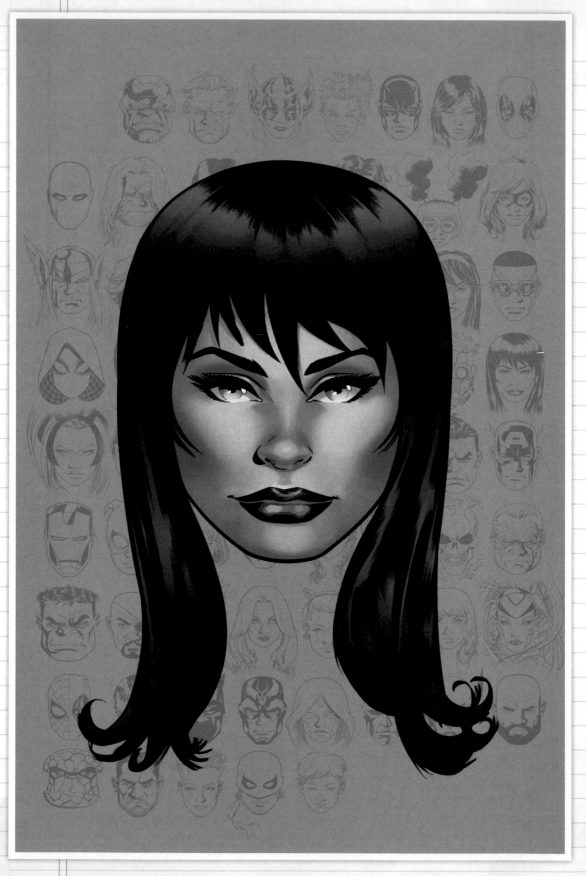

13 LEGACY HEADSHOT VARIANT BY **MIKE** McKONE & **RACHELLE** ROSENBERG

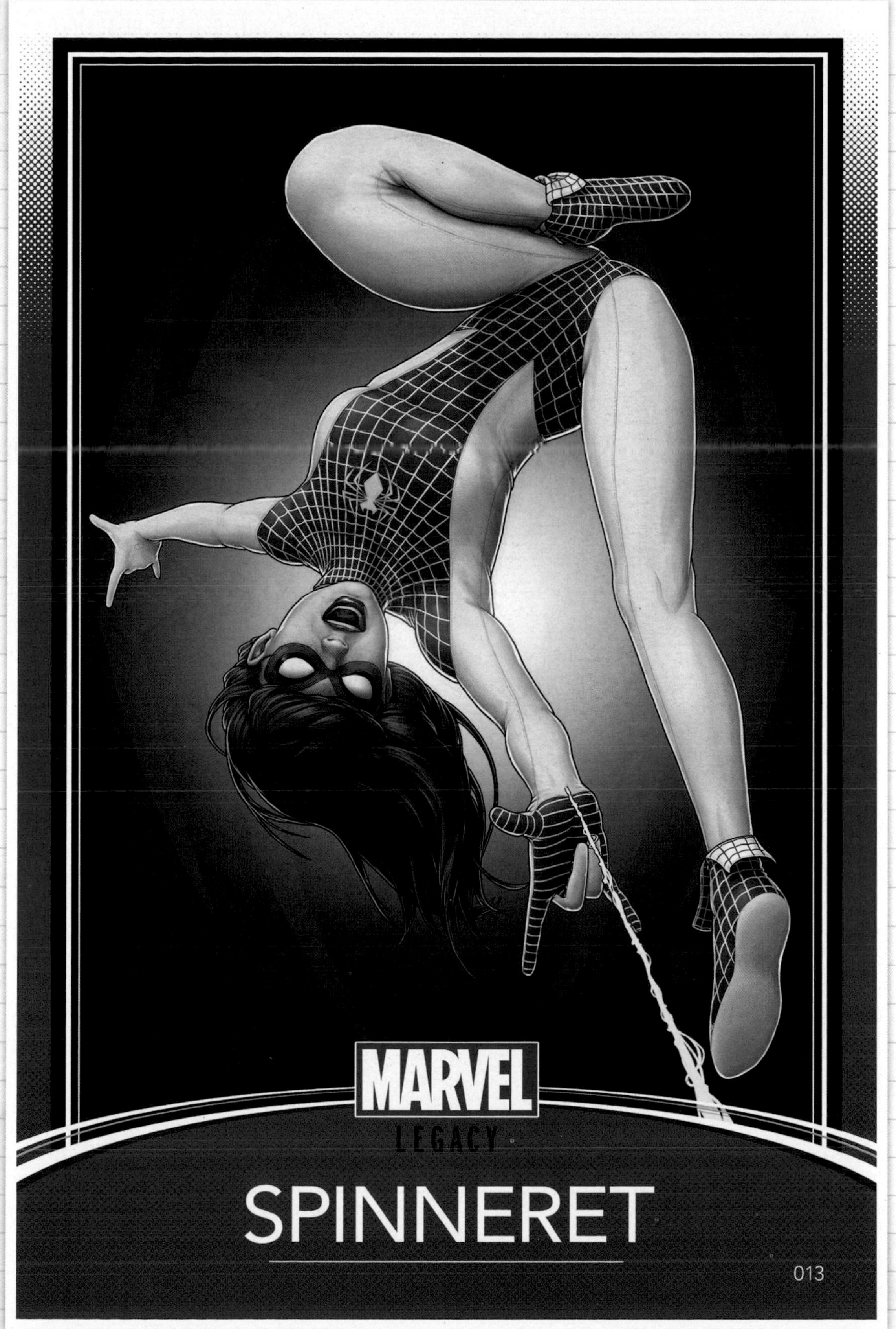
MARVEL
LEGACY
SPINNERET
013

13 TRADING CARD VARIANT BY JOHN TYLER CHRISTOPHER

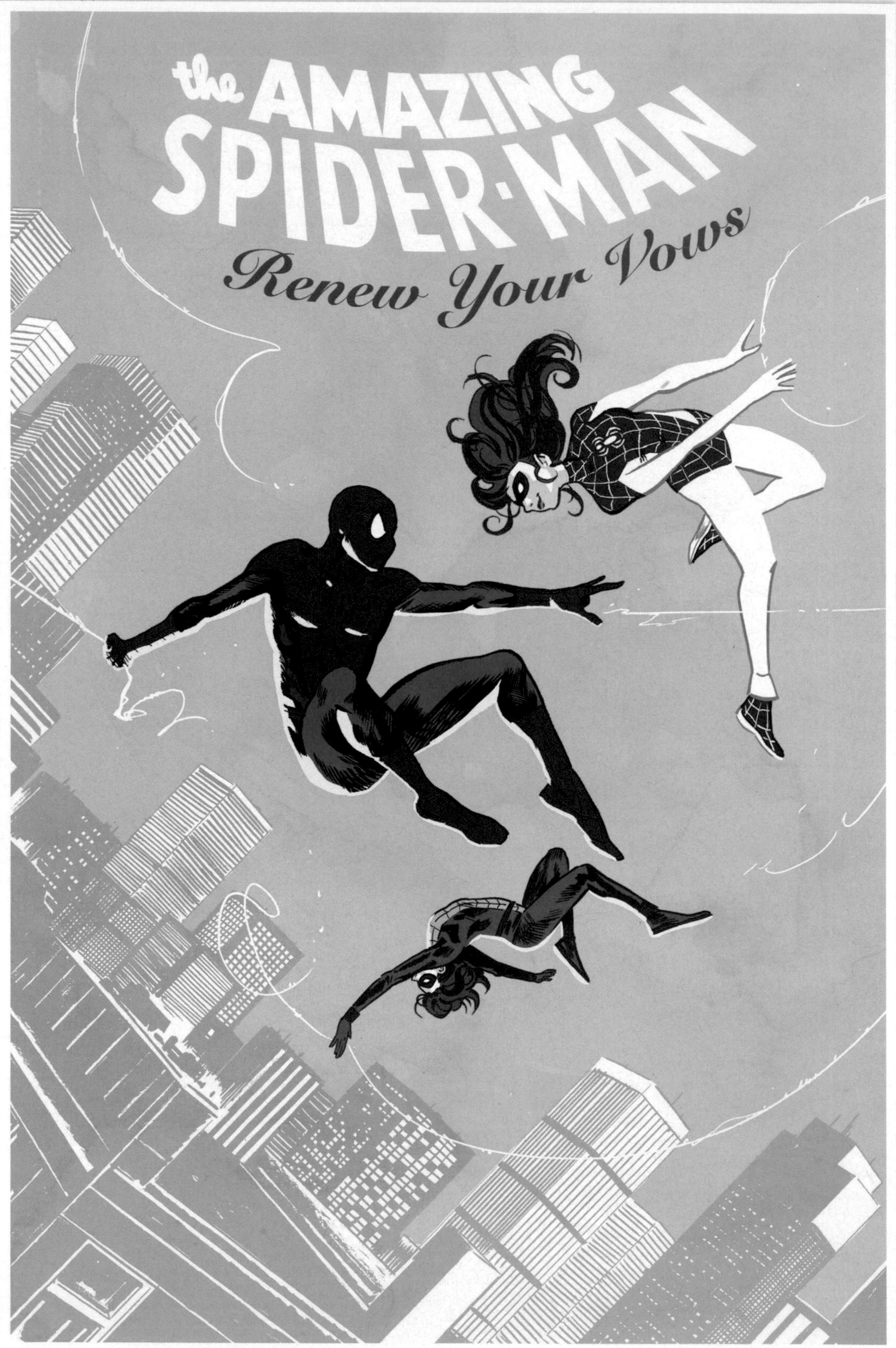
the AMAZING SPIDER-MAN
Renew Your Vows

13 VARIANT BY MICHAEL WALSH

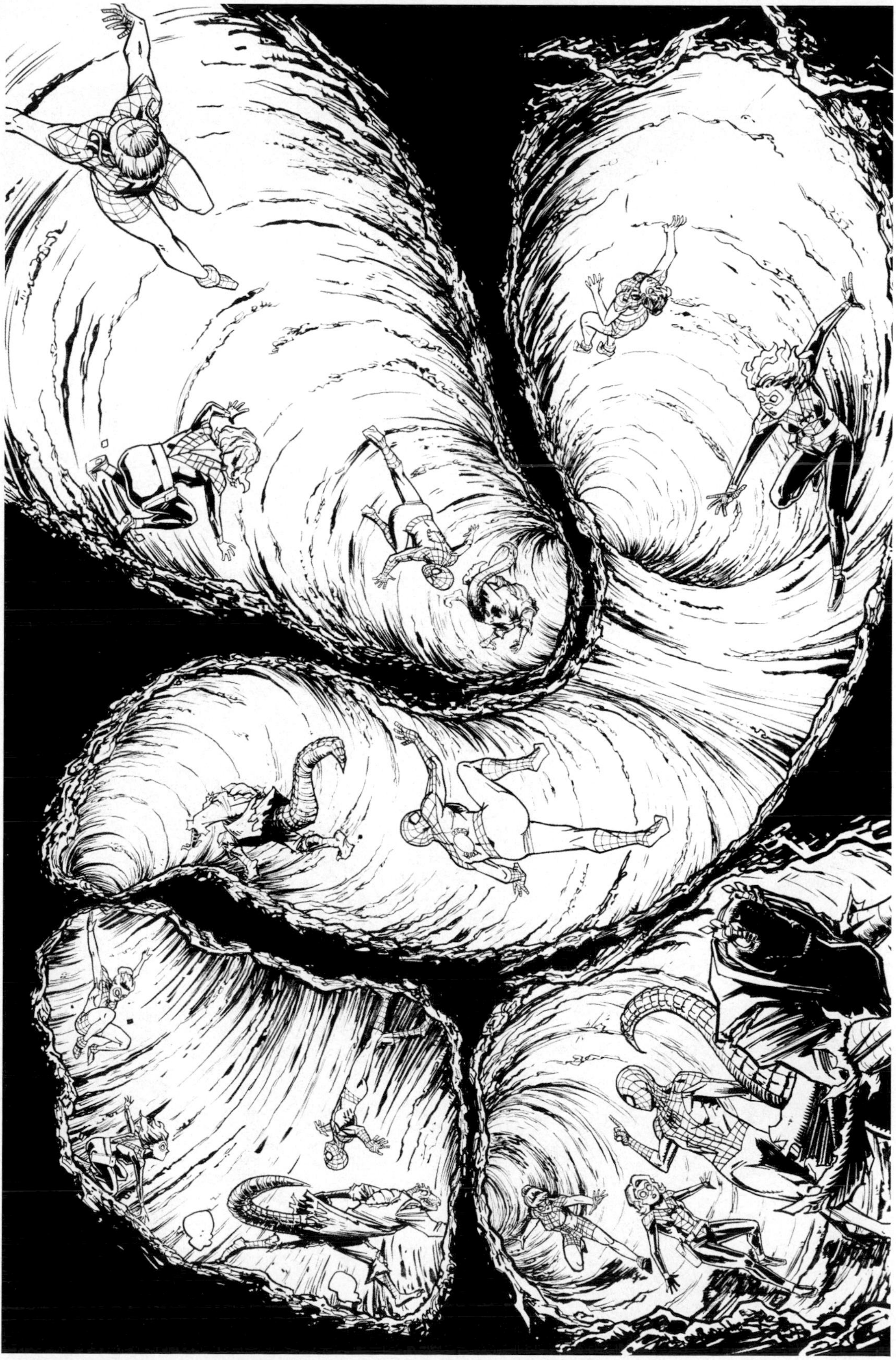

15, PAGE 9 ART BY NICK ROCHE

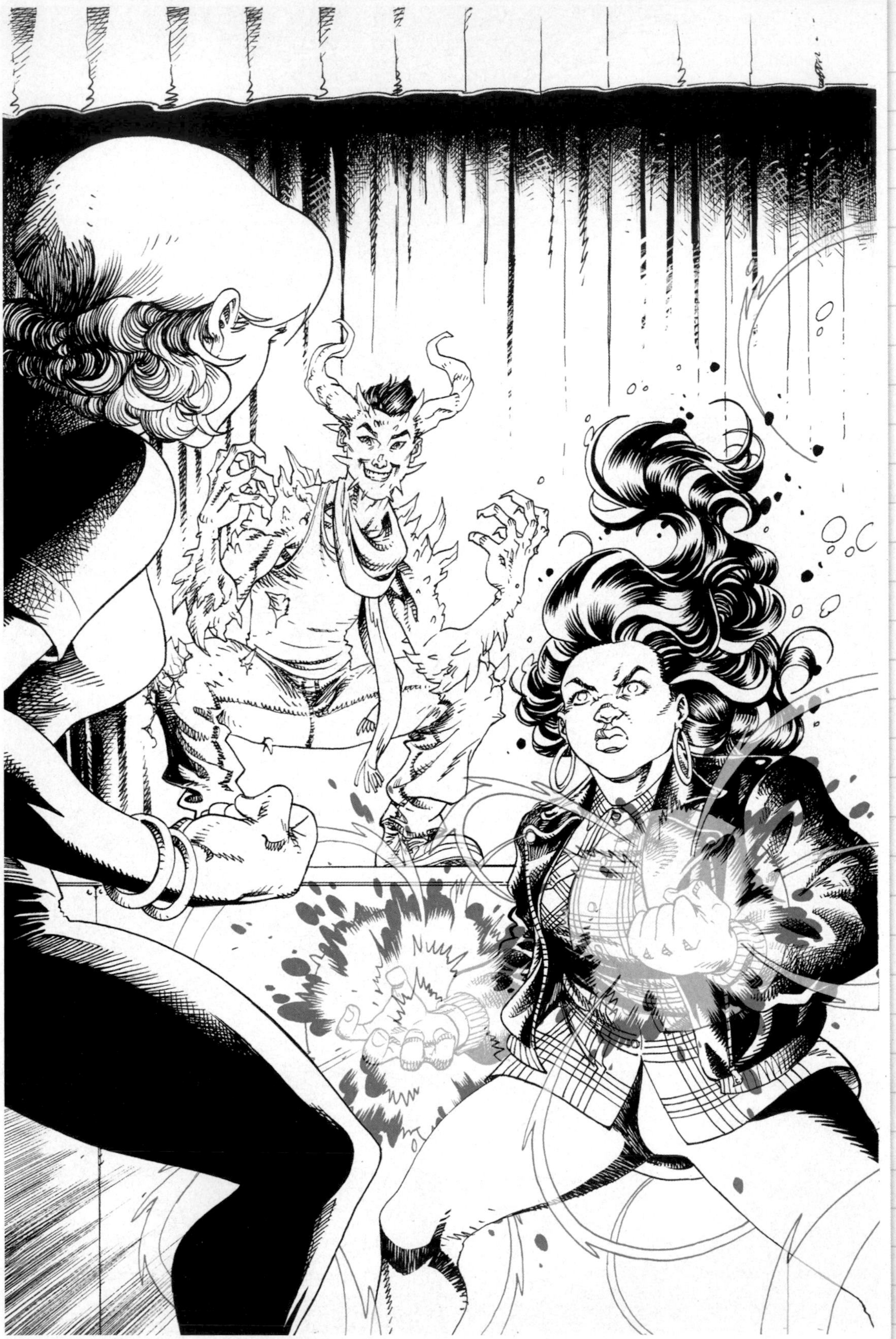

16, PAGE 20 ART BY NATHAN STOCKMAN